Gay Rights at the Ballot Box

GAY RIGHTS
AT THE **BALLOT BOX**

Amy L. Stone

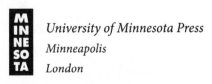
University of Minnesota Press
Minneapolis
London

Portions of this book were previously published by Emerald Group Publishing as "Dominant Tactics in Social Movement Tactical Repertoires: Anti-Gay Ballot Measures, 1974–2008," *Research in Social Movements, Conflict, and Change,* ed. Patrick C. Coy, issue 31 (2011): 141–74.

Published by the University of Minnesota Press
111 Third Avenue South, Suite 290
Minneapolis, MN 55401-2520
http://www.upress.umn.edu

Library of Congress Cataloging-in-Publication Data

Stone, Amy L.
    Gay rights at the ballot box / Amy L. Stone.
    Includes bibliographical references and index.
    ISBN 978-0-8166-7547-0 (hc : alk. paper)
    ISBN 978-0-8166-7548-7 (pb : alk. paper)
    1. Gay rights movement — United States.   2. Gay rights — United States.
3. Constitutional amendments — United States.   4. Referendum — United
States.   I. Title.
    HQ76.8.U5S76   2012
    323.3'2640973 — dc23   2012000010

Printed in the United States of America on acid-free paper

The University of Minnesota is an equal-opportunity educator and employer.

19 18 17 16 15 14 13 12   10 9 8 7 6 5 4 3 2 1

To those within the LGBTQ movement
who persevere in the face of great odds

CONTENTS

ACKNOWLEDGMENTS

THIS BOOK IS THE PRODUCT of more than six years of research on the evolving arena of anti-gay ballot measures. My introduction to Michigan campaigns came in 2002, when I read the local LGBT newspaper headlines about nearby campaigns. First and foremost, this book could not have been finished without the contributions of the 100–plus LGBT organizers and leaders across the country who allowed me to spend hours asking them questions about ballot measure campaigns.

This project began and ended with Glenda Russell, whose personal experience with Colorado ballot measures spans several decades. At the start of this project, Glenda generously allowed me, a stranger to her at the time, to sit in her house and make her dining room dusty during my countless hours of reviewing the Kathleen Russell Files, which were stored in her basement then. To complete my research on Michigan ballot measures I thank many individuals who allowed me to use their own private or organizational files and papers, including Kathleen Russell, Lynn D'Orio, Lisa Zuber, Sean Drate, Joann Willcock, Rudy Sera, Lori Thom, Elizabeth Warren Eddins, and Beth Bashert. Tim Retzloff unexpectedly helped me with archival documents about older Michigan LGBT rights ordinances, information I would not have found otherwise. This early research was supported by my University of Michigan undergraduate research assistants, Julie Parow, Caroline Roberts, Eleanor Hillock, Christine Dewaelsche, and Nicole DuPuis. Last but not least, I learned everything I know about the anti-gay Religious Right from Gayle Rubin.

This project required the assistance of archivists across the country. I worked at the Bentley Historical Library and Special Collections at the University of Michigan, Michigan State University's Special Collection on American Radicalism, Cornell University Human Sexuality Collection, and the GLBT Historical Society. I received funding from the Phil Zwickler Memorial Research Grant, the University of Michigan Sociology Department Dissertation Grant, the Tom and Mary Turner Junior Faculty Fellowship, and Faculty Advancement Funds at Trinity University.

Many readers, both academic and activist, gave input on drafts of this book, from its early stages as a dissertation to its most recent iteration. My dissertation committee (Karin Martin, Anne Herrmann, Michael Kennedy, Anthony Chen, and Barry Adam) gave me both support and autonomy as a graduate student to complete my research on Michigan campaigns. This book was shaped by comments from readers Beth Bashert, Cara Bergstrom, Mary Bernstein, Chris Bobel, K. L. Broad, Dara Bryant, Tony Chen, Pat Coy, Gene Deerman, David Dobbie, Tina Fetner, Jerome Himmelstein, Anna Kirkland, Carla Pfeffer, Jo Reger, Glenda Russell, Meredith McGuire, Tanya Saunders, Eve Shapiro, David Spener, and Mayer Zald. My dear friend Denise Stallcup fixed my worst inaccuracies and awkward language with her patient copyediting. My editor, Jason Weidemann, was enthusiastic about this project from the start.

I am thankful for a loving tribe and family who supported me through the insanity of book writing, including the members of the Department of Sociology and Anthropology at Trinity University, who encouraged me to leave the office on occasion. My immediate and extended family—especially Thomas Stone, Karen Stone, Lenelle Reade, Nathan Reade, Kris Reade, and Eleonore Schlef—planted the seeds for this book when they encouraged me to become an avid reader and dreamer as a child. This book could not have been completed without the encouragement of Amy Fried, Denise Stallcup, Saundra Lamb, Angelita Diaz, Jasmine Dennis, Marla Godron, Andrea Mote, Kellye Green, Tara Wright, and Gale McCommons, along with my tribe in San Antonio and San Francisco. Stephanie Garb, Kris Herzog, and Bill Grindatti are dear to my heart and endlessly supportive of my work (along with being tolerant of my writing angst). Tila Tapp endured years of venting about the Religious Right, neglected housework, and brain-fried company, for which she deserves a medal. Lucy the puppy supervised me through a long summer of writing; without breaks to play fetch and a small dog sleeping on my foot, this book would not have been completed.

ABBREVIATIONS

ACLU	American Civil Liberties Union
ADF	Alliance Defense Fund
AFA	American Family Association
BARF	Bend Alliance of Religious Fundamentalists
CFV	Colorado for Family Values
COST	Citizens Opposing Special Treatment
DOMA	Defense of Marriage Act
EMU	Eastern Michigan University
ENDA	Employment Non-Discrimination Act
EPOC	Equal Protection Ordinance Coalition
EQCA	Equality California
ERA	Equal Rights Amendment
FAQ	frequently asked questions
FRC	Family Research Council
FTMC	Freedom to Marry Coalition
GAA	Gay Activists Alliance
GLAD	Gay and Lesbian Advocates and Defenders
GLSTN	Gay, Lesbian, and Straight Teachers Network
GLVF	Gay and Lesbian Victory Fund
GOTV	get out the vote
GRSR	*Gay Rights, Special Rights*
HDG	human dignity group
HIV/AIDS	human immunodeficiency virus/acquired immunodeficiency syndrome
HRC	Human Rights Campaign
HRCF	Human Rights Campaign Fund

ICA	Idaho Citizens Alliance
IRB	Institutional Review Board
KAD	Kalamazoo Against Discrimination
KOHR	Keep Our Human Rights
LACROP	Lesbian Avengers Civil Rights Organizing Project
LGBTQ	lesbian, gay, bisexual, transgender, queer
MCER	Maine Coalition for Equal Rights
MCHD	Michigan Campaign for Human Dignity
MWD	Maine Won't Discriminate
NAACP	National Association for the Advancement of Colored People
NAMBLA	North American Man/Boy Love Association
NARAL	National Abortion Rights Action League
NEA	National Endowment for the Arts
NGLTF	National Gay and Lesbian Task Force
NGTF	National Gay Task Force
NOM	National Organization for Marriage
NOW	National Organization for Women
OAC	Oregonians Against Cunnilingus
OCA	Oregon Citizens Alliance
PAC	political action committee
PFLAG	Parents and Friends of Lesbians and Gays
PV	persuadable voter
ROP	Rural Organizing Project
SCAT	Seattle Committee Against Thirteen
SMO	social movement organization
SOC PAC	Save Our Communities Political Action Committee
SOME	Save Our Moral Ethics
TVC	Traditional Values Coalition
YCFE	Ypsilanti Campaign for Equality

WINNING (BUT MOSTLY LOSING) AT THE BALLOT BOX

NOVEMBER 4, 2008. The world watched as promising young, progressive Senator Barack Obama was elected president of the United States, sweeping the state of California. That same night, newscasters reported that Californians had passed Proposition 8, a statewide constitutional amendment that banned same-sex marriage. The California Supreme Court had recognized same-sex marriage rights earlier that year, and more than eighteen thousand same-sex marriages had already been conducted when Proposition 8 was passed. To the surprise of many, the supporters of Proposition 8 successfully defeated the largest lesbian, gay, bisexual, and transgender (LGBT) campaign in U.S. history, a campaign that dwarfed any other ballot issue campaign that had come before it.

California LGBT activists had been preparing for this vote for years.[1] Local LGBT organizations had been working in coalition with national organizations for almost four years to plan for a potential anti-gay marriage initiative in California. The organizers of the campaign to fight Proposition 8 spent $43.3 million, shattering campaign-spending records. LGBT activists had run campaigns in twenty-four other states to fight same-sex marriage initiatives; the campaign to fight Proposition 8 spent more than all of the other campaigns combined.[2] Several senior professional consultants served as advisers to the campaign field operation. Many of these advisers had been working on gay and lesbian issues for a decade, and the campaign utilized nearly fifty thousand volunteers. The California campaign managers benefited from the lessons learned from at least two previous campaigns against LGBT rights in California, initiatives against same-sex marriage in other states, and the increasing number of ballot issue campaigns used to pass progressive initiatives. The campaign used focus groups and polling to develop its messages, which it used in radio and television ads and scripts that volunteers read when they contacted voters by phone.

When Proposition 8 failed at the ballot box, protests were held across the country, and LGBT activists immediately mobilized in California and nationally to plan for their next step, a 2010 or 2012 ballot measure. Many criticized the tactics used in the campaign. Critics suggested that the Proposition 8 campaign had not sufficiently reached out to African American and Latino voters. There was also criticism that the campaign was "closeted" and failed to adequately feature gay men and lesbians in radio and television ads. Members of the LGBT community complained that the campaign did not value community input and had been too hierarchical in its decision making. Some of the materials used, such as the tight scripts for volunteers when calling voters, were criticized for being too narrowly focused on one message or, conversely, for not being disciplined or focused enough.[3]

June 7, 1977. A national audience watched as voters in Dade County, Florida, passed a referendum to overturn a local newly created gay-rights law. The campaign against the referendum was largely made up of gay men. Those involved faced sharp internal disagreements over how closeted their approach should be. Money for the campaign came from supportive gay men and lesbians in cities as far away as San Francisco and New York, largely owing to the visibility of the referendum's Religious Right spokeswoman, former beauty queen Anita Bryant. Those campaigning did not have the benefit of lessons learned, as did the California campaign three decades later. In 1977, there had been only one similar referendum campaign, in Boulder, Colorado, three years earlier. None of the Dade County gay activists had experience with campaign politics and had to go all the way to New York City to find a campaign consultant, Ethan Geto, and to San Francisco to hire Jim Foster, the founder of San Francisco's Alice B. Toklas Democratic Club, the first national gay Democratic club.[4] Only two fledgling national gay organizations, the underfunded National Gay Task Force and Lambda Legal Defense and Education Fund, existed in 1977, and the campaign could count on little support from them. Harvey Milk, the first openly gay man to be elected to public office in California, would not be elected until November. Anti-gay policies and laws were ubiquitous across the country, including sodomy laws in most states. The majority of Americans reported not knowing someone who was gay or lesbian.[5]

Nationwide, the LGBT community mourned the losses they suffered with the passage of the 1977 referendum in Miami–Dade County and the passage of Proposition 8 in California, more than three decades later. They saw both losses as a sign that the movement was losing ground in the fight against the Right. Between 1974 and 2009, the Religious Right placed 146 anti-gay ballot measures on the ballot, using direct democracy to success-fully fight LGBT legislative gains on both the state and local level. Direct democracy is the limited ability of citizens in most states to rescind legis-lation by referendum or to create new laws with an initiative or constitu-tional amendment.[6] The Religious Right is far more successful at the ballot box, where it can rely on voters' homophobia, than in the legislative or judicial arenas.[7] Thus, the anti-gay Right has strategically engaged in con-stant attempts to derail LGBT rights not just through the use of referen-dums to rescind local gay-rights laws, but also with initiatives that attempt to ban same-sex marriage, fire gay and lesbian teachers, and eliminate the potential for future LGBT rights legislation. The approach of the LGBT movement for the past thirty years has been to respond to legislation initi-ated by the Right by taking a largely defensive position, with few victories.

The Religious Right is only one of a number of social movements increasingly looking to the referendum and initiative process to legislate change. In November 2008, the pro-life movement created restrictions on minors having abortions, the environmental movement supported clean energy, and the animal-rights movement regulated living space for farm animals. In a single election, 21 percent of all statewide initiatives across the country were sponsored by an identifiable social movement. Despite the many movements on both the Left and the Right using direct democ-racy, there has been little research on the relationship between ballot mea-sure campaigns and social movements.

There is a long history of social movements using the referendum and initiative process, and indeed the establishment of an initiative process in most states was the result of pressure by the Progressive and Populist movements. Yet we know little about the relationship between ballot mea-sure campaigns and social movements. Do such campaigns further social movement goals? Do they sustain existing social movement ideologies and identities? How do different organizations within a larger social movement interact with ballot measure campaigns? And can ballot measure campaigns hijack social movement goals? This book analyzes the relationship between ballot measure campaigns and social movements by using the LGBT movement as a case study.

Campaigns and Movements: A Sociological Approach

Ballot measure campaigns are short-lived political campaigns that arise to support or defeat direct legislation. Direct legislation uses the process of referendums and initiatives to allow citizens to either defeat existing legislation or propose new legislation.[8] For example, if your local city council passed a new zoning ordinance, in many cities you could collect petitions filled with signatures of eligible voters in order to place that ordinance on the ballot in a referendum for voters to decide. If you wanted to create your own law—say, making your city an alcohol-free "dry" city—you could file your petition with the city clerk, gather signatures, and submit the signatures to be counted in order to place your law on the ballot as an initiative. These same processes apply on the state level, as in many states voters are allowed to rescind or propose new laws, even going so far as to amend the state constitution. In addition, the legislature can put advisory votes or constitutional amendments on the ballot in many states. The ballot measure campaigns that arise in response to referendums and initiatives engage in activities such as persuading constituents to vote for a cause and changing public opinion about an issue within a short time period, typically less than six months.

A *social movement,* on the other hand, operates on a larger scale. According to scholar Mario Diani, social movements involve a large number of "individuals, groups and/or organisations, engaged in political and/or cultural conflict, on the basis of a shared collective identity."[9] When most people think of a U.S. social movement, national movements such as the civil rights, environmental, animal-rights, or pro-life movements come to mind. Within any one of these social movements coexist different strategies, identities, ideas about success, ideological approaches, and types of activism, from direct-action protest on the street to lobbying Congress. Social movement goals may include the transformation of culture or politics, or both.[10] For example, within the U.S. second-wave feminist movement, feminists wanted to change cultural expectations of gender with the encouragement of nonsexist language, such as substituting "firefighter" for "fireman." Feminists also wanted to change laws and public policies, such as creating a law to prohibit discrimination against women in educational settings. With every social movement there are multiple social movement organizations (SMOs), formal organizations that further the goals of the movement.[11] Within these organizations, activists are drawn together to create a common collective identity, a "shared definition of a group that derives from members' common interests, experiences, and solidarity."[12]

In her research on ballot measure campaigns in Maine, sociologist Kimberly Clarke Simmons delineates some of the differences between ballot issue campaigns and social movements, and the relationship between them. She suggests that social movements generally have unclear starting and ending times, whereas ballot measure campaign organizations have "discrete temporal boundaries."[13] Typically, there are a number of SMOs that address a social movement issue, such as poverty or reproductive choice, and the leaders of these SMOs are hired or elected through a clear process. However, to fight ballot measures, typically one campaign is created to represent the whole community, and the leaders of that campaign are selected by a small, nonrepresentative group of individuals. In the case of LGBT ballot issue campaigns, the campaign is pressured to defend the rights of *all* LGBT citizens in its area. Thus, campaigns both claim a lot of authority over the progress of the movement and also are new, short-term organizations that select their leaders through an unclear process.[14]

Many LGBT activists have articulated the difference between ballot measure campaigns and the larger social movement. For local activists, campaigns often become the most visible, exciting face of the LGBT movement. One national campaign organizer suggested that LGBT community members project all their expectations about the movement onto local campaigns, and the campaign cannot possibly live up to those expectations. There is extraordinary pressure on campaign activists to both succeed at the ballot box and, concurrently, run a movement, as ballot measures become a vote on the community as a whole. According to a campaign consultant, tensions arise in many ballot issue campaigns because "of a lack of real movement in most of the country. In the absence of a movement, the campaigns become the movement."[15] In places where no existing social movement organizing is occurring, a ballot measure campaign attracts all the local movement energy, and additionally all the pressure to operate as a social movement. This campaign consultant went on to suggest the error in pressuring campaigns to be social movements:

> Campaigns are incapable of serving in that role. Campaigns freeze a moment in time. It's like taking a picture of the organizing in the community. You learn to accept that the campaign cannot change the picture, it took too many years to make in the first place to try to change it in one year. Campaigns, at best, simply try to emphasize the best parts of the picture in order to take votes . . . campaigns are tools of the movement, not the movement itself, nor should they ever become that to us or we will be badly damaged by them.[16]

For this campaign consultant, making a campaign a movement could harm the movement itself, both through the campaign's potential loss at the ballot box and as a result of the inability of campaigns to lead long-term transformative politics. However, campaigns are also reflective of the size and strength of the movement at a given moment; they "tak[e] a picture of the organizing in the community" at a particular time.

The sociological study of social movements rarely addresses ballot measure campaigns. When those campaigns are addressed, it is usually only in relation to social movement framing or messaging.[17] Political scientists often analyze direct legislation as a battle between the Right and the Left, a continuation of normal politics with the adverse involvement of interest groups and political candidates — not necessarily as an extension of social movement activism. They often focus their analysis on issues like voter behavior and rates of winning, along with the long-term impact of direct democracy on minority rights.[18] Scholars miss out on better understanding both ballot measure campaigns and social movements by ignoring the relationship between them. Social movements on both the Right and the Left are increasingly using direct democracy to further their goals. The lack of connection between the analysis of ballot issue campaigns and social movements has ignored the way in which these campaigns cultivate broad public support for social movements. Additionally, to date, analysis has failed to appreciate the political strategies of campaigns.[19]

This book demonstrates that the relationship between ballot measure campaigns and social movements is both complementary and contradictory. Through examining the history of campaigns to fight anti-gay ballot measures, I demonstrate that as social movements grow they are more capable of supporting large-scale ballot measure campaigns. As movements grow larger, strong national organizations help spread models of how to run campaigns to local activists. This process provides new insight into the spread of tactics within a social movement. Ballot measure campaigns may also support the growth of social movements. Social movements and ballot measure campaigns are interrelated—the growth of one often leads to the growth of the other. However, ballot measure campaigns and social movements can also operate in contradictory relationships to one another. As noted in the quote from the campaign consultant, social movement activists may place unreasonable demands on campaigns. Ballot measure campaigns can unwittingly undo work around racial coalition building and remedying marginalization in the movement, such as resolving issues around transgender inclusion. Although tactics may lead to a win at the ballot box, some campaigns may actually set movement goals back.

Building Campaigns and Movements

In 1998, local LGBT and heterosexual community members in Ypsilanti, Michigan, formed a campaign to fight an impending referendum on their newly passed nondiscrimination ordinance, which included protections for sexual orientation and gender identity. Apart from a few individuals who had worked on city council campaigns, these community members knew little about how to run a campaign, much less a ballot measure campaign addressing a controversial issue. The Ypsilanti campaign was well organized, employing such professional techniques as voter identification through door-to-door canvassing and phone banking; disciplined messaging developed from polling and focus groups that took the approach that discrimination against gays was always wrong; and a thorough "get out the vote" (GOTV) effort. To develop these techniques, Ypsilanti activists relied on advice both from staff members of national LGBT organizations and from LGBT campaign activists from distant states, such as Oregon and Maine.

The Ypsilanti campaign used a set of tactics common to campaigns fighting anti-gay referendums and initiatives in the 1990s. Because many of these tactics lead to successful campaigns, they continue to be used. The tactics were spread from campaign to campaign in training sessions offered by national organizations like the National Gay and Lesbian Task Force (NGLTF) and the Human Rights Campaign (HRC). Campaigns still obtain legal advice from Lambda Legal Defense and Education Fund and ask for advice from activists who have led similar campaigns and used the same tactics. After the Ypsilanti campaign ended, a few campaign leaders created a statewide organization, Michigan Equality, which still exists more than a decade later, to support electoral and ballot measure politics in Michigan.

Movement and ballot measure campaigns can mutually support one another. I argue that by developing a social movement infrastructure, which includes strong national and statewide organizations, training programs, and an effective fund-raising donor pool, movements support the development of campaign tactics and ways of effectively running campaigns. This book analyzes the development of a model way of running campaigns, and a set of tactics that were supported by the development of a movement infrastructure.

Conversely, many ballot measure campaigns reinforced and supported this movement structure by becoming permanent SMOs. For example, many campaigns to fight statewide ballot measures developed into statewide organizations, which supported further organizing. Ballot measure campaigns may recruit new volunteers and train new leaders, which supports long-term social movement projects and organizations.

Social Movements Make Campaigns

Since the first referendum in Boulder, Colorado, in 1974, national LGBT organizations and local campaigns have worked together to develop a set of tactics that are now the norm for LGBT campaigns: tactics such as disciplined political messaging, pre-ballot legal challenges, professional polls to evaluate potential messages, voter identification of supporters through phone banking and door knocking with an army of volunteers, and "get out the vote" to maximize the use of supporters on election day. These tactics rely on a growing industry of professionals with experience in ballot measure campaigns, particularly those focusing on LGBT issues. The campaign tactics make it possible for local community groups to evolve into effective professional campaigns, devoted to a win on election day and a victory against the Religious Right.

However, these campaign tactics would not have developed without support from a movement infrastructure. I argue throughout this book that campaigns are made, not born. Many of these tactics are widely used in other electoral campaigns. However, their adoption by LGBT campaigns was neither inevitable nor determined by the structure of campaign politics. Local LGBT campaigns adopted these tactics because the larger social movement became more politically savvy about electoral politics. The movement grew enough infrastructure — which was founded on organizations, financial resources, and "people power" — to support large campaigns. This reliance on a set of model tactics grew over time as the Religious Right escalated its use of direct democracy. In response, national and statewide LGBT organizations supported and spread these tactics, and several critical victories and defeats demonstrated their effectiveness.

Tactics: What Are They?

Scholars have long theorized about social movement strategies and tactics. Strategies are the general plan of action or blueprint that social movement activists use to "turn what we have into what we need to get what we want."[20] Tactics, however, are the specific ways activists achieve their strategic plan. For example, activists may identify one of their strategies as a desire to get media visibility for a social movement issue; they must then choose among such tactics as protest on the street, guerrilla theater, or a press conference to make that happen. Social movement scholars have examined tactics from a variety of perspectives, including how tactics are created (tactical innovation) and spread (tactical dissemination) between social movements and activists.

How do activists choose a tactic? As demonstrated by the Ypsilanti campaign mentioned earlier, they clearly do not reinvent the wheel each time they engage in activism; rather, they adopt tactics from a repertoire, a set of available tactics that are limited by both geography and the time period.[21] Tactical repertoires provide a "tool kit" of tactics available to social movement activists at a given place and time. This "tool kit" includes a range of possibilities that can be chosen, at will, by political actors but does not privilege one tactic as being better than another.[22] If campaign activists have a repertoire of available tactics, how do they choose voter identification over direct-action protest? Francesca Polletta argues that the existing literature on repertoires fails to account "for how particular strategies, tactics or claims come to be part of an established repertoire" with little explanation for "the process by which options are ruled in and out of consideration in activists' strategic decision making."[23] Tactics may be selected by a rational accounting of efficacy but are also selected through emotion, culture, habit, collective identity, and "tactical tastes."[24] The level of organization of collective actors may also matter, as does the structural power of activists.[25]

This book contributes to the literature on social movement tactics by examining the development of dominant tactics, tactics that are not just tactics available within an existing tactical repertoire but dominant tactics that others in the movement expect of social movement organizations and actors. For example, in the late 1990s, within ballot measure campaigns, voter identification became a campaign tactic that was not only available to activists but expected, as it was thought to be essential for successful campaigns. For activists, voter identification was synonymous with winning, and campaigns that did not use this tactic were publicly criticized as ineffective and disorganized. Such tactics become dominant because they are considered the most effective by political actors, and as a result they spread throughout the movement. This research builds on existing literature in social movement theory to analyze three reasons why tactics become dominant in campaigns: (1) their use in critical victories and defeats, (2) the escalation of countermovement or Religious Right activity, and (3) the involvement of increasingly institutionalized national social movement organizations in the development of a movement infrastructure.

It would be easy to say that campaigns select tactics because they have proven to be the most successful. However, ballot measure campaigns are complex. A victory may be the result of innumerable factors, from voter apathy to an inactive Religious Right to a well-run media campaign. How do activists know which tactics will be most successful for their particular campaign? Ironically, social movement scholars have paid little attention to the role of victories and defeats in the selection of tactics. Holly McCammon, in her work on women's suffrage, was one of the first scholars to theorize that activists changed their tactics based on political defeats.[26]

Loss analysis alone is not sufficient to understand the impact of a particular tactic on a campaign; a victory at the ballot box may be an ambiguous event and open to interpretation, and activists may disagree about what makes a campaign victorious, and whether or not the ultimate result of the campaign was a step forward for the movement. Sometimes there is consensus on whether a campaign was a success or a failure, but political actors' understandings of outcomes and competing definitions of success inform whether or not an event will be understood within a social movement as a victory or defeat.[27] A common issue in ballot measure campaigns is that defeating the Religious Right on election day may be a pyrrhic victory, as it may leave a bitter legacy of divisions and broken coalitions.

Countermovement escalation also influences which tactics are used, and how tactics become dominant. My research suggests that campaign tactics become dominant tactics when the countermovement escalates its activity. A countermovement rises in opposition to an existing social movement, such as the rise of the pro-life movement in response to pro-choice advances such as *Roe v. Wade*. One major question in the study of movement–countermovement interactions is how "coupled" movements and countermovements are, particularly "to what degree are one movement's agenda, tactics, and the venues in which it operates determined by its opposition?"[28] Existing studies suggest that movement–countermovement interactions motivate social movements to engage in constant tactical innovation, not focus on one set of tactics.[29] As a social movement tries a new tactic, countermovements would neutralize that tactic with "effective tactical counters," requiring the movement to engage in a new round of tactical innovation.[30]

In addition to the role of countermovements, defeats, and victories, I argue that the most important determinant of the creation and spread of dominant tactics is the development of a stronger social movement infrastructure. This social movement infrastructure includes, most importantly, stable, long-lasting national, regional, statewide, and local organizations to support ballot measure campaigns and keep the momentum of the movement going between campaigns. Social movement theory suggests that organizations play an important role in both developing and disseminating tactics.[31] In the LGBT movement, national organizations developed training programs for activists, sent staff members to work on local campaigns, and provided an institutional memory of past campaign tactics. In this study, the data suggests that national organizations rarely innovated. Most tactical innovations occurred in local or statewide campaigns, and were then spread through connections between organizations and social networks between activists.[32] In the LGBT movement, national and statewide organizations selected the most effective tactics at the local level to spread across the country.

Social movements and the development of a social movement infrastructure are critical in the development of ballot measure campaigns. Specifically, a strong social movement infrastructure facilitates the development and dissemination of dominant tactics, tactics that are not only available to social movement activists but expected.

Campaigns Build a Social Movement

Campaigns can also further social movement goals, helping build the same movement infrastructure that ballot measure campaigns depend on to win. The two most common ways that campaigns build a social movement is by increasing people power by mobilizing new activists and by developing SMOs. Ballot measure campaigns can also help social movements progress by passing legislation through initiatives that would otherwise have been difficult, although it is rare for LGBT rights measures to be more successful at the ballot than in the legislature.[33]

Ballot measure campaigns increase support for a social movement by creating a large, visible campaign that is powered by hundreds, if not thousands, of volunteers, and many donors. The use of volunteers can increase support for a social movement by "drawing 'spectators,' or those who normally watch politics rather than actively participate, into the fight on your side . . . there are few better tools to give your issue increased visibility and media coverage than a divisive initiative."[34] These volunteers may be recruited as leaders, board members, donors, or regular volunteers to support ongoing local or national SMOs. Campaign tactics such as voter identification can create lists of pro-LGBT voters who can be mobilized during local and statewide elections, increasing the power of the LGBT vote and helping the movement meet legislative goals.

In areas that lack political SMOs, the campaign may turn into an SMO after election day. With leftover funds, an active base of volunteers, and energy developed during the campaign, the campaign may develop into a lasting organization. Such a development is common in both local and statewide campaigns.[35] Indeed, since 1974 more than a dozen statewide organizations and countless other local organizations have been founded out of campaigns. It may be easier for victorious campaigns to create these organizations, as they are not as subject to post-campaign movement infighting. Even in unsuccessful campaigns, movement infrastructure may be developed in response to the climate of the ballot measure, rather than emerging directly out of the campaign. For example, in Colorado after the anti-gay Amendment 2 won in 1992, chapters of Parents and Friends of Lesbians and Gays (PFLAG) sprouted up across the state, local public libraries increased their holdings of LGBT books, and a task force to address the climate for LGBT individuals on campus was created at the University of Colorado at Boulder.[36] Thus, during both victories and tragic losses, ballot measure campaigns may contribute to developing a social movement infrastructure.

However, building social movement infrastructure from campaigns is difficult, as activists may struggle with post-campaign burnout and dissent. Even so, many LGBT activists argue that it is necessary. In 1993, one NGLTF staff member emphasized the need for infrastructure development after a tour of a statewide ballot measure campaign:

> This tour [of a statewide campaign] reminded me of the short-comings of the gay movement in general: lack of grassroots infrastructure means electoral campaigns become the movement and the repository of all the frustrations and hopes of gay people. We need to use these loathsome initiatives as an opportunity to organize long-term and way beyond election day. Of course, it is too much to ask field office personnel to (1) direct a winning field campaign, (2) be a spokesperson for all gays and (3) build a grassroots gay movement, all the while making sure phonebanking volunteers show up and are motivated, political coalitions are built and nurtured, the media is taken care of, the [opposition] is kept on the defense, concerned citizens on our side don't freak out, campaign messages are moved, crises are averted, someone brings the coffee and donuts, and the Advil is well stocked. The more I work on these battles the more I realize that long-term movement building must be a focus of the national gay movement, with real resources committed to the grassroots.[37]

This staff member's observation suggests that the overwhelming nature of campaigns makes it difficult to run a campaign while simultaneously building and sustaining a movement infrastructure and doing grassroots organizing. Yet, without a movement infrastructure in place, "electoral campaigns become the movement and the repository of all the frustrations and hopes of gay people."

Campaigns and movements support each other, developing in the best of times a complementary relationship. The strength and power of a social movement infrastructure supports ballot measure campaigns, and campaigns in turn help develop a stronger social movement infrastructure. However, as I demonstrate throughout this book, ballot measure campaigns and social movements have a contradictory relationship, and support each other at their peril.

Rolling Back Social Movement Gains

One of my first interviews for this project was with a board member of a ballot measure campaign who told me two things before I turned on the recorder. The first was that LGBT rights lose when they go to the ballot box; the ballot box was a dangerous place for those rights and should be avoided at all costs. The second was that campaigns were not and could not be a movement; if they tried to be a movement, they would lose the campaign. Later in the interview, this organizer explained that campaigns to fight referendums and initiatives had to be focused solely on winning on election day, employing a narrow range of tactics with intensity during the short period of time that most campaigns run. If campaigns became distracted with "movement issues," such as affirming collective identities, long-term coalition building, education, and direct action, they would lose at the ballot box. Her job as a leader, she explained, was to prevent the campaign from being derailed by these "movement issues" in order to win on election day.

One of my last interviews was with an activist from a different state who is a lesbian of color, and who described feeling shut out by the campaign decision-making process. She described the leadership of the campaign as full of "elitist, we-know-better-than-you-do professional gays." This activist described the importance of inclusivity and grassroots organizing to sustain the community after the campaign, particularly in the face of a potential loss. She was one of the few people of color involved in the campaign and ultimately, as a result of feeling excluded, she left the campaign.

Just as the relationship between ballot measure campaigns and social movements can be supportive and complementary, campaigns and movements can also weaken each other. The first activist quoted in this section was concerned that movement issues would harm the ballot measure campaign, pushing the campaign to do too many different things rather than focus on winning. Indeed, many campaign leaders I interviewed argued that too many movement issues would distract campaigns during the limited campaign time period. The second activist's account of her involvement in a campaign suggests that ballot measures can harm social movements by undoing existing coalitions and increasing marginalization within the social movement.

Although campaigns are supported by social movements, they can also roll back social movement gains. Campaigns can strain social movement resources, drawing resources away from other organizations that are already strapped for cash, and pulling support away from like-minded political candidates in the same election. If too many resources are spent on a campaign and too few on "maintaining other movement organizations and projects, the campaigns become the centerpiece of the movement and when finished the movement may be in disrepair."[38]

Ballot measure campaigns can potentially harm social movements by increasing movement infighting or dissent.[39] LGBT campaigns increase movement dissent and marginalize direct action and queer activism. Queer activism emerged in the early 1990s as "an anti-identity ethos that implicitly celebrated the proliferation of identities — especially bisexual and transgender identities — while explicitly questioning the utility of all identity categories themselves."[40] Queer activism challenges campaign work by celebrating proliferating identities within the movement and the importance of proud, diverse representations of the LGBT community. Queer activists are often critical of the homonormativity within campaign politics, or the incorporation of heteronormative ideals such as binary gender systems and procreation into LGBT activism. For example, in many campaign messages, if LGBT lives are represented at all, they are typically white, gender-normative, middle-class, gay men or lesbians in monogamous, procreative relationships. In so representing the LGBT community, diversity within the movement is stifled and community members who are less palatable to mainstream voters — such as drag queens, transgender women, or leather-men — are hidden from view. The use of *gay* in the title of this book rather than LGBTQ or queer is not incidental. Campaign politics is rarely queer politics.

Queer activists and other community members, particularly social justice–oriented activists, criticize the underlying logic of campaign activism. Although campaigns can and often do support the movement infrastructure, dominant campaign tactics are also an instrumental approach to activism. Jean Hardisty defines instrumental approaches as short-term campaigns that employ a "task-oriented approach."[41] In campaign work, activists refer to this instrumental approach as the "50 percent + 1" approach, referring to the necessity in campaigns to get 50 percent of the vote plus one additional voter in order to achieve a majority and win. This instrumental organizing employs "shrewd political strategies . . . that may carry the day, but leave behind no coalition, no momentum towards other issues or causes, and no raised consciousness or expectations."[42] These tactics that "carry the day" may include professional polling that recommends that political messaging include no discussion of LGBT life.

In this book, I argue that the biggest rollback to LGBT movement gains is the creation of a legitimacy crisis for the movement when campaigns reinforce what scholar Jane Ward calls "instrumental conceptualizations of difference."[43] There is a long and problematic history within the LGBT movement of marginalizing both racial minorities and transgender individuals. Ballot measure campaigns face expectations by the local LGBT community that they will engage in strong racial coalition building and visible transgender inclusion as part of social movement progress in alleviating these issues.[44] Yet many ballot measure campaigns address this marginalization only if they believe it is directly and apparently beneficial to a win on election day. Ward suggests that even progressive activists often use "instrumental conceptualizations of difference, privileging those forms of difference that have the most currency in a neoliberal world and stifling differences that can't be easily represented, professionalized, or commodified."[45] This book shows that although instrumental tactics lead LGBT campaigns to victory at the ballot box, they reinforce this use of "instrumental conceptualizations of difference," particularly regarding racial

coalition building and transgender inclusion, which creates larger problems for the movement.

Thus, as I demonstrate throughout this book, the relationship between
ballot measure campaigns and social movements is an ambiguous one. At
times complementary, at times contradictory, campaigns and movements
engage in a constant, complex dance of engagement.

Studying Campaigns

Campaigns are ephemeral. They come, they go. And they leave behind
few traces after election day. Until recently, at the end of a campaign most
campaign flyers and internal documents were stored (if kept at all) in a
leader's musty basement. Accordingly, while writing this book, I spent a
lot of time sitting in musty basements, digging through archival files of
national organizations, searching small-town newspapers online and on
microfiche, and speaking directly with campaign organizers. Most of my
archival information came from special collections at the Cornell University Human Sexuality Collection, University of Michigan Special Collection, and the Gay and Lesbian Historical Society of Northern California,
along with many other smaller archives. Through my archival and newspaper data collection, I created a database of all recorded attempted ballot
measures, which I analyze throughout this book. As this project began
as a dissertation on transgender inclusion in LGBT organizing in Michigan, I have a great deal of detail on campaigns from this state, where I sat
for hours in the living rooms of organizers digging through dusty files. I
have also e-mailed dozens of leaders of statewide organizations and contacted small-town newspapers in Oregon for information not available on
microfiche.

Between 2004 and 2010, I interviewed more than one hundred individuals involved in ballot measure politics: campaign leaders, professional
consultants, fieldworkers in national organizations, and the occasional
disgruntled community member, city clerk, and member of the Religious
Right. Sixty-eight of these interviews were with LGBT organizers and
community members in Michigan, which allows me to provide detailed
analysis of a winning streak in this state, along with detailed case studies on the role of racial coalition building and transgender inclusion in

campaigns. The remaining interviews are with national organization field-workers, professional consultants, and leaders of key ballot measure campaigns. The interviews throughout this manuscript were conducted under three different Institutional Review Boards at two different institutions. Many of my earlier interviews with Michigan activists were confidential by requirement, whereas more recent interviews allowed interviewees to choose whether they wanted to make all or part of the interview confidential. When at all possible, I identify the speaker. However, at other times it is necessary to be vague about the identity of the speaker to honor a request for confidentiality.

In addition to my work in the archives and in interviews, I attended three training sessions on how to run campaigns by the National Gay and Lesbian Task Force between 2002 and 2010, including the 2006 Midwest Power Summit, and served as a phone-banking volunteer on two Michigan campaigns.

Overview of Chapters

This book begins by documenting the history of anti-gay ballot measures in the United States. It then provides an analysis of how the LGBT movement learned how to create campaigns to fight anti-gay ballot measures. Chapter 1 provides a detailed background of the ways in which the Religious Right has used direct democracy to limit LGBT rights from 1974 to 2009. This chapter uses an innovative dataset that includes both direct legislation that was attempted by the Religious Right and direct legislation that was put before the voters. These attempted and successful examples of direct legislation demonstrate the constant tactical innovation of the anti-gay Right as activists experimented with referendums, legal-restrictive initiatives like Colorado Amendment 2, "stealth" initiatives that did not even mention sexual orientation, and eventually same-sex marriage bans.

The next four chapters analyze how, from 1974 to 2009, the LGBT movement developed tactics to fight these ballot measures, while engaged in reconciling the at times contradictory relationship between movements and campaigns. Between 1974 and 1991, the movement was young and weak. Local campaigns tried many tactics to win campaigns, and many of these tactics were abandoned later as ineffective.

In the critical time period from 1992 to 1996, the anti-gay Right barraged the LGBT movement with many ballot measures of varying types. The movement responded by developing a stronger movement infrastructure, including field programs in national organizations and a new industry of campaign professionals. This movement infrastructure, along with a victorious campaign in Oregon in 1992, was used to create a "model campaign," which slowly gathered credence among activists, despite dissent. From 1997 to 2003, these model campaign tactics became widely adopted and strongly supported (indeed, expected) within the national movement. Ballot measure campaigns and social movements began to support the development of movement infrastructure in a reiterative fashion. This time period includes a winning streak in ballot measure campaigns, which I analyze with a short case study of Michigan, one of the "winningest states" of the time. This winning streak came to an abrupt end in 2004, when statewide ballot measures to ban same-sex marriage led to a series of devastating defeats between 2004 and 2009. During this time, the LGBT movement reconsidered both campaign tactics and the relationship between ballot measure campaigns and the larger social movement.

Chapter 6 analyzes the relationship between ballot measure campaigns and social movements. It focuses on the ways that ballot measure campaigns may roll back movement gains by analyzing racial coalition building and transgender inclusion during campaigns.

The Conclusion discusses the relationship between social movements and ballot measure campaigns in both the LGBT movement and other movements.

CHAPTER 1

FROM ANITA BRYANT TO CALIFORNIA PROPOSITION 8
THE RELIGIOUS RIGHT'S ATTACK ON LGBT RIGHTS

> If prostitution is the world's oldest profession, antigay politics is
> among the world's oldest obsessions.
>
> Sean Cahill, *The Politics of Same-Sex Marriage*

DIRECT DEMOCRACY, or the proposal and passage of laws through voters rather than legislators, has been a longtime tool of social movements, including those working to derail or restrict minority rights. The anti-gay Religious Right, a movement birthed in the late 1970s that had become a national movement by the early 1990s, has used direct democracy as a tool to effectively roll back LGBT rights. By fighting LGBT rights at the ballot box, the Religious Right has mobilized interested local activists, affected public opinion, and grown as a movement. This chapter documents the history of how the Religious Right used the ballot box to fight LGBT rights from 1974 to 2009. Although the remainder of the book analyzes the LGBT movement, this chapter focuses exclusively on the Religious Right and its long history of using the referendum and initiative process.

This chapter analyzes both the escalation in direct democracy and the increasing tactical innovation of the Religious Right. Many scholars have described the strength of the Religious Right as its constant strategic and tactical innovation.[1] The tactics used by the Right from 1974 to 2009 included everything from the most virulently moralist homophobic attacks to legalistic arguments about changing civil rights laws. Religious Right activists used several different types of direct democracy, from simple referendums that rescind a newly passed law to initiatives that twist legal language to restrict LGBT rights in both the present and the future. Similar to other social movements that use direct democracy to further their goals, the anti-gay Religious Right has used the referendum and initiative process both to further its own goals and to restrict another movement's gains.

1

The Politics of Direct Democracy

Social movements have used direct democracy since it was spread like wildfire by Progressive and Populist activists, who established initiatives in most western states in the early twentieth century as an attempt to circumvent corrupt, partisan state legislatures and educate voters on social issues. For these activists, citizen-sponsored initiatives would make the legislatures accountable to the general public. And indeed, early initiatives were used to pass laws on child welfare, workday length, and prohibition.[2] This trend of social movements using the referendum and initiative process has persisted to this day. It has allowed citizens to vote on abortion, medical marijuana, euthanasia, tax laws, environmental preservation, hunting, gun control, living wages, child labor, nuclear freeze, and health care—all initiatives sponsored by single-interest groups within a larger social movement. For example, the November 2008 ballot included statewide initiatives sponsored by the Religious Right, the animal-rights movement, the marijuana legalization movement, and the pro-life movement.[3]

With direct democracy, citizens can use referendums to overturn existing legislation or can propose new laws with initiatives, including constitutional and charter amendments. Although all states except Delaware allow (and at times require) the legislature to place laws on the ballot, only twenty-seven allow for a citizen-initiated referendum or initiative process. In many cases, this process allows citizens to propose constitutional amendments. Most of these states are located in the western and midwestern part of the United States, as early Progressive and Populist activism focused on these states. However, local cities and towns often have their own referendum and/or initiative process, even if it is not permitted on the state level; for example, Texas does not allow citizens to put referendums or initiatives on the ballot, but residents of Austin and Houston have voted on LGBT-inclusive fair-housing laws and domestic partnership benefits.

The use of the statewide initiative process in particular has changed dramatically over time, as demonstrated in Figure 1, influenced by several social forces. First, the contemporary resurgence in initiative use is often attributed to the success in 1978 of California's Proposition 13 to reduce property taxes.[4] The initiative process has also been stimulated by the rise of professional consultants and an initiative industry, which makes it easier for local activists to collect petitions for referendums and initiatives.[5]

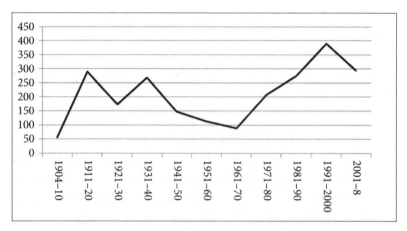

Figure 1. Statewide initiatives by decade, 1904–2008. Data from the Initiative and Referendum Institute.

Other trends, such as the use of initiatives by legislators during campaigning and the increasing use of counterproposals or competing measures, have increased the use of initiative process.[6] State laws about petition signature requirements, requirements (or lack thereof) for legislative approval, and time to collect petitions make it easy to put initiatives on the ballot in states such as California, Colorado, and Oregon, which boast the highest number of referendums and initiatives.[7]

With this growth in statewide initiatives have come concerns about the impact of direct democracy on civil rights. Direct democracy tends to be devastating for the civil rights of minorities. In general, "civil rights laws seek to shift political power from the majority to the minority, creating a conflict steeped in self-interest. Where the civil rights of a political minority are at stake, the absence of the representative filter opens the door to the tyranny."[8] This danger of tyranny has been demonstrated throughout history. In the wake of the Civil War, residents of Georgetown and the city of Washington, D.C., voted on a referendum, the Black Suffrage Bill, to prevent newly emancipated blacks from becoming enfranchised.[9] A statewide referendum in Ohio in 1917 disenfranchised women from their newly won right to vote.[10] In 1946, a California statewide initiative to create a Fair Employment Practice law to protect racial minorities against employment discrimination lost two to one.[11] In 1993, Cincinnati, Ohio, voters decided whether gay men and lesbians would be permanently exempt from future nondiscrimination laws.[12] Californians voted against affirmative action in 1996, the rights of illegal immigrants in 1994, and bilingual education in 1998.[13]

Direct democracy's effect on minorities can be alleviated through intervention by the legislature or judiciary. When Washington, D.C., and Georgetown voters elected in a landslide to rescind the newly acquired suffrage of black men in 1865, their vote was quickly overturned by Congress. States with little judicial or legislative review of ballot measures, such as California and Oregon, face more extreme ballot measures, such that voters have cast ballots in favor of quarantining individuals with HIV/ AIDS, withholding medical treatment from illegal immigrants, and firing gay teachers. Although all of these initiatives either did not pass at the ballot box or were later declared unconstitutional by the courts, votes such as these can have psychological consequences for minorities and divert the resources of social movements.[14]

Not all minority rights are rescinded at the ballot box. For example, the women's suffrage movement achieved women's right to vote in many states long before the national suffrage amendment, often through the initiative process. However, LGBT rights are likely to both be on the ballot and be rescinded. Indeed, counting all 158 referendums and initiatives that made it to the ballot box, voters rejected LGBT rights in 70 percent of all direct legislative measures.[15] Although not all of these ballot measures were sponsored directly by the anti-gay Right, the vast majority were.

Direct Democracy and the Religious Right

The Religious Right is a "broad coalition of pro-family organizations and individuals who have come together to struggle for a conservative Christian vision in the political realm."[16] Scholars of the Right have traced the emergence of the New Right to the Cold War and Barry Goldwater's run for president in 1964. The anti-gay Religious Right, however, emerged within the New Right from the rising involvement of evangelical Christians in politics in 1970s, specifically the emergence of the pro-life movement in response to *Roe v. Wade*, the development of the antifeminist movement to defeat the Equal Rights Amendment (ERA), and mobilization to respond to the growth of the lesbian and gay movement.[17] In a survey of Religious Right literature, Didi Herman notes that evangelical Christian journals did not acknowledge the lesbian and gay movement until the 1960s and then did not encourage countermovement activities against the movement until the late 1980s.[18]

Direct democracy is an important arena of contention for interactions between the Religious Right and the LGBT movement because of its frequent use by the anti-gay Right.[19] The Right has achieved more tangible success in its fight against gay rights using the initiative process than either the judiciary or the legislative process.[20] At the ballot box, activists can repeal local legislation and create new legislation by mobilizing public opinion and homophobia rather than navigating the complexities of either the courts or legislatures. Beyond changing public policy, "antigay political entrepreneurs compete in a game that involves building political capital, establishing and mobilizing a base of supporters, moving mass opinions about gays and lesbians, and, eventually, constraining the discretion of elected legislators."[21] Anti-gay leader Kelly Walton, who led an unsuccessful initiative campaign to limit future LGBT rights laws in Idaho, bragged that his campaign was "able to rob left-wing candidates of precious campaign money that was devoted to this initiative."[22] Although later chapters explore the ways that ballot measure campaigns can mobilize LGBT activists and create LGBT organizations, Religious Right–sponsored ballot measures also have negative consequences for the LGBT movement. In her book *How the Religious Right Shaped Lesbian and Gay Activism*, Tina Fetner describes how anti-gay activists have effectively diverted the agenda of the LGBT movement for the last thirty years, frequently through the use of direct democracy. Instead of pursuing its own agenda to achieve legislative or public policy advances, the LGBT movement has continually found itself spending time, money, and energy organizing local communities to defeat referendums and initiatives, and many of those campaigns do little to advance gay rights.

One of the ways that the anti-gay Right is so effective at diverting the agenda of the LGBT movement is through the ongoing tactical innovation in its use of the referendum and initiative process. In this tactical innovation, the Religious Right continually tried new techniques to win at the ballot box, spurring the LGBT movement to respond to an array of tactics over the last thirty-five years.

Tactical Innovation

Between 1974 and 2009 the Religious Right attempted more than 245 referendums and initiatives across the country. These included referendums to rescind small town nondiscrimination ordinances that included sexual orientation and/or gender identity, virulent statewide anti-gay initiatives, and initiatives to create constitutional amendments banning same-sex marriage. The Religious Right constantly altered its use of direct democracy during these years, changing the type (e.g., referendums, constitutional amendments), subject (e.g., gay teachers, same-sex marriage), and level (e.g., statewide, local) of referendums and initiatives. This rapid and continuous tactical innovation is common for countermovements that are trying to catch another social movement off guard with new, effective tactics.[23] By continually changing the nature of the electoral battle, the Right may force the LGBT movement to engage in continuous tactical innovation as well.

The largest tactical change was moving from an almost exclusive use of referendums to an almost exclusive use of initiatives to fight LGBT rights. Scholar John Green refers to referendums as "reactive opposition" or a response to the gains of the LGBT movement.[24] Nondiscrimination legislation, either at the state or local level, has been an effective tool of the LGBT movement to establish protections against discrimination in public accommodations, employment and housing for sexual orientation and/ or gender identity in the absence of federal legislation.[25] Religious Right activists respond to this legislation by attempting to rescind it with a referendum, playing "defense" to the LGBT movement. However, initiatives are forms of "proactive opposition" or playing "offense as defense" in the fight against LGBT rights.[26] As one anti-gay activist proclaimed, "We want to take the battle to the enemy."[27] With initiatives, Religious Right activists had more options for tactical innovation in the language and type of initiative. Initiatives were also more effective at diverting the agenda of the LGBT movement. However, initiatives were often reactive in their own way, a response to failed Religious Right legislation or advances of the LGBT movement.

Although referendums were a response to existing gains by the LGBT movement, such as domestic partnerships or nondiscrimination ordinances, with an initiative the Religious Right could address a wide range of subjects, including any of the following: gay adoption, teachers, or foster parents; media depictions of homosexuality; homosexuality in the school curriculum; affirmative action for LGBT individuals; and access to marriage for same-sex couples. Some of these initiatives were attempts to constrain future LGBT rights legislation or provide a radical departure from the state's existing policies.[28] The two most common types of initiatives are "legal-restrictive initiatives" and marriage or partnership initiatives. Legal-restrictive initiatives are attempts to constrain future LGBT rights legislation by limiting government support for homosexuality or the possibility of passing LGBT rights legislation in the future, along with typically eliminating any existing protections. Thirty-one percent of all attempted direct legislation by the Religious Right has been the use of legal-restrictive initiatives of one form or another. Marriage or partnership initiatives are attempts to constrain or repeal legislation that granted relationship recognition rights—such as domestic partnerships, civil unions, and marriage—to same-sex couples, which account overall for 25 percent of all attempted direct legislation by the anti-gay Right. Even within both of these commonly used initiatives, there was tactical innovation in the language and legal implications of each initiative. Additional initiative topics include HIV/AIDS (3.3 percent); an exclusive focus on schools, teachers, or adoption (4.4 percent); and other miscellaneous topics (0.8 percent).

Other tactical innovations included the changing level of direct legislation from the local level (i.e., town, city, or county) to the state level. Although most attempted direct legislation occurred on the local level (63 percent), as the anti-gay Religious Right grew in strength and resources, more direct legislation was attempted on the state level (37 percent). Anti-gay activists also experimented with campaign tactics such as political language, coalition building with new groups, and the level of visible homophobia in their messaging and leadership.

Attempted and Successful Direct Legislation

The preceding account of tactical innovation includes both direct legislation that made it to the ballot box and direct legislation that was merely attempted by anti-gay activists. There have been many studies, primarily in political science, on anti-gay referendums and initiatives that come before voters.[29] With one exception, existing studies of anti-gay direct democracy only examine referendums and initiatives that make it to the ballot box.[30] I assert that we cannot fully understand the tactical innovation of the Religious Right without analyzing both attempted ballot measures and those that made it successfully to the ballot box.

Attempted ballot measures either were submitted to the relevant city or state clerk for approval (where applicable) or attracted attention in the local newspaper when petitions were publicly collected yet did not make it to the ballot box.[31] These anti-gay referendums and initiatives included any direct legislation, local or statewide, that either explicitly targeted LGBT rights or was fought by the LGBT movement.[32] *Successful* ballot measures made it to the ballot box. In this chapter, *passed* direct legislation refers to a positive outcome for the Religious Right.

In general, it is common for direct legislation to not make it past the petition collection process. For example, in California, of all attempted statewide initiatives filed, only 26 percent made it to the ballot, and 8 percent were passed by voters.[33] In this dataset of anti-gay ballot measures, 60 percent of all direct legislation attempted by the anti-gay Right made it to the ballot box. And in a survey of local nondiscrimination ordinances from 1972 to 1993, more than one out of three passed ordinances that include sexual orientation was challenged in efforts to overturn it.[34] If anything, this data suggests an underestimation of attempted anti-gay direct legislation.[35]

Examining only successful referendums and initiatives obscures tactical innovation in both the Religious Right and the LGBT movement. For example, a rash of legal-restrictive initiatives in 1992 has often been described by scholars and activists alike as a new, suddenly developed tactical innovation of the anti-gay Right. However, the Religious Right had been unsuccessfully experimenting with special rights language in initiatives for at least eight years. Even if these attempted initiatives did not appear before voters, they provided the foundation for future tactical innovation by the anti-gay Right. As demonstrated in the remainder of the book, the LGBT movement innovated with pre-ballot legal challenges and other tactics to keep direct legislation off the ballot, an innovation that is lost when only successful direct legislation is examined. And even if the Religious Right could not succeed in getting an initiative on the ballot, the local LGBT community may still have mobilized significant time, energy, and money in anticipation of the initiative.

The Religious Right innovated with direct legislation not just through repeated attempts at new language or type of initiative but also by innovating within a certain geographic area.

Battleground States

Although the Religious Right sponsored referendums and initiatives from Maine to Hawaii, a few states bore the brunt of anti-gay organizing. More than two-thirds of all attempted referendums and initiatives between 1974 and 2009 took place in seven states — Oregon, California, Michigan, Florida, Washington, Maine, and Colorado — as demonstrated by Figure 2.[36] In these battleground states, LGBT rights were contested at the ballot box in surges of Religious Right opposition, concentrated in the 1990s. Although other states were the site of critical ballot measure battles — such as Cincinnati, Ohio, in 1993 and Hawaii in 1998 — these seven battleground states became center stage. These states were disproportionately targeted owing to the ease of their direct legislation requirements and the strength of the Religious Right affiliate.

According to David Magleby, political scientist and eminent scholar of direct legislation, the different rates of statewide initiatives can be directly attributed to the ease of signature requirements in different states.[37] The Religious Right targeted these battleground states because of the ease of getting referendums or initiatives on the ballot. Many of these states have a lax citizen initiative process in which citizens frequently propose initiatives with low signature requirements and limited pre-ballot judicial review. With only one exception, the battleground states for anti-gay activity mirror the states with the most general statewide initiative activity. Oregon, California, and Colorado are the top three states for statewide initiatives. Michigan and Washington fall in the top ten states, and Maine falls in the top twenty.[38] Florida does not fit into this pattern; however, most successful referendums and initiatives in Florida have occurred at the local, not statewide, level.

As I will demonstrate later in this chapter, battleground states only developed with the emergence of a strong statewide anti-gay organization, often an affiliate of a larger national organization. Periods of intense anti-gay organizing at the ballot box have historically been led by one strong Religious Right organization within that state; for example, the Traditional

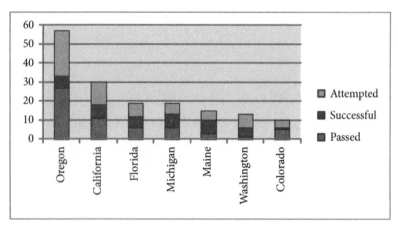

Figure 2. Battleground states, 1974–2009.

Values Coalition in California in the late 1980s, the Oregon Citizens Alliance in the 1990s, and the American Family Association in Michigan and Florida all spearheaded a flurry of local attempted anti-gay referendums and initiatives. In Colorado, Colorado for Family Values and other groups supported by the Colorado Springs organization Focus on the Family led several anti-gay referendums and initiatives. In some of these states, an anti-gay campaign industry developed supporting this organization, such as in Oregon, "where the drafting, circulation, and qualification of antigay initiatives became something of a cottage industry."[39] Through the coordinated efforts of one group, the Religious Right can flood LGBT communities with anti-gay ballot initiatives, depleting resources and dividing group efforts.

Ironically, because of the nature of LGBT campaign tactical development documented in chapters 3 and 4 of this book, battleground states became losing states for the anti-gay Right after 1996. Although Religious Right activists passed the majority of their sponsored legislation before 1996, after 1996 their ability to win in battleground states declined dramatically. In general, the Religious Right passes legislation at a much higher rate in non-battleground states (88 percent) than battleground states (62 percent). And the anti-gay Right has the lowest rate of success in states such as Maine, Washington, and Michigan. Yet, even with the failing rates over time in battleground states, these states were often ground zero for tactical innovation, as anti-gay activists experimented with new ways of passing referendums and initiatives.

A Short History of the Anti-Gay Right at the Ballot Box

As demonstrated in Figure 3, the numbers of attempted, successful, and passed direct legislation waned and waxed as the anti-gay Right grew in strength and organization, focused on the ballot box as an important arena of contention, and innovated with new types of direct legislation. Transitions from one time period to the next are often marked with a significant victory or defeat for either movement. Overall, the Religious Right had periods of consistent success in getting direct democracy measures on the ballot and passed. The movement also had periods of intense tactical innovation in which many referendums and initiatives were attempted but did not successfully end up on the ballot.

The use of referendums and initiatives by the Religious Right can be divided up into five distinct time periods based on the number and type of direct democracy measures. From 1974 to 1987, the anti-gay Right developed into a national social movement, and Right-sponsored ballot measures were primarily referendums that were reactive to the gains of the LGBT movement. From 1988 to 1992, the anti-gay Right grew as a movement, as it sponsored and supported more statewide initiatives and innovated tactically with the development of proactive opposition, the legal-restrictive initiative. From 1993 to 1996, anti-gay activists across the country attempted legal-restrictive initiatives, ultimately abandoning the tactic as a statewide initiative after it was defeated in the Supreme Court

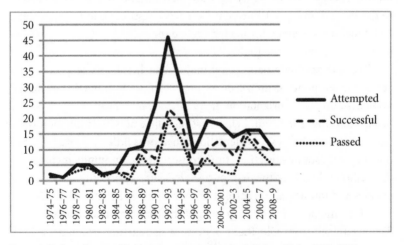

Figure 3. Referendums and initiatives sponsored by the Religious Right, 1974–2009.

case *Romer v. Evans* in 1996. From 1997 to 2003, the anti-gay Right tried a wide range of tactics, ultimately growing into the marriage movement focused on restricting access to marriage for same-sex couples. Initiatives to ban same-sex marriage became the primary focus of anti-gay activism from 2004 to 2009. The following sections document the growth and change of the anti-gay Religious Right as a movement and the tactical innovation in its use of direct legislation over time.

1974–87 Referendums

In 1974, the anti-gay Religious Right was not yet a national movement; anti-gay activism grew out of small, localized social networks that ran through Christian churches and radio and television shows. Initially, anti-gay activism was led by dominant figures such as Anita Bryant, and this activism fizzled out quickly when those figures stepped down. But by 1987, an organized anti-gay Religious Right existed, a national movement connected through networks between local and statewide organizations that grew during this period. Anti-gay referendums sponsored by Religious Right activists were both a cause and a consequence of growing anti-gay social networks. As the movement grew in strength, it became less reactive to the gains of the LGBT movement through using referendums and instead began its own tactical innovation to curb LGBT rights. During this time period, of the twenty-nine attempted ballot measures, 75 percent were referendums and 10 percent were legal-restrictive initiatives. These ballot measures were highly likely to get on the ballot box (65 percent) and result in a victory for the Right (73 percent).

The anti-gay Right had not yet mobilized when LGBT activists began passing local, nondiscrimination ordinances that prohibited discrimination based on sexual orientation. In 1972, lesbian and gay college students in East Lansing, Michigan, helped pass the first nondiscrimination ordinance that included sexual orientation. There was little organized opposition, beyond routine objections from conservative community members or the Catholic church, to the first fourteen local gay rights ordinances passed in cities and municipalities across the country between 1972 and 1974.[40]

This time period saw the growth of the New Right, a movement that distanced itself from Old Right politics of segregation and aligned itself instead with big business, moral traditionalism, and the revival of the

Republican party.[41] In the early 1970s, the New Right had not yet mobilized white evangelical Christians who would constitute the majority of anti-gay activists. Although connected through a growing network of radio shows, churches, and television shows like Jerry Falwell's *The Old Time Gospel Hour*, many white fundamentalist Christians at the time refrained from involvement in the secular political world.[42]

There were signs during this time, however small, that anti-gay Religious Right organizing would grow to challenge the LGBT movement. In 1974, in Boulder, Colorado, a bitterly divisive referendum overturned a newly passed nondiscrimination ordinance that included protection for sexual orientation. Although the referendum led to a recall drive against the city's mayor and a closeted city council member, the opposition was mainly routine, coming from a few outraged individuals and the membership of certain churches. Glenda Russell, a lesbian resident of Boulder, remembers that "there was enough antipathy for homosexuality floating around in general that you didn't need a campaign."[43] Unlike Miami Dade in 1977, the Boulder referendum received scant national attention.[44] The next year, the California Coalition of Concerned Citizens filed petitions for a ballot initiative to overturn the recent repeal of California's sodomy law, alarming local gays into creating their own organization, hiring a campaign manager, and beginning fund-raising.[45] Neither of these attempts resulted in the rise of prominent leaders on the Right or the growth of an anti-gay organization.

Bryant and Briggs, 1977–79

However, when Anita Bryant, former Miss America contestant and spokesperson for Florida orange juice, mobilized her followers in opposition to the newly passed nondiscrimination ordinance in Miami–Dade County, Florida, her role in the opposition received national visibility.[46] Bryant's campaign persuaded voters with language about religious rights and influence on local children, implying that all gay men were pedophiles and looking to recruit children. This referendum in 1977 was the beginning of the first wave of anti-gay activism, a series of referendum campaigns that lasted for two years and were led by figureheads like Bryant.[47]

The Dade County victory emboldened Religious Right activists nationally; they sponsored a spate of referendums in cities across the country in 1978, many of which were visibly and economically supported by the

Anita Bryant Ministries, Protect America's Children, with Anita Bryant herself as a spokesperson. Within two years, ordinances were overturned by referendum in Wichita, Kansas; Eugene, Oregon; and St. Paul, Minnesota. Religious Right activists were unsuccessful in their attempt to overturn the Seattle, Washington, ordinance but threatened many more newly passed ordinances across the nation. The media attention garnered by Bryant brought the use of referendums to the attention of local religious activists as a tool to respond to the growing number of local and state laws that prohibited discrimination based on sexual orientation.[48] Referendums became the most common tactic, accounting for more than 75 percent of all attempted and successful uses of direct democracy by the anti-gay Right between 1974 and 1987.

This initial wave of referendums also gave birth to the first innovative initiative sponsored by the burgeoning anti-gay Religious Right. The California Defend Our Children Initiative was a response to a 1975 California law that protected gay and lesbian teachers from being fired. California State Senator John Briggs, who worked with Anita Bryant in Dade County, sponsored this initiative, popularly called the Briggs Initiative, that would have required the firing of teachers who were lesbian or gay, or who advocated homosexuality.[49] Overwhelmingly opposed by teachers' unions and then-Governor Ronald Reagan, the Briggs Initiative lost at the ballot box by a million votes.[50]

Despite its successes, this first wave of anti-gay organizing died quickly and left few lasting resources. The first campaigns lacked political sophistication, rarely used new technologies like direct mail, and had difficulty mobilizing politically apathetic fundamentalists and evangelicals.[51] In addition, these campaigns relied too heavily on Bryant and Briggs as figureheads, and faltered as both leaders experienced personal issues such as Bryant's divorce. However, some networks and organizations were created that would become important in the next wave of anti-gay organizing. Activism in California and in Florida strengthened an anti-gay activist network, including the formation of groups like Christian Voice, "a major Christian Right electoral vehicle of the 1980s," and Focus on the Family.[52] These early organizations rallied against a range of issues, including abortion, sex education, and feminism, but were home to early anti-gay organizing as well. These early campaigns also trained future Religious Right leaders such as Jerry Falwell, who worked in the Dade County campaign and soon founded the Moral Majority, an anti-gay organization that would mobilize the Right in the 1980s.[53] The executive director of the Briggs campaign, California Defend Our Children, was the Reverend Lou Sheldon, who later founded the Traditional Values Coalition (TVC), an anti-gay organization that sponsored referendums and initiatives across California in the 1980s.[54] Although not yet a national movement, the Religious Right entered the 1980s with more networks among a few key anti-gay religious leaders along with national attention from the Miami Dade and Briggs campaigns.

Growing Organizations, 1980–87

The election of Ronald Reagan in 1980, which combined the mobilization of evangelical Christians with "the political arousal of conservative economic elites," ushered in a new era of Religious Right organizing.[55] The second wave of anti-gay organizing, from 1980 to 1987, demonstrated the beginnings of a national anti-gay and (increasingly) "pro-family" movement, as national anti-gay organizations grew stronger and more supportive of both local activism and national legislation. As HIV/AIDS spread in the United States, the Religious Right harnessed panic and fear about AIDS to increase fund-raising and anti-gay animosity.

During this time, the New Right started and developed major organizations that contributed to anti-gay activism. Jerry Falwell's organization the Moral Majority "marked the religious right's official entrance into interest-group politics."[56] Anti-gay organizations drew strength from the growing pro-life and antifeminist movements, including Phyllis Schlafly's decade-long attack on the Equal Rights Amendment (ERA) through her organization Eagle Forum.[57] These early Right organizations were able to grow on the voting power and political mobilization of Christian evangelicals. For example, the Moral Majority mobilized and registered evangelical voters in 1980 for Reagan's election.[58]

In the wake of Reagan's election, the initial focus of Religious Right organizations was passing federal legislation to reinstate school prayer, redirect government funding, and restrict abortion. An example of this legislation was the unsuccessful Family Protection Act of 1981, which was sponsored by Nevada Republican Senator Paul Laxalt. Often referred to as a "Christmas tree for the New Right," the Family Protection Act included provisions for school prayer, the restriction of minors' access to abortion, parental control over textbooks, traditional roles for women, opposing federal statutes on child abuse, and prohibiting the promotion or support of homosexuality by the government.[59] The bill was "designed to strengthen the American family... to preserve [its] integrity to foster and protect [its] viability by emphasizing family responsibilities in education, tax assistance, religion and other areas related to the family and to promote the virtues of the family."[60] After limited success on the federal level for its "moral issues agenda," the Right moved "from an exclusive focus on making policy change at the federal level and, instead, dug their heels in for a long, multi-faceted struggle" that included direct action protests and local electoral politics.[61]

To develop strength for this struggle, growing Right organizations drew on emerging technologies, such as direct-mail fund-raising.[62] Millionaire Richard A. Viguerie helped develop computer lists of New Right voters to use in innovative direct-mail fund-raising by diverse Right organizations such as the Conservative Caucus and the Committee for Survival of Free Congress, often coordinating fund-raising for local campaigns through letter-writing campaigns.[63] Toward the end of the 1980s, Falwell and the Moral Majority sent direct mail that used AIDS and anti-gay sentiments to raise money. For example, in a 1987 fund-raising letter, Falwell asserted that gay men donate blood because "they know they are going to die—and they are going to take as many people with them as they can."[64]

Using fear of AIDS to raise funds was indicative of the growing use of public-health (and eventually legal) messaging during referendum and initiative campaigns. Embedding public-health concerns within a growing pro-family and family values message, the anti-gay Right steered away from explicitly religious justifications for their activism. Paul Cameron, a psychologist who resigned from membership in the American Psychological Association in 1983 while under an ethics investigation, pioneered this public-health approach. Cameron conducted questionable survey research on gay men and their sex habits, generating bogus statistics, including one that reported the average life expectancy of a gay man as thirty-nine years. Cameron made his debut during a 1981 debate over the Lincoln, Nebraska, gay rights ordinance, where he introduced these statistics, along with invented stories about child victims of homosexual pedophiles.[65] After the Lincoln ordinance was rescinded in a referendum, Cameron assisted other referendum campaigns, including the Committee for Public Awareness, which was formed to repeal two gay rights laws in Houston in 1984.[66] Some local activists also experimented with legal messages that claimed gay men and lesbians were trying to usurp civil rights laws. For example, in 1980, a San Jose, California, Religious Right group asserted that two local referendums on gay rights "are not civil rights issues at all. Instead they give gay people special privileges, opportunities, and job considerations because of their sexual lifestyle. Gays feel their sexual choice makes them a special minority deserving of special treatment and protection."[67]

With a new arsenal of language opposing LGBT rights, local anti-gay activists used referendums liberally, and successfully placed nine referendums on the ballot during this time period while attempting four others. Local activists also innovated with initiative language that would prevent gay rights ordinances in the future and restrict support for LGBT rights by public officials. An initiative developed in 1982 in Austin, Texas, would have allowed discrimination based on sexual orientation in housing by using convoluted, confusing language: it stated that "it shall not be unlawful to deny housing on the basis of sexual orientation," thereby preempting a local fair-housing ordinance.[68] The Austin initiative was not passed by voters, and lost 65–35 in the most dramatic defeat of the 1980s. In 1986, a Washington State group attempted both a statewide and a local initiative in King County that would eliminate "special rights" for gay men and lesbians. The statewide initiative was a response to failed legislation sponsored by State Representative Glenn Dobbs that would have overturned state and local gay rights ordinances and prevented both the government and schools from hiring gays. This failed legislation was likely inspired by the failed Family Protection Act.[69] The Washington Religious Right was unable to get either of these initiatives on the ballot owing to legal challenges and insufficient petitions.[70] Consistent with the Briggs initiative, these initiatives were responsive to either successful LGBT legislation or to failed Religious Right legislation.

Reflecting the growing trend of legislative candidates to use the initiative process to garner public attention and advance their own causes, radical activist Lyndon LaRouche sponsored a statewide HIV/AIDS initiative in California in 1986. Proposition 64, commonly known as the LaRouche Initiative, mandated state reporting of individuals with AIDS, the inclusion of AIDS in quarantine and isolation statutes, and a limitation on the occupations open to individuals with AIDS. LaRouche was a campaign spokesman, and he asserted during a radio interview that "A person with AIDS running around is like a person with a machine gun running around shooting up a neighborhood."[71] Even after the initiative failed at the ballot box, 29 percent to 71 percent, LaRouche asserted that "what I represent is a growing movement . . . the movement is coming strong all the time."[72]

Although the LaRouche Initiative mimicked the Briggs Initiative in both its radical departure from state policy and its vitriolic language, this wave of anti-gay organizing was stronger than the earlier Briggs and Bryant wave. Even with little coordination of campaigns by national organizations, campaigns shared resources; for example, many campaigns used psychologist Paul Cameron or Judi Wilson, a consultant who had worked on the 1977 and 1980 Miami Dade campaigns.[73] Toward the end of this time period, anti-gay activism became more concentrated in a few states, often in response to growing LGBT activism. Some of this organizing in battleground states was coordinated by growing regional organizations, such as the Traditional Values Coalition (TVC) in California. There were also signs of increasing anti-gay tactical innovation in the use of direct mail and development of political messaging.

1988–92 Innovative Initiatives

In 1988, as Ronald Reagan finished his second presidential term, the New Right was left with a void in presidential leadership. The New Right was both growing exponentially and experiencing a decline of such major anti-gay organizations as the Moral Majority and Christian Voice.[74] In this contradictory period, the New Right became more focused on opposing LGBT rights, particularly through proactive opposition. Through a series of tactical innovations, anti-gay activists developed the legal-restrictive initiative, which would curb government recognition of LGBT rights. This period culminated in two statewide legal-restrictive initiatives in Oregon and Colorado in 1992. Of the forty-one attempted ballot measures during this time period, most were either referendums on nondiscrimination legislation (48.8 percent) or legal-restrictive initiatives (24.4 percent), although the Right also sponsored initiatives to restrict the rights of people with AIDS (14 percent) and to eliminate newly passed domestic partnership laws (9.7 percent). Slightly more than half of the ballot measures made it to the ballot box and 57 percent ended in a victory for the Right.

This activism was led by a new national organization, the Christian Coalition, and a growing anti-gay industry. After Pat Robertson briefly ran for the Republican nomination for president, he used his list of evangelical supporters to start the most important national Right organization of the late 1980s, the Christian Coalition.[75] To complement the Christian Coalition, a whole industry of anti-gay Religious Right leaders, organizations, and literature arose to address both HIV/AIDS and the growing strength of the LGBT movement. These anti-gay organizations increased their involvement in grassroots politics as part of a shift in focus within the New Right from national to local politics. This local focus included "stealth" campaigns to get Right-supportive city council and school-board members elected.[76] According to scholar Sara Diamond, "For the Christian Right, the strategic lesson of the 1980s was to keep one figurative foot inside formal Republican Party circles and another planted firmly within evangelical churches."[77]

With the increasing attention to AIDS and growing strength of anti-gay organizations, opposition to LGBT rights became more central to the mainstream Christian agenda, expressed through both anti-gay ballot initiatives and public efforts to curtail any federal funding that was supportive of LGBT rights or individuals. Two examples of the latter trend are opposition to federally funded safer sex materials that express approval of homosexuality and the defunding of the NEA Four, four artists whose National Endowment for the Arts funding was revoked owing to the controversial nature of their art, which in many cases focused on gay or lesbian themes. These activities brought anti-gay politics firmly into mainstream Christianity, demonstrated by the increased space given to anti-gay rhetoric in the early 1990s in mainstream Christian journals.[78] This anti-gay activism culminated in the 1992 Republican National Convention, where anti-gay rhetoric was subsumed under a focus on "family values."[79] The Republican convention was a rallying call on the Right to fight LGBT advances supported by the Democratic Party.

The anti-gay Right increasingly sponsored referendums to rescind existing LGBT rights legislation, including domestic partnership rights in San Francisco. In 1988, the LGBT community in Oregon faced the Oregon Citizens Alliance (OCA) for the first time, as the OCA sponsored the first successful statewide initiative to rescind the governor's executive order prohibiting discrimination based on sexual orientation.[80] The growth of these referendums and their location in increasingly battleground states demonstrates the growing power and involvement of established anti-gay Right organizations. For example, in California the TVC became involved in anti-gay referendums and initiatives in the late 1980s. It provided support for ballot measures across the state, including three statewide initiatives to target people with HIV/AIDS and the repeal of nondiscrimination protection for individuals with AIDS in Concord, California, in 1989.[81] After the Concord vote, a TVC spokesperson remarked: "This shows that it is possible to repeal the laws. We're not going to go city by city, county by county repealing laws, but there could be a few more soon."[82] In other cities, groups modeled themselves after the TVC, as in Irvine, where the anti-gay campaign, the Irvine Values Coalition, used the Reverend Sheldon as a public spokesman.[83] The Christian Coalition supported a 1990 battle over an anti-gay initiative in Broward County, Florida. It boasted in its national fund-raising letters that it "led the charge" and "won a major political victory" in Broward County, encouraging activists in other states to "duplicate this success in your city and state and throughout the nation."[84]

At the end of the 1980s, the Religious Right shifted focus from the use of referendums to a period of rapid innovation in use of the initiative process. Although the anti-gay Right had experimented with a few unsuccessful initiatives in the 1970s and early 1980s, 1988 to 1992 was an intense four-year period of innovating that resulted in the legal-restrictive initiative. The legal-restrictive initiative was an attempt to create an initiative that would restrict the ability of the government, whether local or statewide, to pass LGBT rights laws or support homosexuality more broadly. Many of these attempted initiatives included provisions to both eliminate existing LGBT rights laws and prevent future ones. One of the first attempts to restrict future government support of LGBT rights was in 1978 in Seattle, an initiative that both repealed the existing ordinance and prohibited all future action on the part of city officials to grant rights based on sexual orientation.[85] Rather than respond directly to the growing power of the LGBT movement in passing local legislation with referendums, the use of these initiatives in the late 1980s showed the anti-gay Right going on the offensive.

During the tactical innovation to develop this initiative, anti-gay activists attempted a series of draconian initiatives that were inspired by the failed Family Protection Act in Washington in 1986, and the NEA fight.

In 1991, ten out of eighteen direct-democracy measures were attempted initiatives, the first time that initiatives had outnumbered referendums as a tactic of the Religious Right. These initiatives included unsuccessful attempts to require voter approval for LGBT rights laws in Maine, California, and St. Paul, Minnesota, and to prohibit the government from promoting homosexuality in the California cities of Irvine, Concord, and Riverside. These initiatives were increasingly extreme and draconian, including attempts to make Josephine County, Oregon, an "AIDS-Free Zone" in 1989 and to bar gay and lesbian foster parents in Massachusetts in 1991.[86] Ultimately, none of these initiatives made it to the ballot box, either because of petition collection problems or because they were defeated during pre-ballot legal challenges.

In 1992, these attempts to craft a legal-restrictive initiative bore fruit as anti-gay activists successfully sponsored legal-restrictive initiatives in two cities and two states.[87] In Oregon, the Oregon Citizens Alliance (OCA) led by vocal anti-gay activist Lon Mabon, sponsored legal-restrictive initiatives in the cities of Corvallis and Springfield.[88] These legal-restrictive initiatives were test cases for the Oregon statewide initiative in November 1992, Ballot Measure 9. This was a broad, moralistic initiative that eliminated future and existing gay rights legislation, paralleled homosexuality with sadomasochistm and pedophilia, and prohibited government promotion of homosexuality.[89] Ballot Measure 9 was one of the most extreme anti-gay initiatives in that it required the firing of lesbian and gay teachers in public schools (along with anyone openly supportive of LGBT rights) and the removal of all books approving of homosexuality from government-funded libraries. OCA tactics were virulently homophobic and often connected to the Oregon far Right. For example, one of the OCA flyers suggested that LGBT activists were inspired by *Mein Kampf*.[90] Although the anti-gay Right did not pass Ballot Measure 9, OCA leader Mabon seemed invigorated by the loss and asserted his plans to pursue future legal-restrictive initiatives.

In the same election, Colorado anti-gay activists sponsored their own statewide initiative. Focus on the Family, a growing anti-gay organization, moved to conservative Colorado Springs in October 1991 and provided support for a new wave of anti-gay ballot initiatives. In 1992, the organization Colorado for Family Values (CFV) sponsored Amendment 2, a legalistic initiative that eliminated future and existing gay rights laws in the state. CFV had originally mobilized to defeat an ordinance in conservative

Colorado Springs. Colorado Amendment 2 distinguished between "true" minorities and gays by using legal language about "protected classes" and "minority status." This initiative was "not an aberration; rather, Amendment 2 was a logical progression in a national, concerted [Religious Right] antigay effort of over two decades' duration."[91] The advisory board of CFV included anti-gay leaders from all over the country, including representatives from TVC, Concerned Women for America, Focus on the Family, and the Eagle Forum.[92] When Colorado Amendment 2 passed in a narrow victory, it launched CFV into the limelight.

One innovation that is typically attributed to CFV politics is the use of a secular, legalistic argument about LGBT rights, which gained popularity after Colorado Amendment 2. This legalistic argument about how LGBT rights were "special rights" usurping the rights of others displaced religious language opposing gay rights with a language of "secularism and accommodationist pluralism."[93] Religious Right activists had used references to preferential treatment and special rights since the 1970s.[94] Some of this language was developed when Lou Sheldon of the TVC and Pat Robertson of the Christian Coalition led a "national summit meeting on homosexuality" that addressed the issue of how lesbian and gay individuals want "special protection over and above the equal rights already given to all Americans."[95] This argument was popularized by a widely distributed article by Tony Marco, mastermind of the Colorado initiative, who questioned whether gays were "oppressed minorities or counterfeits?"[96] Part of this secular argument about "special rights" was a new image of the Religious Right as supportive of civil rights for "deserving" minorities such as African Americans but opposed to "undeserving" minorities such as LGBT activists. The anti-gay Right used special rights political messaging to divide potential political allies by exacerbating existing tensions about race and class in LGBT politics. Through this messaging, the Right reaffirms gayness as whiteness, creating divisions between a presumed white LGBT movement and the presumed heterosexual African American community. For example, in a 1990 Tacoma, Washington, referendum campaign, Religious Right activists suggested that "the only valid civil rights are determined by race, religion and nationality," and in 1991 antigay activists attempting a referendum in Pittsburgh stated that gay rights laws "will make it harder for blacks to get jobs in Pittsburgh (because) there will be a well-organized and affluent special interest group ahead of them."[97] The next section gives a more detailed overview of the development of Marco's treatise into racialized political messaging about race and LGBT rights.

The 1992 Republican National Convention sparked a culture war when the Republican "pro-family" platform included a multipronged attack on LGBT rights in legislation, public education, and the arts.[98] The 1992 Republican convention, together with Colorado Amendment 2 and Oregon Ballot Measure 9, was a sign of growing anti-gay movement power. As national and local organizations coordinated their efforts and shared strategy, the Right moved into the most aggressive period of anti-gay organizing to date.

1993–96 Special Rights Initiatives

Buoyed by a surge of energy at the 1992 Republican Convention and the passage of Colorado Amendment 2, along with the growing opposition to the election of President Bill Clinton and Republican takeover of Congress in 1994, the Right escalated its use of direct legislation from 1993 to 1996, attempting more referendums and initiatives than ever before. Many scholars suggest that this time period marked a resurgence of the New Right, which included large-scale mobilization of anti-gay activists in battleground states.[99] In the mid-1990s, national organizations like the Christian Coalition swelled to more than 1 million members and a $25 million annual budget.[100] A growing anti-gay cottage industry produced videos, pamphlets, and books as resources for anti-gay activists. The anti-gay Right gained more public support and visibility than at any other time in U.S. history by addressing federal issues such as gays in the military and the threat of same-sex marriage in Hawaii in 1993. There was also an explosion of political connections between national and state activists owing to the use of the legal-restrictive initiative during this time period.

Between 1993 and 1996, anti-gay activists attempted legal-restrictive initiatives in thirteen states and more than thirty cities and towns.[101] Of the seventy-nine attempted ballot measures during this time period, legal-restrictive initiatives (70.9 percent) dramatically outnumbered referendums (19.0 percent).[102] However, only half of all attempted ballot measures made it to the voters. These included initiatives modeled after Colorado

Amendment 2 or Oregon Ballot Measure 9 and attempts to create a new type of statewide "stealth" initiative. Few statewide initiatives made it to the ballot box, but the presence of active Religious Right organizations collecting petitions for legal-restrictive initiatives in thirteen states mobilized LGBT activists across the country.

After the defeat of Ballot Measure 9, Lon Mabon and the OCA began building momentum for a 1994 Oregon statewide ballot initiative, Measure 12, by supporting more than thirty anti-gay initiatives in small towns across Oregon.[103]

> Mabon hoped the local ballot initiatives would bring the issue of gay rights to small-town Oregon, the OCA's core constituency, relatively free of the hype and posturing of statewide, media-driven campaigns. He cultivated leaders who were known in their communities, who had broad networks of contacts that they could tap, and learned hundreds of people's names by heart, calling them and writing them personal letters to elicit their support. This "plain folks" populist style appealed to a constituency that distrusted the media, and large institutions in general.[104]

The OCA consistently won these rural initiatives, which often took place in areas with little or no visible LGBT community.[105] The new initiatives in 1994 mirrored Ballot Measure 9 but adopted more legalistic language from Colorado Amendment 2 by reducing the parallels between homosexuality and bestiality in favor of prohibiting the government from "advising or teaching children, students, employees that homosexuality equates legally or socially with race, other protected classifications." Even with these changes in language, this initiative did not pass in Oregon.

During this intense period of anti-gay organizing, regional associations like OCA and CFV expanded their influence beyond Oregon and Colorado. OCA created affiliates in Nevada, Washington, and Idaho that attempted statewide legal-restrictive initiatives. Only Idaho's initiative successfully made it to the ballot and was defeated by Idaho voters. Because of the success of Amendment 2, CFV was influential in encouraging activists in other states to use Amendment 2 language for their own statewide initiatives. CFV provided training sessions for activists across the country in 1994 and directly supported both statewide and local initiatives, including the infamous Cincinnati Issue 3 in 1993. Cincinnati was the only city outside of Oregon to pass a legal-restrictive initiative during this time period. Using Colorado Amendment 2 language and CFV funding and training, Cincinnati Religious Right activists passed a local legal-restrictive initiative in a contentious campaign.[106] CFV also influenced the activism of the Florida affiliate of the American Family Association (AFA), which became active in ballot initiatives and attempted several statewide anti-gay initiatives. AFA and CFV together influenced other statewide ballot initiatives, such as those in Maine, which were ostensibly run by a Maine-based organization that used the language and tactics of all three other organizations.

The spread of the legal-restrictive initiative as a tactic was owing to the appeal of a proactive strategy that would stymie the LGBT movement's push for rights on the local and state level, eliminating the necessity of referendums. The use of the legal-restrictive initiative, particularly the version that was used in Colorado, marked a shift in anti-gay Right tactics beyond the type of direct legislation. The language used to defend these initiatives became more racialized and secular. The level of homophobia and religious extremism evident in campaigns also changed.

Gay Rights, Special Rights

In the opening of the film *Gay Rights, Special Rights (GRSR)*, the well-known footage of Martin Luther King Jr. orating the "I Have a Dream" speech is overlaid with ominous concerns about gay rights usurping civil rights for racial minorities. This video, created by the pairing of the Reverend Lou Sheldon from the TVC with Jeremiah Films in Hemet, California, signaled a shift in Religious Right tactics from using moralistic and religious language to racialized legalistic messaging. Indeed, the premise of most legal-restrictive initiatives was that sexual orientation could not and should not be a protected class status like race. This racialized language sidesteps the history of Old Right support of segregation and the New Right opposition to affirmative action.[107] This racialized language was coupled with dissent within the Religious Right about religious extremism and homophobia.

This racialized argument about special rights, popularized by Tony Marco of CFV, included three arguments for opposition to LGBT rights.

The first was that gays did not qualify for minority status because of their wealth, power, and lack of discrimination. Discrimination against gays was portrayed as a deceptive, liberal hoax, and Religious Right literature often used examples of the funding of LGBT initiative campaigns to illustrate the wealth of gays. Anti-gay campaign literature frequently used a graph illustrating the supposed differences in income between African Americans and wealthy gay men, a graph based on literature used by CFV in Amendment 2 (see Figure 4).[108] The emphasis on these traits is because of the Supreme Court definition of a protected class status, which requires a history of political powerlessness and insidious discrimination, along with immutability or inability to change.[109] In this argument, anti-gay activists "sought to portray the lesbian and gay movement as an elite cadre of well-to-do professionals insinuating themselves into the fabric of American institutional life."[110] Being gay or lesbian was also changeable, unlike "real" minorities. According to OCA leader Lon Mabon, "I don't think you're ever going to show that homosexuality is an unchangeable characteristic. It's not like being Caucasian or African American, which gender you were born with, or whether you're Irish or German or whatever. Those are things that are immutable."[111]

The second argument was that gays wanted more rights than other individuals, or "special rights." These "special rights" would give them more rights than average citizens. Religious Right literature was careful (most of the time) not to position the Right as opposed to civil rights for African Americans, but rather against the special rights of gays. This argument juxtaposes deserving blacks who have experienced discrimination with gays as an undeserving group. For example, in West Palm Beach, Florida, in 1995, opponents asserted that the "U.S. Constitution guarantees equal protection. Anything else is a special right. Some people, like blacks, deserve special rights, such as those in the 1964 Civil Rights Act, because of long history of discrimination. Homosexuals are not deserving of a special law."[112] This argument builds on misconceptions about civil rights protections. In this misconception, civil rights inherently take rights away from someone else, in a zero-sum game.

The third argument was that not only did gays want special rights but their rights would ultimately usurp rights from legitimate minorities such as blacks by rendering civil rights gains meaningless. To make this claim, campaign literature included civil rights master frames, such as "this is a

"Gay Rights" Opposition to Amendment 2
Boils Down to Three Phony Arguments...

1) FEEL SORRY FOR US... THEN GIVE US SPECIAL RIGHTS.

BUT - are "gays" really hurting? Consider these facts:

	Average Household Income	% College Graduates	% Managerial/ Professional Positions	% Overseas Travel
"GAYS"	$55,430	59.9%	49.0%	65.8%
AVG.AM.	$32,144	18.0%	15.9%	14.0%
DISADV. AFRICAN AMERICANS	$12,166	5.0%	1-2%	1%

(*Acc. to U.S. Census Bureau, Simmons Market Research , Statistical Abstract, U.S., 1990)

*2) WE GAVE BLACK PEOPLE, WOMEN AND THE HANDICAPPED SPECIAL RIGHTS --
NOW, WHY NOT "GAYS"?*

BUT -- do "gays" qualify for special rights like these groups do?

To qualify for special rights, groups must be (a) disadvantaged, (b) not defined by behavior and (c) politically powerless. Women, blacks and the handicapped all meet those qualifications. Do you think "gays" meet them? Why shouldn't they have to, like the others did? Homosexuality is behavior or desire. If we give behavior or desire special rights, who'll be next -- drug addicts, pedophiles or prostitutes?

*3) "GAYS" SAY THEY DON'T WANT SPECIAL RIGHTS -- THEY JUST WANT TO BE LIKE
EVERYONE ELSE.*

BUT -- are they telling the truth?

Rabbi Steven Foster (Co-Chairman of EPOC, the "gay rights" campaign against Amendment 2) says he thinks homosexuals deserve special minority status. Amendment 2 doesn't change "gays" present status -- it just prevents special rights for "gays." According to Colorado's most prominent Civil Rights leaders, "gays" already have the same basic rights as anyone else. That means they are equal right now. Amendment 2 means they'll stay equal, not special.

VOTE "YES!" ON AMENDMENT 2!

Paid for by Colorado for Family Values. Will Perkins, Executive Board Chairman. Kevin Tebedo. director.)

Figure 4. Political messaging from Colorado for Family Values.

hijacking of the freedom train" and phrases such as "equal rights, not special rights," along with invoking Dr. Martin Luther King Jr. and his family. To reinforce this claim of injury to African Americans, campaign literature began using African American and other racial minority spokespeople in their literature in the 1990s. Anti-gay activists also engaged in their own racial coalition building with African American pastors. In Cincinnati Issue 3 in 1993, African Americans were targeted by Issue 3 proponents and featured prominently in Issue 3 literature.[113] A leader of the Cincinnati anti-gay campaign noted that "A key ingredient to victory is winning the Black vote. Our spokesperson was the President of the Black Baptist Ministerial Association. Even with a Black spokesperson, the Black vote was split evenly, which was our goal."[114] To reinforce the supposed antagonism between African American and LGBT communities, anti-gay literature consistently portrayed white gay men and lesbians, often making white gay men the dominant representation of public LGBT life. The absence of LGBT people of color in anti-gay literature becomes "a telling indication both of the intrinsic whiteness of homosexuality and of the threat that gay rights may pose to the rights of other 'others.'"[115]

Similar to Cameron's public-health messaging, this legalistic language was often coupled with voyeuristic images from LGBT community events. In videos such as *GRSR,* which were commonly used during initiative campaigns, the perfunctory legalistic arguments about civil rights law were juxtaposed with wild depictions of the "gay lifestyle." Between clips of minority leaders discussing the differences between the LGBT and civil rights movements, *GRSR* includes clips of the March on Washington in 1993 showing kissing gay men, polyamorous bisexuals, queer leathermen, and parading transsexuals and drag queens. In *GRSR,* transgender participants in the march became a spectacle to convince voters of the dangers of LGBT rights. The anti-gay Right had long used marginalized groups within the LGBT movement, such as the North American Man/Boy Love Association (NAMBLA), to bolster arguments against LGBT rights. The specter of cross-dressing teachers and babysitters was occasionally used in anti-gay literature before 1992.[116] In the late 1990s, the anti-gay Right used changes within the LGBT movement, such as the increasing inclusion of transgender protections in nondiscrimination legislation, to create effective smear tactics. These tactics often focused on transgender access to bathrooms, suggesting that transgender individuals were really "men in dresses" looking to victimize helpless women in the bathroom. These tactics emerged in the St. Paul, Minnesota, ordinance in 1990 and quickly spread across the country.[117] For example, during OCA's 1991 opposition to the Portland, Oregon, antidiscrimination ordinance, activists passed out

flyers at hearings that had a photograph of a male teacher in a dress stand-
ing in a classroom, with the following message: "If gay rights becomes law,
what prevents this type of thing from happening?"[118] Since the mid-1990s,
Religious Right groups have begun using these tactics for a week or two
during referendum and initiative campaigns, regardless of whether or not
there are transgender protections written into local ordinances.[119]

Some of these shock and awe campaigns were controversial even
within the Right, as anti-gay activists re-formed their image to address a
mainstream audience. Although scholar John C. Green asserts that proactive opposition like legal-restrictive initiatives are led by the most "hard-
core specialists in antigay politics," some Right "organizations publicly
downplay hostility to homosexuals, and some Christian Right leaders have
criticized their colleagues for their strident antigay rhetoric."[120] Although
many leaders were ministers and evangelical Christians, the image of the
Right became increasingly less religious and more "pro-family." Some anti-
gay activists criticized the crude tactics and defamatory rhetoric of the
OCA and its affiliate, Idaho Citizens Alliance. Many anti-gay activists realized that this extremism could be the downfall of a campaign. The dangers
of extremism were aptly demonstrated in Idaho, when the revelation that
Jeremiah Films had not only produced *Gay Rights, Special Rights* but also a
series of anti-Mormon films led to Mormon opposition to the initiative.[121]
Some campaigns avoided associations with controversial psychologist Paul
Cameron after public criticism of his research during Colorado Amendment 2. And OCA activist Scott Lively's claim that gays were Holocaust
perpetrators put the OCA under attack in the Oregon media. When Maine
faced an initiative in 1995, the leader of the preeminent group of Maine
religious conservatives criticized that anti-gay campaign, remarking that
"This must not become a campaign calculated to arouse hatred or fear of
any group of our fellow citizens" and suggesting that the campaign should
be different than those in Oregon and Idaho.[122]

This kinder, gentler, civil rights–supportive anti-gay Right was an effective ballot box tactic. The use of special rights language may simultaneously gain the support of African American and liberal voters alike and
appeal to the anxiety of working-class voters who did not benefit from the
gains of the civil rights movement.[123] This special rights messaging "allows
the leaders of the right's campaign to present themselves as the defenders

of 'deserving' people, such as people of color and working-class people [which] . . . helps create and maintain a wedge of resentment between groups who might otherwise be political allies."[124]

The "Magic Bullet"?

Although the special rights language was an excellent tactical innovation for the anti-gay Right, the legal-restrictive initiative was not. The legal-restrictive initiative was responsible for a surge of anti-gay activism at this time that encouraged activists all over the country to attempt their own initiative. However, outside of Oregon, legal-restrictive initiatives were difficult to get on the ballot box (only a third were successful) and were rarely passed by voters. Outside of Oregon, only four legal-restrictive initiatives made it onto the ballot, and the legal-restrictive initiative never succeeded again on the state level, only passing in municipalities like Cincinnati and Alachua County, Florida. The difficulty in getting these initiatives on the ballot can be attributed to both lackluster organizing and pre-ballot legal challenges. For example, Florida and Maine activists innovated with a "stealth" legal-restrictive initiative that did not mention sexual orientation but rather created a list of approved categories to include in state and local nondiscrimination legislation.[125] However, Florida courts would not allow the initiative to go on the ballot because of constitutionality issues.[126] Other initiatives were voided after the fact, such as the invalidation of Alachua County's legal-restrictive initiative with a post-ballot legal challenge.[127] The use of Religious Right state-level legal-restrictive initiatives ended abruptly in 1996 with the overturn of Colorado Amendment 2 by the Supreme Court in *Romer v. Evans,* which affirmed the legitimacy of sexual orientation as a minority-group category.[128] These initiatives were not popular because "Antigay forces have more success asking voters to return to some recent status quo than they have asking voters to depart from it."[129] However, these initiatives were successful in recruiting anti-gay followers and building a stronger Religious Right movement.

Even with the triumph of *Romer v. Evans,* Religious Right and LGBT activists alike anticipated a new battleground for referendums and initiatives. A prominent LGBT organizer predicted in 1995 that "[the next] big issues will be marriage, adoption and immigration. Politicians are going to pit us against women, infants and children, sodomy or milk."[130] And indeed, the Right had already begun mobilizing against same-sex marriage after the 1993 Hawaii Supreme Court case, *Baehr v. Lewin,* which opened the door for same-sex marriage in Hawaii.[131] This decision set off a wave of Right-inspired panic across the country, as the Full Faith and Credit Clause of the U.S. Constitution requires states to recognize marriages conducted in other states. Politicians responded to this panic by passing both the national Defense of Marriage Act (DOMA) in 1996 and fifteen state-level DOMAs in 1995 and 1996 in states such as Arizona, Georgia, Idaho, Michigan, and Utah. These statewide laws against same-sex marriage were successful as "the legislation not only served as a rallying point for conservatives, but also divided liberal legislators from their gay constituents."[132] Although this mobilization around same-sex marriage rallied anti-gay activists, it had not yet reached the ballot box.

1997–2003: Innovating Same-Sex Marriage Initiatives

Between 1997 and 2003, there were several subtle shifts in the anti-gay Right, including the development of the marriage and fatherhood movements and a growing ex-gay movement. The growing strength of the marriage movement included the use of direct legislation to restrict access to marriage for same-sex couples, culminating in the wave of initiatives in the 2004 presidential election to write same-sex marriage bans into state constitutions. During this period, these marriage bans accounted for more than a third of all attempted ballot measures. However, almost half of all fifty-three attempted ballot measures were still referendums and 15.1 percent were local legal-restrictive initiatives. Almost 60 percent of attempted ballot measures made it to the ballot box; but, for the first time, the Religious Right lost more than half of all such measures.

Welfare reform in 1996 that promoted the formation and maintenance of two-parent households also funded marriage promotion programs and encouraged the development of two overlapping movements, the fatherhood and marriage movements.[133] The fatherhood movement is a men's movement that grew through the development of SMOs like the Promise Keepers, a Christian men's organization devoted to traditional gender roles in the family. The Promise Keepers grew throughout the 1990s, had an estimated 3.5 million members in 1999, and waned in influence, membership, and funding shortly after that.[134] Government-sponsored marriage promotion programs that disproportionately targeted white middle class

Christian families put money into marriage movement coffers.[135] Organizations devoted exclusively to the promotion of heterosexual marriage and restriction of same-sex marriage arose during this time, including the Alliance for Marriage, a Virginia-based organization founded by Matt Daniels. Both the marriage movement and traditional anti-gay organizations became connected with ex-gay organizations, predominately Christian organizations that promised to convert gays and lesbians to heterosexuality. The most visible presence of the ex-gay movement was the 1998 "Truth in Love Campaign," which included a four hundred thousand–dollar ad campaign in the summer of 1998 in three major newspapers sponsored by a coalition of fourteen organizations, including the ubiquitous Christian Coalition.[136] The marriage movement also increasingly mobilized Mormon congregations and organizations, as Mormons contributed money and manpower to campaigns against same-sex marriage across the country.[137]

The anti-gay movement was galvanized into action by a series of Right and LGBT victories around marriage. Anti-gay activists were encouraged by the passage of both DOMA and welfare reform in 1996, along with election of George W. Bush to the presidency in 2000. The growing reality of access to marriage for same-sex couples also roused the marriage movement. LGBT advances during this time include the legalization of same-sex civil unions in Vermont in 1999 and the double victory in 2003 of the overturn of sodomy laws in the Supreme Court case *Lawrence v. Texas* coupled with the Massachusetts Supreme Judicial Court ruling in *Goodridge v. Department of Public Health* that established the right of same-sex couples to marry.[138] Before the Massachusetts verdict, the marriage movement organized the Marriage Protection Week in October 2003, sponsored by twenty-nine organizations, including Concerned Women for America, Focus on the Family, the Family Research Council (FRC), and the TVC. As evidence of the growing monetary power of these organizations, the largest thirteen organizations that sponsored the weeklong event had a combined budget of $217 million.[139] The anti-gay Right also began to rally around the Federal Marriage Amendment, a proposed constitutional amendment that would restrict marriage to between a man and a woman. The bill was first proposed in 2002 by the Alliance for Marriage and it gathered steam in 2003 and 2004.

It was inevitable that same-sex marriage would make its way to the ballot box. Indeed, Religious Right activists had been challenging marriage recognition rights like domestic partnerships for a decade. The first vote on domestic partnership benefits was in 1989 in San Francisco as a referendum to challenge a recently passed ordinance.[140] And some legal-restrictive initiatives in the early 1990s included a prohibition of same-sex marriage as part of their list of demands. However, it was not until the late 1990s that the use of initiatives to ban same-sex marriage proliferated on the state level.[141] The first statewide votes on same-sex marriage occurred in Alaska and Hawaii in 1998 in response to state court cases about same-sex marriage.[142] The Religious Right in Alaska and Hawaii framed same-sex marriage as an invasion from the mainland with disastrous consequences for the whole nation. The Alaska Family Coalition sent fund-raising letters across the country, emphasizing that "Ballot Measure No. 2 will *overrule* the liberal judges and *protect* marriage and the family not only in Alaska, but also in your state."[143] These two initiatives were followed by marriage bans in four states, including the Knight Initiative in 2000 in California and an expansive anti-gay initiative (called a "super-DOMA") that eliminated both same-sex marriage and domestic partnerships in Nebraska.[144]

Marriage bans were a winning tactic, as they were more likely to get on the ballot, pass in favor of the anti-gay Right, and mobilize new activists into the marriage movement than either referendums or legal-restrictive initiatives. The Christian Coalition and AFA became increasingly involved in local and statewide referendums at this time, including attempts to revoke recently passed ordinances in Miami–Dade County in 2002 and Ypsilanti, Michigan, in 1998, neither of which was successful. The Christian Coalition was involved in the defeat of Maine's gay rights law in a referendum in 1998.[145] However, there were signs that the anti-gay Right was becoming less effective at winning referendums, as it won only 44 percent of the referendums during this time period that made it to the ballot box.

Religious Right attempts to sponsor and win legal-restrictive initiatives on the local level were also a dismal failure. In 1997, a federal appeals court upheld the language of Cincinnati Issue 3, which created an opening for legal-restrictive initiatives to be passed in cities and towns. From 1998 until 2002, these initiatives were attempted in Michigan, a new site of anti-gay activity with the growth of an AFA affiliate under the leadership of Gary Glen, along with initiatives in Falmouth, Maine, and Colorado Springs, Colorado. The legal-restrictive initiative was abandoned after a triple defeat of initiatives in the Michigan cities of Ypsilanti, Kalamazoo, and Traverse City in 2001 and 2002, coupled with a failed OCA-sponsored

Oregon initiative in 2000 that would have prohibited schools from discussing or encouraging homosexuality.

Besides winning at the ballot box, marriage bans fulfilled the promises that legal-restrictive initiatives never could. They circumvented future LGBT rights, as all initiatives were passed in states that did not yet allow same-sex marriage. Anti-gay activists were successful at sponsoring statewide initiatives either through petitions or through the legislature. And many of these marriage bans took place in non-battleground states, such as Nebraska and Nevada, where voters were unaccustomed to voting on LGBT rights. Anti-gay activists were also able to pass most of these marriage bans as constitutional amendments, a surefire guarantee that statewide DOMAs would not be overturned in state courts as being unconstitutional.

2004–9 Same-Sex Marriage Initiatives

Just as the Massachusetts legislature was preparing to issue its first marriage licenses to same-sex couples in the winter of 2004, a flurry of same-sex marriages took place across the country. The mayor of San Francisco, Gavin Newsom, allowed more than four thousand same-sex couples to marry in February, flooding the media with images of couples marrying at San Francisco City Hall and setting off alarms. The marriages were quickly curtailed by litigation by the Alliance Defense Fund, a national coalition of Right lawyers.[146] But the seeming growing success of the LGBT movement in passing same-sex marriages led to the largest wave of anti-marriage activity ever in 2004. The biggest tactical shift was from legislative statutes that restricted marriage to heterosexual couples to constitutional amendments, passed either by the legislature or by the voters. The Right received an additional boost by the overturning of legalized same-sex marriage by Proposition 8 in California in 2008 and Question 1 in Maine in 2009. Almost all of the forty-five attempted ballot measures during this period were initiatives to restrict same-sex marriage or domestic partnerships (80 percent); most ballot measures easily made it to the ballot box (82.2 percent) and were passed by voters (81.1 percent).

The opposition to same-sex marriage dominated the anti-gay Religious Right agenda during this time period through the push for a Federal Marriage Amendment, legislative activity, fending off LGBT litigation or sponsoring their own, using marriage as an effective political wedge in the 2004 and 2008 presidential elections, and marriage ban initiatives. Organizations devoted to marriage such as the National Organization for Marriage (NOM)[147] and Americans United to Preserve Marriage have grown as major anti-gay organizations like the Christian Coalition are declining.[148] The success of the Right in fighting marriage benefits for same-sex couples at the ballot box during this time period also encouraged an explosion of statewide initiatives to restrict abortion and affirmative action. In the November 2008 election alone there were five attempted and three successful statewide initiatives to restrict abortion.

This time period has easily been the most successful one for the anti-gay Right. Although it won more direct legislation between 1993 and 1996 (84.6 percent versus 88.1 percent), most of these victories were in small rural towns in Oregon, and all were annulled by the state courts and legislature. However, the anti-gay Right has been able to pass constitutional amendments and initiatives that restrict access to marriage and other relationship recognition benefits for same-sex couples. These initiatives are statewide, difficult to revoke without revisiting the ballot box, and pass by a large margin.

One of the largest tactical shifts was the use of two overlapping draconian tactics: super-DOMAs, which extend restrictions of same-sex marriage to domestic partnerships or anything "like" marriage, and constitutional amendments, which write the definition of marriage into the state constitution. Most super-DOMAs are also constitutional amendments. The use of a constitutional amendment was a powerful Religious Right tactic that stymied the use of the legislative (and in many cases the judicial) system to overturn anti-gay legislation and frequently could only be retracted by a return to the ballot box. In 2004 alone, twelve states voted on constitutional amendments, and in nine states those amendments were a super-DOMA, solidifying the use of both tactics.[149]

The Right won all of these marriage bans, with the exception of a super-DOMA in Arizona in 2006 that was narrowly defeated. This was only a temporary defeat. In 2008, Arizona voters passed Proposition 102, the Marriage Protection Amendment, which defined marriage as between a man and a woman. The Right also lost a 2009 referendum in Washington State to repeal domestic partnership benefits.

The two most significant victories by the Right at this time were California Proposition 8 in 2008 and Maine Question 1 in 2009, both of which overturned legal same-sex marriage granted by either the courts or the legislature. The most publicly visible of these constitutional amendments was California Proposition 8, which countered a 2008 decision by the California Supreme Court to allow same-sex marriage. Political Research Associate analyst Surina Khan describes the Proposition 8 campaign as a "shrewd, media-savvy, well-funded and well-organized grassroots movement that understood California's complex geographic and political landscape."[150] With record-breaking fund-raising of more than $40 million from across the country, the campaign was a "well-funded operation that rivaled any major electoral campaign in its scope and complexity."[151] According to Frank Schubert, political operative and campaign manager for the Yes on 8 campaign, the campaign set ambitious goals:

> Our ability to organize a massive volunteer effort through religious denominations gave us a huge advantage, and we set ambitious goals: to conduct a statewide Voter ID canvass of every voter; to distribute 1.25 million yard signs and an equal number of bumper strips; to have our volunteers re-contact every undecided, soft yes and soft no voter; and to have 100,000 volunteers, five per voting precinct, working on Election Day to make sure every identified Yes on 8 voter would vote. All of these goals, and more, were achieved.[152]

Yes on 8 grew into the largest anti-gay campaign thus far in history. Part of its power was the coordination of Mormon, Catholic, and Protestant opposition to same-sex marriage.[153] The tactics used in California were emulated in Maine, and to some extent Washington, as similar political messaging and strategies were used in both states.

King and King

The commercial begins with a young girl in pigtails coming home from school into her kitchen, carrying the children's book *King and King*. She announces to her shocked mother, "Mom, guess what I learned in school today? I learned how a prince married a prince and *I* can marry a princess."[154] The television ad goes on to warn California voters that in Massachusetts schoolchildren in the second grade have already learned that "gay marriage" is acceptable, and their parents have no control over what they are learning in school. Building on issues about parental control and sex education, this political messaging used during the California Proposition 8 campaign was one of many strategic messages developed to convince voters to approve bans on same-sex marriage. This marriage messaging rivals special rights messaging in its political effectiveness.[155]

In a survey of newspaper accounts of same-sex marriage, scholar Shauna Fisher found that the most common arguments against same-sex marriage are those about the protection of marriage as an institution, morality, public opposition to same-sex marriage, and the importance of heterosexual marriage for raising children. These arguments are often coupled with the depiction of courts and judges as antidemocratic "activists."[156] In more liberal states, these messages included using gay male spokespeople to assert that same-sex couples did not need the rights and benefits of marriage.[157] This messaging often weakened moderate and liberal voters by suggesting that the Right was supportive of civil unions but not marriage for same-sex couples.[158] For example, a political ad on the Yes on 8 Web site depicted a heterosexual family who were close friends with their gay neighbors but opposed extending the benefits of marriage to them. The ad described how the parents, Jan and Tom, were relieved to find out that their neighbors would get the same benefits of marriage with a domestic partnership, and thus they felt comfortable voting for Proposition 8.[159]

The most common and lasting arguments are about the sanctity of marriage as an institution and the ways that giving same-sex couples access to marriage would radically alter and/or diminish the institution. However, even Right political organizers admit that in more liberal states "soft supporters" are easily swayed by messaging about children and the unanticipated consequences of allowing the legalization of same-sex marriage. Indeed, in early polling for the Yes on 8 campaign by the firm Lawrence Research, more than 60 percent of "No" supporters polled changed their mind when confronted with information about how health-education teachers would have to teach children about same-sex marriage.[160] The danger of LGBT rights to children is an old political message that can be traced back to the early Miami–Dade County referendum in 1977, where the anti-gay campaign was called Save Our Children. Legal-restrictive initiatives also focused on children, although that was not a central focus. For example, three Oregon statewide ballot initiatives (1992, 1994, and 2000) included provisions to prevent schools from promoting homosexuality to children. Some of the most popular messaging during marriage bans was using pro-LGBT children's literature, which has always been criticized and attacked by the Right, to demonstrate the perils of same-sex marriage. The first marriage ban campaign in Hawaii aired a commercial showing a young boy reading from *Daddy's Wedding*, a pro-gay children's book. The commercial warned voters about the impact on children of same-sex marriage.[161] This messaging was used in other campaigns, including Oregon Measure 36 in 2004 and Maine Question 1 in 2009. This messaging includes warning voters that if same-sex marriage is legal, children will learn about gay sex and be forced to attend their teacher's lesbian wedding. Schubert of Yes on 8 suggested that this messaging was a strategic way of appearing less homophobic and focusing on the unintended "consequences" of same-sex marriage for children rather than criticizing same-sex couples who wanted to get married.[162] Like special rights messaging, messaging about children and marriage represents a trend within the anti-gay Right to target more moderate and liberal voters, raise legalistic or ethical issues rather than moral issues, and engage in "homophobia lite" rather than far-Right attacks on LGBT rights.

Some political pundits have suggested at the close of the decade that the wave of same-sex marriages allowed by courts and state legislatures in 2009 signified the waning influence of the anti-gay Right. For example, in Frank Rich's column in the *New York Times* in April 2009 he remarks that the recently created organization National Organization for Marriage's expensive ad "Gathering Storm" about same-sex marriage "bookmarks a historic turning point in the demise of America's anti-gay movement" as "its release was the only loud protest anywhere in America to the news that same-sex marriage had been legalized in Iowa and Vermont."[163] There are some concerns in the Right that attention to same-sex marriage may be displaced by the faltering economy, health care legislation, and anti-Obama activity by groups like the Tea Party. The anti-gay movement may be losing traction in the Republican Party, although that was hardly evidenced by the anti-gay rhetoric present in the recruitment of voters by Republican hopefuls at the annual Values Voters Summit in 2010, sponsored by the long-standing anti-gay research think tank Family Research Council.[164] And the National Organization for Marriage began a campaign in 2011 to unseat New York legislators who passed a bill legalizing same-sex marriage.

The future of anti-gay ballot measures is unclear. It is evident that the anti-gay Right may abandon local referendums and initiatives, as it was unable to pass almost all local referendums and initiatives sponsored in this time period, including a defeat of a legal-restrictive initiative in Topeka, Kansas, the home of Fred Phelps's Westboro Baptist Church. As we will see in chapter 5, the Right may face a new round of LGBT-sponsored initiatives to annul these constitutional amendments that restrict access to marriage for same-sex couples.

The anti-gay Right may be innovating with new types of anti-gay ballot measures as well. A successful 2008 initiative against gay and lesbian adoption in Arkansas, which was written broadly to include all cohabiting nonmarried couples, potentially could have inspired a round of anti-gay adoption initiatives outside of battleground states. However, in 2011, the Arkansas Supreme Court unanimously overturned the initiative as unconstitutional. Religious freedom initiatives, which do not explicitly mention LGBT issues, may allow individuals to circumvent statewide or local nondiscrimination protections for LGBT citizens. Religious freedom initiatives were pilot-tested by the Religious Right in North Dakota and Florida in 2012.

A Long, Weary Battle

It took the Religious Right more than a decade to develop a strong anti-gay movement, a movement that only began to use direct democracy systematically in the early 1990s. Yet, direct legislation became a central arena of contention for the Religious Right. This direct legislation served a variety of functions for the movement.

> In addition to banning legal protections and family recognition for gay people and same-sex couples, they play a myriad of other roles: they can have a "priming" effect by making gay rights a more salient issue in voter decision making; they can mobilize the Christian Right's base of conservative voters; the mobilization of moderates and liberals to resist antigay ballot questions can starve such candidates of campaign funds; they can make gay rights issues politically radioactive; and they can serve as a hook to bring in new audiences to hear the Christian Right's broader conservative and theocratic policy agenda.[165]

Similar to the relationship between the LGBT movement and ballot measure campaigns, campaigns served as a way to build movement power and infrastructure for the Religious Right.

Direct legislation also became an arena that allowed for the continuous development of new tactics to be used against the LGBT movement. These tactics ranged from referendums to annul local ordinances to proactive opposition to eliminate the possibility of same-sex marriage. Over time, the Religious Right repeatedly altered its tactics to more effectively stymie gains by the LGBT movement, changing the subject and level of ballot measures and innovating with more politically sophisticated messaging.

How did the LGBT movement respond to this series of tactical innovations? Scholars such as David Meyer and Suzanne Staggenborg theorize that "*interactions between opposing movements prevent the complete institutionalization of tactics by either side.*"[166] Doug McAdam suggests that movements have to develop continual new rounds of tactical innovation owing to such innovation by the countermovement.[167]

The remainder of this book demonstrates that, contrary to existing theories about movement–countermovement interaction, this tactical innovation propelled the LGBT movement to develop a set of campaign tactics, field programs in national LGBT organizations, and statewide organizations in battleground states. Although these tactics were challenged and slightly altered by the LGBT movement after 2004 when marriage bans became common, dominant models of how to run campaigns were developed and solidified even in the midst of Religious Right escalation and tactical innovation.

CHAPTER 2

AN UPHILL BATTLE IN THE 70s AND 80s
BUILDING LGBT MOVEMENT INFRASTRUCTURE

> The results in [Miami] Dade County that night roused many homo-
> sexuals, and the gay movement, as nothing had before. It was
> a turning point for gay men and lesbians who years later would
> trace their own coming out or interest in gay politics to the Anita
> Bryant victory. In the days after the repeal, there were marches
> in cities large and small, from Los Angeles to Indianapolis; from
> San Francisco, where thousands of people marched through to
> Union Square chanting "Out of the bars and into the streets,"
> to New Orleans; from Boston to Houston. Gay Pride marches
> that month saw record turnouts. Jeanne Cordova always marked
> the vote as the beginning of a migration of lesbians back into
> the gay rights movement. Gay organizations popped up all over
> the country; existing ones saw their membership rolls swell. The
> National Gay Task Force saw its membership double in just four
> months.
>
> Dudley Clendinen and Adam Nagourney, *Out for Good:*
> *The Struggle to Build a Gay Rights Movement in America*

WHEN GAY AND LESBIAN RESIDENTS of Boulder, Colorado, were faced
with a referendum on their recently passed nondiscrimination ordinance
in 1974, they had no models to look to from previous campaigns. There
were no former leaders of LGBT campaigns to call. The campaign had to
persuade voters to support gay rights at a time when more than 70 percent of the nation believed that homosexuality was always wrong.[1] The
two existing national organizations, Lambda Legal and the Task Force,
were weak, poorly funded, and newly created. Indeed, there was not yet a
real national LGBT movement; scattered, individual organizations across
the country would not coalesce into a national movement until the 1979
National March on Washington for Lesbian and Gay Rights.[2]

This early campaign marked the beginning of almost two decades of struggle, as LGBT activists fought anti-gay ballot measures across the country, and frequently lost. In the late 1980s, several AIDS initiatives were on the ballot in California that tested the fund-raising, energy, and strength of LGBT organizing. Several cities faced multiple initiatives in the same city or a spate of direct legislation concentrated in one part of the state. For example, between 1978 and 1991, voters in St. Paul voted on two referendums sponsored by the Religious Right and one initiative sponsored by the LGBT movement, along with witnessing petition collecting for an initiative by the Right in 1991 that would have required all gay rights issues to go before the voters. And in Oregon, LGBT residents faced down the OCA for the first time in 1988 in a statewide initiative.

As the Religious Right experimented with referendums and different types of initiatives, local LGBT groups scrambled to respond. With underfunded national organizations, pressing concerns like HIV/AIDS, and few good models to follow, the movement's initial response to Religious Right–sponsored ballot measures was weak. Part of this weakness resulted from the absence of a real social movement infrastructure, especially strong national and statewide organizations, to support local campaigns. In addition, fighting ballot measures was not high on the agenda of movement leaders, because, during the late 1970s to early 1990s, ballot measures were sporadic and infrequent; other issues, such as the repeal of sodomy laws and addressing HIV/AIDS, took precedence. Despite this lack of infrastructure, as the epigraph at the beginning of this chapter suggests, these ballot measures did help draw activists together into a national movement, encouraging connections between LGBT individuals in cities across the country who were facing ballot measures.

As the relationship between social movements and campaigns was developing during this time period, activists struggled to develop a set of winning tactics and fought one anti-gay ballot measure after another. This was a time of tactical innovation and experimentation in which activists tried direct-action protests, new forms of political messaging about privacy, LGBT-sponsored initiatives, and professional polling. They sought to develop tactics, such as political messaging about LGBT rights, that were in accordance with movement goals. They learned by trial and error. Some tactics that were considered important during this time period were later dismissed as ineffective. An examination of failed tactics is important given the lack of scholarly literature on tactical failure.[3] Such an examination reveals much about how activists make decisions about which tactics are "winning" tactics and which are not.

This chapter analyzes what these early campaigns tell us about tactical innovation, and about how we can understand why activists select from within a set of tactics to determine which are the winning ones. I suggest that the development of movement infrastructure plays a strong role in the development of dominant tactics, and analyzing activists' interpretation of victories and defeats is critical to understanding why some tactics are used over and over again. This innovation took place at a time when the realities of ballot measure campaigns were becoming clearly evident, teaching the LGBT movement a series of painful lessons about the nature of the ballot box.

Early Lessons

The wake-up call for the LGBT movement came shortly after early campaigns in Miami–Dade County in 1977 and the spate of referendums in St. Paul, Wichita, and Eugene in the spring of 1978. It quickly became clear that the Religious Right had discovered a number of effective tactics in its fight against LGBT rights. It also became clear that local politics was national politics, as local victories and defeats had consequences for the national movement. For example, before the LaRouche Initiative, Tom Stoddard, the executive director of Lambda Legal, suggested that "Because of California's size, and because it is one of the two states most heavily affected by AIDS, the initiative will be to some degree a barometer of public opinion on the issue . . . A bad result will haunt us all."[4]

The first, and most painful, lesson was how easy it was to lose a ballot measure. Many early referendum battles involved time-consuming campaigns, only to see voters overwhelmingly reject LGBT rights. Even in the Miami–Dade County campaign, Task Force directors predicted a loss, despite polling to the contrary. "Discussions with civil rights leaders from other organizations and movements, and with public opinion pollsters and analysts, led us early in the Dade County campaign over a year ago to the conclusion that we were not likely to win referenda *at this early stage* of our movement and campaign to educate the public."[5] Even at this early stage, a victory or defeat at the ballot box was taken as evidence of the growing strength or weakness of the larger movement, as this analysis suggests.

The second (contradictory) lesson was that even when campaigns were won, they did not result in a change to the status quo. They did not necessarily advance movement goals. LGBT residents of the city or state in question retained a law that had already been passed or prevented a virulently anti-gay initiative from becoming law. But these residents were left with few *new* rights once the battle was over. For the LGBT movement, direct legislation is typically both defensive and regressive, offering few genuine civil rights gains even when the campaign wins, just maintenance of the status quo.[6] For example, when activists successfully defeat a virulently homophobic initiative such as the Briggs Initiative in California, which would have led to the firing of gay and lesbian teachers, the community is left with no additional rights after election day.

Sometimes, however, winning a ballot measure was effective in cutting short tactical innovations of the Religious Right. Campaigns could contribute to movement goals by preventing the advance of the Religious Right. Movement leaders perceived these initiatives as test cases and feared that, if successful, the Right would pursue such initiatives across the country. There was general awareness that the Right was innovating with new types of ballot measures, and sometimes retaining the status quo meant preventing the Right from spawning a new wave of anti-gay ballot measures. Before the Austin election, Task Force executive director Lucia Valeska stated:

> We have to win the Austin battle, since it is the first time anywhere that voters have been asked to approve a law explicitly permitting private, non-governmental discrimination against gay people. *A victory of this kind by our enemies would be a terrible, terrible precedent and example.* It's bad enough when they succeed in repealing laws meant to give us equal protection, but this one, like the "Family Protection Act," singles us out for discrimination. It's a license for bigotry.[7]

When campaigns did defeat these initiatives, the defeats were all interpreted as setbacks for the Right. For example, after the defeat of the La-Rouche AIDS initiative, Bruce Decker, the chairman of the California State

AIDS Advisory Task Force, proclaimed it a victory over the advancing Right: "We have thrown a very, very cold bucket of water on this witch," he said, invoking the defeat of the Wicked Witch by Dorothy in *The Wizard of Oz*.[8]

An additional lesson was that local campaigns had national consequences. Dade County is the most obvious example. Social movement scholar Tina Fetner has documented the ways in which Dade County's defeat shifted the way LGBT activists elsewhere framed the need for LGBT rights to the greater public, permanently altering the growing movement.[9] Other campaigns, however, were also important. In St. Paul in 1991 a referendum campaign member asserted that "The importance of this vote cannot be overstated. Beyond its obvious ramifications for St. Paulites, the veto has broader implications at the metro, state and national levels . . . both our friends and our foes are watching this vote as a litmus test to see if the gay community indeed has the political muscle it claims to have."[10] When Santa Clara County faced two referendums in 1980, local activists stressed the importance of the campaign "in a traditionally liberal area, to the entire nation. All eyes will be on Santa Clara County, only 50 miles from San Francisco, to provide direction."[11] As the importance of local battles became clear, activists across the country realized the need for clear, decisive tactics to defeat anti-gay ballot measures.

Faced with these difficult lessons, campaign workers were creative in finding ways to fight ballot measures. As it became increasingly evident how important victory was to the larger movement and to local communities, activists sought to develop the most effective tactics to fight them.

Innovative Tactics

Between 1974 and 1991, activists across the country experimented with a wide range of tactics, from ballot box avoidance techniques to professional polls for messaging development to LGBT-sponsored initiatives. Innovation in the LGBT movement has come almost exclusively from local and statewide campaigns, as activists across the country fought the anti-gay Right. There was no consistent logic to these attempts. Indeed, many tactics contradicted one another; some activists developed tactics to avoid the ballot box entirely, whereas others worked to propose their own LGBT rights ballot measures. There was uncertainty about how ballot campaigns fit into movement tensions between assimilationist and liberationist politics. Thus, campaigns also varied in whether or not they employed a professional approach to campaigning or a direct-action approach. No single approach predominated.

Ballot Box Avoidance

Because of the high probability of losing at the ballot box, one of the earliest and most lasting tactical approaches was to avoid the ballot box entirely. Ballot box avoidance tactics either keep direct legislation off the ballot or delay the ballot measure. The LGBT movement avoided the ballot box in two ways: pre-ballot legal challenges, and counterpetitioning. Pre-ballot legal challenges sought to disqualify either circulating or submitted petitions from the Religious Right through use of the judicial system. Petitions could be challenged based on procedural issues such as the title or text, constitutional issues based on the content, or signature verification to eliminate ineligible signatures. Other tactics included post-ballot legal challenges and campaign law challenges to existing campaigns, such as misleading campaign messaging.

Counterpetitioning is a direct-action tactic in which pro-LGBT advocates confront and educate both voters who are considering signing petitions and petition collectors. These advocates may also encourage voters to decline to sign petitions through media coverage or direct mailings. Both of these tactics take advantage of the period of several months during which petitions are being circulated to qualify a referendum or initiative for the ballot. Both tactics also require LGBT activists to mobilize and organize before petitions can qualify for the ballot.

Both pre-ballot legal challenges and counterpetitioning were pursued between 1974 and 1991. Early on, activists searched in vain for ways to permanently avoid the ballot box. Shortly after the Dade County defeat, National Gay Task Force staff members were inspired by a Supreme Court decision invalidating a referendum to rescind a California fair-housing law. Task Force staff consulted with national legal organizations such as the American Civil Liberties Union (ACLU) on the possibility of challenging gay rights referendums in federal courts.[12] ACLU representatives affirmed the lack of potential for constitutional challenge to local referendums and instead recommended challenging referendums on procedural issues, such as petition collection practices.[13] There were some early attempts as well to stall the opposition with legal tactics. In Seattle, in 1978, gay and lesbian activists challenged their opponents' defamatory and malicious messaging by using fair-campaign laws. Task Force directors forwarded information about Seattle's tactic to LGBT organizations in other cities that were facing a ballot measure. The Task Force encouraged local campaigns to consider the tactic for media reasons as well, as "it will serve to publicize and dramatize the false statements made by gay-rights opponents in the referenda campaigns."[14] Procedural challenges on the subject or on collection practices of petitioners were the most effective. In 1986, King County, Washington, avoided a referendum on an ordinance when courts struck down the petitions because of deception by petition collectors on the subject of the referendum. That same year, the first attempt of the Davis, California, Religious Right to submit referendum petitions was deflected by citing a clerical error.[15] There were also attempts to challenge early initiatives on constitutional issues, including a challenge to the 1978 Briggs Initiative by pre-ballot lawsuits on grounds of constitutionality and free speech.[16] These constitutional challenges became more effective as the Religious Right innovated with legal-restrictive initiatives in the late 1980s and early 1990s. For example, in 1991 in Riverside, California, a proposed initiative prohibiting future gay rights laws and government support of homosexuality was rejected by the California appellate court, eliminating both the Riverside initiative and copycat initiatives attempted in Irvine and Concord.[17] Even when they did not eliminate the ballot measure, pre-ballot legal challenges could delay or distract the Religious Right and generate free media coverage for the LGBT campaign. Sometimes just the threat of a pre-ballot legal challenge could prevent a referendum. In 1991, in Pittsburgh, the threat of a lawsuit challenging the petition procedures of a Religious Right organization led the group to withdraw its petitions for a referendum rather than face a court battle.

Counterpetitioning, described as "on-the-spot democratic activism," was reportedly developed during an attempted legal-restrictive initiative in the 1980s in Seattle. Seattle-area activists engaged in loosely coordinated efforts to discourage voters from signing Religious Right petitions.[18] There had been similar attempts at counterleafleting in 1978 by the Seattle Committee Against Thirteen (SCAT), a splinter campaign from the more mainstream Seattle campaign, during a referendum battle, launching a monthlong counterleafleting in areas where the opposition was gathering petition signatures.[19] Building on the logic of gay liberationist "zaps" and direct-action protests of the 1970s, this early counterpetitioning was described by activists as "peaceful, creative, and uniquely effective at educating the public."[20]

Counterpetitioning reemerged as the Bigot Busters organization in Oregon, created by activists when the OCA was collecting petitions for a referendum in Portland in 1991. Bigot Busters deployed volunteers to sites where petitions were being collected to discourage voters from signing petitions and petitioners from collecting petitions, or to encourage local business owners to disallow petition collections on their property.[21] Bigot Busters may have played a role in the failure of the OCA to collect enough petitions.[22] The logic of Bigot Busters fit a time period in the late 1980s in which the tactics of direct-action groups such as ACT UP and Queer Nation were popular.

An additional way of avoiding the ballot box was to alter the state or city rules for ballot measures by requiring more signatures, shortening the signature collection period, or restricting the ability of citizens to vote on civil rights laws. In the late 1970s, LGBT activists in many cities considered altering the referendum process to eliminate votes on civil rights issues more generally, or LGBT rights issues specifically.[23] This tactic may have been a response to attempts by local Religious Right organizations to create a new referendum process in anticipation of LGBT legislation in cities such as Washington, D.C.[24] Washington activists in the late 1970s considered an amendment to the city charter to prohibit such referendums.[25] National organizations like the National Gay Task Force and the ACLU recommended that "vulnerable jurisdictions" that were a potential target of a referendum should introduce language restricting the use of the referendum process.[26]

This tactic evolved into an initiative to restrict the direct democracy process in St. Paul, Minnesota. A gay rights ordinance in 1978 in St. Paul had been eliminated in one of the first referendums. In 1988, LGBT activists in St. Paul sponsored their own initiative, which attempted to rewrite the city charter to prohibit referendums against civil rights laws. Modeling their effort after Boulder's successful initiative, the activists' original plan had been to amend the city's ordinance to include sexual orientation by initiative.[27] Instead, they were the first to place the alteration of the

referendum process to a vote. City council members were visibly supportive, and the council president argued in a letter to the public that "there
are some issues that are so fundamental that they should not be subject
to a direct popular vote." However, Religious Right claims that the process
would take away voters' rights and the "essence of democracy" ultimately
won the day, and the initiative was defeated 55–44.[28] Some activists suggested that the wording of the initiative was confusing, and many supporters thought they were voting for the amendment by voting no (instead of
yes), a common issue in ballot campaigns.[29] The initiative lost by a large
margin, and this tactic was not attempted by other LGBT groups. Scholar
Sarah Soule suggests that it is just as important to understand why innovations do not spread from one group to the next as it is to understand the
spread of successful tactics.[30] In this case, the overwhelming defeat of the
St. Paul initiative may have inhibited the spread of the innovation.

With ballot box avoidance tactics and the alteration of direct democracy, LGBT activists had to work hard to avoid appearing undemocratic
and averting the "will of the people." Such tactics gave the Right the opportunity to easily position itself as being victimized by the LGBT movement,
as its campaigns were being charged with a lawsuit, annoyed during the
petition collection process, and prevented from sponsoring a ballot measure at all. Nevertheless, these innovative tactics would be critical as they
spread to other campaigns in the next decade.

Sponsoring Ballot Measures

In contrast to the St. Paul initiative, some activists and organizations sponsored their own ballot measure, typically an initiative to create an LGBT
rights law. Rather than avoiding the ballot box, these activists proposed their
own initiative, often in cities with unresponsive city council members. This
tactic was largely ineffective yet still spread throughout this time period.

One of the first votes on LGBT rights was in Ypsilanti, Michigan, in
1975, when local progressive activists sponsored an initiative to establish
a nondiscrimination ordinance that included sexual orientation, after the
city council had ignored a proposed ordinance. The initiative failed 64–36
after a controversial campaign.[31] Between 1975 and 1980, LGBT groups in
three cities sponsored initiatives, all of which were dramatically defeated.
These initiatives included Miami Dade County, where gay activist Bob Kunst

and a small group of volunteers gathered enough petitions in 1978 to place the local ordinance on the ballot again. The Dade County initiative was not widely supported by either local or national LGBT organizations. A spokesperson for the campaign that had fought Anita Bryant in 1977 stated that "the timing is bad and . . . the campaign is bringing on more injurious sentiment towards us."[32] National leaders were concerned that the Dade County initiative would distract gays and lesbians from the fight against the Briggs Initiative in California.[33]

However, in 1987 a victorious LGBT-sponsored initiative in Boulder, Colorado, encouraged activists to sponsor their own initiatives. Between 1988 and 1991, at least eight initiatives were attempted, including a state-wide initiative in California in 1991. With the exception of a San Francisco domestic partnership initiative, other LGBT-sponsored initiatives failed miserably at the ballot box, often by more than a twenty-point spread.

Yet this failing tactic had ongoing appeal because it was compatible with activists' goals of being more proactive in their fight against the anti-gay Right.[34] They also could cling to their two victories as evidence that this tactic was viable nationally. However, efforts to sponsor LGBT rights initiatives were quickly overshadowed by the approach of avoiding the ballot box whenever possible. And both avoidance and pursuit of the ballot box tactics were overshadowed by the complication of fighting anti-gay ballot measures.

Running a Campaign

Most ballot measures were sponsored by the Religious Right and could not be deterred by ballot box avoidance tactics. The LGBT movement ran a lot of campaigns during this time period, and it experimented with tactics. This section will focus on two important tactics during this time period — voter contact and messaging. Of course, campaign tactics were not the only campaign issues; campaigns also had to negotiate hiring and managing paid staff (if they were lucky), fund-raising, securing the endorsements of political allies, and creating a pool of volunteers. Some activists began to have a clearer grasp of the resources required to run an effective campaign, from the number of volunteers to the amount of money that had to be raised. But voter contact and messaging were important tactical innovations, and their importance to campaigns persisted long past this time period.

These tactics generated tension in the relationship between the campaign and the social movement. Campaign members debated questions such as whether or not campaigns should support national movement goals of gay and lesbian visibility or focus their messaging on campaign arguments about privacy and government interference, which were thought to better appeal to moderate voters. Campaigns splintered over the issue of whether or not they should include radical and liberationist tactics such as nonhierarchical decision making and in-your-face messaging. Even in early campaigns in Dade County, Seattle, and Eugene, there was dissent about the role of direct-action tactics; Dade County and Seattle both saw splinter campaign organizations that took a more radical approach.[35] The debates raging in the larger movement about assimilationist versus radical approaches to activism were reflected within campaigns.

Voter Contact and Get Out the Vote

Systematic voter contact through voter identification and get out the vote (GOTV) efforts would not become part of model campaign tactics until after 1992. However, a few campaigns between 1974 and 1991 experimented with types of voter contact. One of the realities of Religious Right–sponsored ballot measures is that the Right begins the campaign with a stack of petitions filled with signatures of supporters. Before the ballot measure even qualifies to go on the ballot, anti-gay campaigns already have a list of voters who can be contacted and rallied to support the cause.[36] In addition, Religious Right activists could mobilize through churches, whose members were organized into membership lists and brought together for weekly meetings. LGBT campaigns worked within a social movement that often did not maintain a list of supporters. An existing LGBT organization may have a short list of supporters of that organization, a fraction of the local LGBT community; but to get a majority and win the election, LGBT campaigns have to mobilize and turn out heterosexual pro-gay voters on election day. As with later campaigns, there were debates about how much energy should be spent on educating voters, which was more time-consuming, instead of just counting and recruiting existing supporters.

Some campaigns during this period did engage in canvassing; campaign supporters would go door to door to speak with residents about the ballot measure. Some campaigns relied on phone banking, in which campaign supporters would call voters. These attempts at voter contact may have been targeted at specific precincts or cities or organized using lists of Democratic voters. For example, Seattle's strategy in the 1978 Citizens to Retain Fair Employment campaign was to "focus the campaign against I-13 [Initiative 13] on the general public, while insuring maximum turnout at the polls from the gay community and its supporters and from historically liberal precincts."[37] And Denver's referendum campaign in 1991 only sent literature to "people who were registered to vote, who vote, and who live in liberal areas."[38] These efforts may or may not have been accompanied by systematic identification of supportive voters, who then could be called before election day to remind them to vote. In the 1978 Eugene, Oregon, campaign, organizers used door-to-door canvassing, and encouraged canvassers to avoid interacting with people who were strongly opposed to gay rights and to use the canvass as an opportunity to educate voters about gay visibility. Many of these early campaigns also engaged in voter registration, which was emphasized less in future campaigns in favor of getting already-registered voters to the polls. But there is little evidence that this voter contact included a system of keeping track of supporters and mobilizing them on election day.[39]

When campaigns did engage in systematic voter contact through voter identification, it was typically in cities or states that had experienced a series of ballot measures, such as California and St. Paul. California statewide campaigns were by necessity large, professional affairs, staffed by paid campaign managers and supported by an industry that was increasingly political savvy about voter contact techniques. In 1991, the St. Paul LGBT community faced its third ballot measure, another referendum on the newly passed nondiscrimination ordinance. The third campaign won, 55 to 45, and was the biggest campaign of the three. Campaign chair B. J. Metzger compared that campaign with earlier ones: "We had a lot of volunteers who got out the vote and handed out lots of literature. I think we reached more voters this time with our message, and we were able to counter the misinformation the opposition was putting out there."[40] The campaign also ran a phone-banking operation with volunteers on twenty-two phones calling thousands of St. Paul voters.[41] They completed their voter identification work early in the campaign, made persuasion calls, and sent literature to undecided voters, and "during the first five days of November [called] thousands of voters and saturated neighborhoods, shopping centers and church parking lots with literature."[42] Although activists would later dismiss some of these tactics — such as putting flyers on parked cars — as ineffective, the St. Paul campaign's approach to saturating voters with information about the campaign would be emulated in future campaigns.

Messaging

Part of this voter contact was clearly messaging, the way that campaigns framed and positioned the issue for voters. According to one political organizer, these messages are typically short sound bites that "create the framework in which a ballot question is considered" through "the use of good messages married to good messengers."[43] Between 1974 and 1991, campaigns experimented with different messages. It was within discussions about messaging that social movement issues such as visibility and assimilation were most pressing.

These messages are often developed by professional campaign consultants who test possible messages on local voters through polling and focus groups. Such polls were used in some early campaigns, such as Seattle in 1978 and almost all California statewide campaigns. A fledgling pro-gay professional campaign consulting industry arose as campaigns used the same few consultants, such as Celinda Lake and Pacy Markman. The polls and focus groups focused on moderate, undecided, potentially persuadable voters. For example, in 1982, the Austin media campaign spent more than fifty-five thousand dollars communicating to moderate voters, emphasizing privacy and general discrimination. The assumptions of Citizens for a United Austin was that "the fundamentalists will come out and vote no matter what, and so will the gays, so we're going to focus our campaign on the moderates in the middle."[44]

This focus on moderate voters led to messaging that was at odds with movement goals of visibility and "coming out" and created a conflicting relationship between the LGBT social movement and campaigns. Austin's messaging about privacy and discrimination in general was effective in early polls, but it raised the ire of many activists, who argued for more gay and lesbian visibility in the campaign. An Austin activist noted in a post-campaign commentary that "it is ironic that in a campaign against anti-gay discrimination, gay people were hardly seen and gay issues were rarely raised."[45] Many campaigns at this time used messaging that avoided addressing LGBT issues and may have even avoided using the words *homosexual* or *gay*.[46] For example, in the 1978 Seattle campaign, Citizens to Retain Fair Employment used privacy language, and asserted in one newspaper ad that "In America one of our most sacred values is the Right to Privacy. Initiative 13 threatens that right!"[47] Many campaigns, such as in St. Paul in 1978, relied on messaging about "human rights" rather than "homosexuality."[48]

In the face of blatantly homophobic accusations by the Right that LGBT individuals were pedophiles and immoral, many activists criticized this closeted messaging as a form of internalized homophobia. The assimilationist approach of the main Seattle campaign led to the creation of the Seattle Committee Against Thirteen, with the intentionally preposterous acronym SCAT. SCAT activists asserted that their campaign was one of "high visibility and public education in combating homophobia. We feel the folly of refusing to openly confront the lies and myths about lesbians and gay men is amply documented by the failure of the essentially civil rights oriented campaigns which have been waged in other cities."[49] Other campaigns, such as Eugene's 1978 referendum campaign, tried to balance closeted messaging to moderate voters with encouraging gay visibility in door-to-door canvassing, as the group's polling had suggested that running a "personal campaign" and "breaking down the myths and stereotypes that surround gay people can be one of our most effective weapons."[50]

Embedded within this debate about gay and lesbian visibility in messaging were disagreements about whether campaign messaging should respond to the opposition's assertions about LGBT life. Many early campaigns spent a lot of time countering such assertions. In 1980, the San Jose, California, campaign spent most of a press release repeating and refuting the opposition's messaging, and the Miami Dade County campaign in 1977 created a "Myths and Lies" flyer to counter the opposition's claims.[51] In 1978, St. Paul activists mailed several leaflets repeating their opposition's messaging about "parents' rights," and asserted: "Sure, parents have rights. But parents' rights aren't on the ballot. Other human rights are."[52] There were disputes within the movement about whether or not this focus on the opposition was being "defensive" and gave the opposition free media access to reiterate the stereotypes about LGBT life. In a 1978 gathering of campaign leaders, one of the purported lessons learned, according to one participant, was that "it is important for us to take the offensive in our campaign rather than being on the defensive."[53] In Denver in 1991, Tim Creekmore, of the Equal Protection Ordinance Coalition

(EPOC), emphasized that "We kept focused on the civil rights law and on not getting caught up in other issues. And we stayed on the offensive."[54]

Campaign organizers also struggled with how to depict the opposition. Several early campaigns used extreme language to describe the Right. For example, a press release from the Live and Let Live Committee in San Jose, California, disparaged the opposition's messaging and leafleting and called it "dishonest," suggesting that "it's taken the so-called 'Moral Majority of Santa Clara County' to bring hard-core pornography back to the pages of our family newspaper."[55] At times, this language negatively impacted the campaign, and, like Bigot Busting tactics, made the LGBT campaign appear undemocratic. When Seattle city officials signed a pledge asking voters to "join with us in saying no to bigotry," it backfired on the campaign when the Religious Right spokesperson claimed that "it's dangerous when the mayor and the president of the City Council go around calling the 22,000 people who signed the (initiative) petition bigots."[56]

There was no clear consensus about how to best develop political messaging that would both make a campaign succeed and advance movement goals about visibility. Indeed, political messaging has been an enduring source of tension between movement and campaign goals. The goal of LGBT visibility often clashed with the need to appeal to moderate voters.

Nonetheless, in the face of much uncertainty, activists all over the country developed creative and politically savvy tactics to fight anti-gay ballot measures. Although many of the elements of later model tactics were present, such as voter identification and professional polling, no developed set of "best practices" on how to run a campaign emerged. Indeed, tactics with contradictory logics coexisted in the absence of a dominant set of tactics.

Choosing Tactics

With this wide range of tactics and approaches to ballot campaigns, how did activists decide which tactics were the most useful? Some tactics quickly fell out of favor (such as the alteration of the referendum process); other tactics (such as door-to-door canvassing) are still used today. In this section, I introduce the interpretation of victories and defeats and the development of a social movement infrastructure as two important keys to understanding how activists select tactics. After each round of ballot measures, movement leaders and LGBT journalists examined victorious campaigns for signs of good tactics and analyzed defeated campaigns for cautionary tales. The development of a social movement infrastructure tells us much about how these tactics may spread from state to state and city to city.

Victories and Defeats

At a 2010 Creating Change workshop, one campaign consultant commented that the selection of campaign tactics is "like oral history . . . after a winning campaign everyone remembers that they used lots of lawn signs, so in the next campaign they believe that lawn signs are *the* key to winning." From 1974 to 1991, when tactics did spread from one group to the next, they were a form of oral history. In order to understand how activists selected among a variety of tactics, it is critical to examine their interpretation of victories and defeats.

In her work on the women's suffrage movement, Holly McCammon argues that political defeats are a more powerful explanation for tactical changes than political opportunities. A big defeat "can send the message to movement actors that current tactics are ineffective and new ones are needed, and thus a defeat, rather than an opportunity, should provide the impetus for change in action."[57] I argue that tactics are selected through their continual use in victorious campaigns, as well as their absence in defeats. These victories and defeats become interpretative events, as activists examine them closely for which tactics did or did not work. In her work on shantytown protests on college campuses in an attempt to get colleges to divest from apartheid South Africa, Sarah Soule suggests that these protests spread as a tactic because students believed it was successful due to its portrayal in the media.[58]

But not all victories are the same, nor are all defeats; they are interpreted differently. Victories and defeats may be more significant to political actors when they are unexpected. For example, activists may expect a victory in cities like Seattle, Eugene, and San Francisco, or in states like California and Massachusetts. Unexpected victories take place in cities or states that are considered too conservative and "unwinnable," during times when other campaigns are losing by large margins, and during times of intense Religious Right mobilization, such as during an LGBT-sponsored initiative in Boulder in 1987 or virulently homophobic AIDS initiatives in California. During this period, there were few unexpected victories: almost all victories were in progressive cities such as San Francisco, Seattle, and Portland. Unexpected defeats can also have a dramatic effect, as evidenced by the response to the failure to defeat a domestic partnership referendum in San Francisco. LGBT activists and journalists analyzed both unexpected victories and defeats in an attempt to understand which tactics influenced the outcome and which lessons to learn. Surprising defeats serve as cautionary tales, warning activists against complacency. They become "the places we should have won but didn't."

There was some useful strategizing after these early campaigns, as activists learned from defeats. For example, in the middle of escalating anti-gay referendums in 1977, activists met at the National Gay Leadership Conference in Denver, organized by national organizations to help the impending Seattle and Briggs Initiative campaigns learn from the experiences of previous campaigns. National Gay Task Force leaders such as cochairpersons Jean O'Leary and Bruce Voeller described the meeting as "the opportunity for sharing technical information" where campaign leaders "met with one another, discussed their experience and distilled the lessons they had learned, so that these facts could be compiled and made available to organizations around the country as referenda arise, and to be of immediate use in California and Seattle."[59] To develop Seattle's plan, campaign leader Charles Brydon also traveled to St. Paul, Wichita, Eugene, and Dade County to meet with other leaders.

There were some important victories during this time. Activists learned from victories in Seattle, Austin, San Francisco, and multiple statewide California initiatives, on both gay rights and AIDS issues. When the Seattle and Briggs Initiative campaigns both defeated anti-gay initiatives in November 1978, LGBT activists tried to identify which tactics made each campaign victorious, whether that was the disapproval of the Briggs Initiative by former Governor Ronald Reagan or the tolerant, liberal voters in Seattle. Newspaper accounts of Seattle's victory focused disproportionately on the disciplined messaging about invasion of privacy and government interference that the main campaign organization used.[60] This explanation for the Seattle victory encouraged local campaigns to use this type of messaging in their own campaign, and indeed, privacy messaging was popular until the early 1980s. A postelection analysis of Austin described it as "the

victory of a well-organized, well-financed campaign over an inept one . . .
it cost $55,000 to convince the public to turn out and defeat it. Freedom is
not cheap."[61] Austin, Briggs, and the LaRouche AIDS initiative in California
were seen as important victories because of their precedent-setting nature.

These victories — particularly, unexpected victories — fueled activists' in-
terpretations of certain tactics as being more effective than others. Although
there was no consensus as to which tactics were the most effective, with
each victory came a new discovery of potentially useful tactics.

Movement Infrastructure

Even with widespread agreement about the efficacy of campaign tactics,
they still may not spread across the country. Campaigns are by their nature
ephemeral organizations, typically formed for six months or less. With high
leadership turnover, particularly during the turbulent 1980s and the HIV/
AIDS crisis, it was difficult to spread information about these campaigns
beyond the immediate context. Although ballot measures can undermine
the progress of a social movement (see chapter 6), successful ballot measure campaigns also depend on the development of a social movement
infrastructure. In his book on the civil rights movement, scholar Kenneth
Andrews examines social movement infrastructures to determine whether
or not the movement has long-term impact. He focuses on three parts of
a social movement infrastructure: resources, organizational infrastructure,
and leadership.[62] For the LGBT movement, the development of campaign
leadership and resources was intimately connected to the development of
social movement organizations. Within these movement organizations,
resources and leadership were mobilized and trained to fight on ballot
measure campaigns. This social movement infrastructure includes, most
importantly, stable long-lasting national, regional, statewide, and local organizations to support ballot measure campaigns and keep the momentum of
the movement going between campaigns. National organizations are social
movement organizations that attempt to operate on a national level, working at the federal level and in several states or regions of the country simultaneously. Regional organizations focus on one region of the country, such as
New England or the Pacific Northwest. Statewide organizations focus their
efforts on one state and organize throughout the state. And local organizations include long-lasting organizations such as community centers, HIV/

AIDS service organizations, chapters of national organizations like Parents and Friends of Lesbians and Gays (PFLAG), and local political groups. In his work on LGBT campaigns, political scientist Donald Haider-Markel argues that the process of institutionalization was a critical part of the growth of the LGBT movement and often grew out of ballot measure campaigns.[63] This institutionalization of political action includes the formalization of bureaucratic organizations.

When the first campaigns began in 1974, the few established organizations were local in nature. Activists in cities and college towns across the country had formed their own political and social organizations that served the needs of their community. National organizations in the LGBT movement were fledgling organizations, and no statewide organizations existed yet. The movement was young and in the process of becoming a national movement.

However, the four national organizations that played a critical role in fighting anti-gay ballot measures were all formed during this time period. Gay lawyer Bill Thom founded Lambda Legal Defense and Education Fund in 1972 and conceived of the organization as the gay and lesbian equivalent of the NAACP (National Association for the Advancement of Colored People) or the ACLU. But Lambda Legal "became its own first client, suing to establish its very right to exist" when New York courts denied the need for a legal voluntary organization for homosexuals.[64] The National Gay and Lesbian Task Force was founded as the National Gay Task Force in 1973 by New York activists Bruce Voeller, Nathalie Rockhill, Ron Gold, and Howard Brown. Voeller, Rockhill, and Gold had worked within the post-Stonewall gay liberationist organization Gay Activists Alliance (GAA). Although it is one of the oldest LGBT national organizations, the Task Force has an organizational identity that gay historian John D'Emilio describes as "elusive." It has both worked with mainstream legislative issues and supported grassroots direct action. Historically, it "exists to fill a void . . . its purpose from its inception has been to do what needs to be done, but what no one else is doing."[65]

Two other national organizations important today were not yet created in 1974. The Human Rights Campaign (HRC) grew out of the efforts of the Gay Rights National Lobby, an organization created in 1978 to lobby Congress. Steve Endean founded the Human Rights Campaign Fund (HRCF) in 1980. From the beginning, HRCF focused on federal politics and issues.

The Gay and Lesbian Victory Fund (GLVF) was founded in 1991, more than a decade after HRCF and the Task Force were founded. GLVF is devoted to helping openly LGBT candidates win elections to local, state, and federal offices through fund-raising, campaign training, and field support.[66]

These national organizations were all weak and underfunded in the 1970s. In the 1980s, national organizations expanded dramatically in response to both the AIDS crisis and the escalating dynamics between the LGBT movement and the Religious Right.[67] All of these organizations grew increasingly professional and formal, even as their staff experienced dramatic funding problems, leadership transitions, and ideological differences. Even with this growth and development, national LGBT organizations were a fraction of the size of their Religious Right counterparts. For example, in the fiscal year from 1980 to 1981, the Task Force's budget was $338,000, whereas the Moral Majority's budget was estimated at more than $56 million.

National organizations were involved in these early LGBT campaigns to the extent their resources allowed. They attempted to coordinate the sharing of campaign resources, spreading new tactical innovations, and some fund-raising, such as the creation of the Tri-Cities Defense Fund in 1978 to raise funds for simultaneous referendums in Wichita, St. Paul, and Eugene. Bruce Voeller of the Task Force traveled to Miami Dade County several times to assist in the 1977 campaign.[68] And Task Force staff members worked with Miami Dade County activists and influenced the national media's reporting of the campaigns, along with rallying national associations like the National Organization for Women (NOW) and the American Federation of Teachers to write press releases in support of the campaign.[69] The Task Force tried to launch a national media education campaign in response to Anita Bryant's win. The organization was also involved in Wichita, meeting with the Homophile Alliance of Sedgwick County, where it brainstormed ideas about challenging the constitutionality of the Wichita referendum on a local or federal level.[70] Lambda Legal assisted local campaigns in using the court system to challenge early referendums and initiatives. The Task Force and HRCF allowed local campaigns to use their fund-raising lists and cultivated social networks among activists. National organizations donated money, contributed advice in person and over the phone, and assisted with fund-raising when possible.

National organizations also collected information about local campaigns, including examples of campaign messaging, messaging polls, and campaign strategic plans, and archived this information for future campaigns. When tactical innovations were considered effective, newly formed national organizations attempted to disseminate tactics to local activists. They served as clearinghouses for information about campaigns, which were often ephemeral organizations that left no records, so that lessons learned from victorious campaigns could be retained from one decade to another. Campaign workers from later campaigns, such as the Denver 1991 referendum, stressed the importance of information they received from the Task Force.[71]

There were few statewide organizations at this time, and the ones that did exist were fledgling organizations in non-battleground states. However, a local movement infrastructure was beginning to develop in many cities. For example, in Seattle, there were several established local lesbian and gay organizations in the 1970s that were used to recruit supporters and leaders for the 1978 campaign. This local infrastructure put Seattle at an advantage in comparison to cities like Wichita that had little local community infrastructure. Areas that faced a referendum may have been more likely to have an established LGBT rights organization, because a local organization might have been formed for the purpose of pursuing a local nondiscrimination ordinance. For example, in California, the Santa Clara Coalition for Human Rights was formed in 1976 and transformed into a campaign to fight a referendum in 1980 on the newly passed nondiscrimination ordinance in Santa Clara County.

At times, campaigns built the movement infrastructure. Many gay historians and activists have remarked on the importance of the Miami–Dade defeat in mobilizing the masses, as evidenced by the epigraph that begins this chapter. According to one Task Force staff member shortly before the defeat, "the backlash in Miami has brought us together and has strengthened us as a national political movement. And it has given us the chance to speak out on the really big issues that concern us. Whether we've won or lost the Miami vote, the challenge will be there. And it will be up to us to meet it."[72]

The Long Road Ahead

It was evident from the beginning that the relationship between ballot measure campaigns and social movements could be both complementary and contradictory. The defeat in Dade County strengthened the movement, drawing interested bystanders into the growing movement. However, the movement infrastructure was not strong enough to support ballot measure campaigns all over the country. Such campaigns also brought to the surface tensions within the movement about the role of visibility, assimilation, and direct action, tensions that would continue to fester. Within this tension between movements and campaigns, activists developed new and innovative tactics to fight anti-gay ballot measures. Although these tactics were at times contradictory, activists used each victory and defeat to re-assess the effectiveness of each tactic.

At the end of 1991, it was clear that something dramatic was happening in the world of Religious Right ballot measures. That year, the LGBT movement was hit with a barrage of attempted ballot measures that were the most draconian the movement had yet seen. Most of these measures were prevented from going to the ballot box, but a growing Religious Right backlash was coming that would dramatically change the nature of ballot measure campaigns.

CHAPTER 3

FIGHTING THE RIGHT IN THE 90s
DEVELOPING SOPHISTICATED CAMPAIGNS

> As the American gay and lesbian movement approaches its
> sixth decade of political activism, it finds itself at a contra-
> dictory juncture: what Dickens would call the best of times
> and the worst of times. On one level, our movement has been
> a staggering, if controversial, success; yet on another level, gay
> and lesbian people remain profoundly stigmatized, struggling
> against the same crises—in health, violence, discrimination and
> social services—that have plagued us for decades . . . A backlash
> against gay rights swells at the same instant we witness the
> widest cultural opening gay people have ever experienced; public
> opinion is deeply divided about how to respond to our emergence
> from the shadows.
>
> Urvashi Vaid, *Virtual Equality:*
> *The Mainstreaming of Gay and Lesbian Liberation*

AS URVASHI VAID OBSERVES, 1992 to 1996 was indeed "the best of times and the worst of times." In the midst of progress in media visibility and in the treatment of HIV/AIDS, the LGBT community was faced with the largest and most dramatic culture war against LGBT rights to date. A growing Religious Right targeted the LGBT movement in the name of "family values"; this right-wing backlash included attempted ballot measures from California to Maine and the use of draconian legal-restrictive initiatives. The LGBT movement struggled internally with issues around inclusivity, as community members who were transgender, bisexual, and people of color pushed for explicit inclusion in the movement. Queer activists also criticized the mainstreaming of the LGBT movement as direct action became contested within the larger movement.

In the electoral arena, the movement was under attack all over the country, as LGBT campaigns in Idaho, Colorado, Oregon, and Maine fought off legal-restrictive initiatives from the statewide level to the smallest rural town. In areas of the country that had little movement infrastructure, many of these campaigns were ones in which "inexperienced social movement organizations led disorganized campaigns to maintain lesbian and gay rights on shoestring budgets."[1] Between 1993 and 1996, for every state, city, or town that faced a ballot measure on election day, there was one additional state, city, or town that mobilized to prevent an attempted ballot measure.

Yet this time period of heightened Religious Right activism also sparked the development of new models on how to run campaigns, including an increasing focus on techniques such as voter identification that were developed after the successful Oregon campaign to fight Ballot Measure 9. For the first time, a model campaign was developed that included tactics that gained credibility nationally and eventually led to their widespread adoption. These model tactics developed in response to a combination of an unexpected victory in Oregon and the dramatic escalation of efforts by the Religious Right at the ballot box. The spread of these tactics was supported by a growing movement infrastructure to support ballot measures campaigns. National organizations developed small field programs to support local campaigns and began to train activists on how to best run campaigns. These smaller campaigns sometimes grew into a statewide organization — an important step, even though many early statewide organizations were weak.

With the use of these model campaign tactics and the increasing professionalization of campaigns came new debates about the relationship between the movement and its campaigns. The model campaign plan assumed that "one campaign fits all" and raised concerns about whether the model could work for both rural and statewide campaigns alike. Increasingly, organizations debated the issue of LGBT visibility and the role of direct action in campaign politics. All winning statewide campaigns during this time period used professional campaign organizers and tactics, such as voter identification. However, there was growing concern about the larger cost of these professional campaigns — the cost to community solidarity, resources, and leadership — and debate about the impact these campaigns had on the larger movement.

This chapter traces the complicated and contradictory development of dominant tactics based on a model campaign and contributing to gaps in social movement theory about how some tactics become preferred over others. The development of this model campaign began with the November 1992 elections.

Turning Points in Oregon and Colorado

In 1992, the LGBT movement faced a turning point as a social movement, and in response organizers changed the way they approached campaigns. It was evident by the Republican National Convention in 1992 that the Right was escalating its attack on LGBT rights.[2] This escalation included two of the most contested anti-gay initiatives in U.S. history thus far: Oregon Ballot Measure 9 and Colorado Amendment 2. Urvashi Vaid, the executive director of the Task Force at the time, noted that "This is the Right's new strategy. They're test-marketing it in Oregon and Colorado. They have a comprehensive agenda to eliminate the gains of the civil rights movement."[3] At this critical moment, many LGBT activists realized the importance of winning (and losing) campaigns and began paying increased attention to which tactics were more effective than others.

LGBT organizers and activists developed this "model campaign" by comparing tactics used in victorious and unsuccessful campaigns. One campaign in particular, No on 9, was analyzed closely for keys to its unexpected victory. Analysis focused on campaign tactics, and generally did not take into consideration other influences that might explain why No on 9 won, suggesting that activists' interpretation of tactical efficacy should be central to the scholarly analysis of tactics. This emphasis on Oregon's tactics demonstrates the importance of both the explanation of victories and support by national organizations in the development of model campaign tactics. The Oregon campaign in 1992 became the model for two reasons: the tactical development between the 1988 and 1992 Oregon campaigns and comparisons between Oregon and Colorado in 1992.

In 1988, the Oregon LGBT community unsuccessfully fought an initiative to rescind the governor's executive order on gay rights.[4] The 1992 Oregon campaign took into account lessons learned by activists in the unsuccessful 1988 campaign. In 1988, Oregonians for Fairness ran a short campaign with extensive fund-raising and clear messaging about "witch hunts" that never mentioned the word *gay*.[5] However, when Oregon was faced with a statewide initiative in 1992, the LGBT community benefited from the earlier campaign experience and was aware of the divisions it had caused in the community. Although initially paralyzed by campaign infighting, the Campaign for a Hate Free Oregon/No on 9 campaign developed into a professional campaign, with an experienced campaign manager and an early start on the campaign season. The focus of the No on 9 campaign field strategy in the last four months included a strong field program with voter identification and GOTV. It was the first statewide LGBT initiative to identify voters en masse, trying to identify a hundred thousand voters' positions on the initiative through phone banking.[6] This narrow focus did not come without controversy, as the No on 9 campaign was criticized for isolating direct-action groups such as Queer Nation and Bigot Busters and running a "straight" or closeted campaign, common issues in campaigns that are addressed later in this chapter.[7]

That same year, a Denver-based LGBT organization ran a campaign that was in sharp contrast to the No on 9 campaign. The organization that ran the Colorado Amendment 2 campaign had no experience organizing a statewide campaign, and took an approach that many activists considered to be "straight" or closeted. The campaign strategy was badly informed by polling that used poorly worded questions and misrepresented voters' support of Amendment 2.[8] Because the organization was initially based in Denver, the campaign had difficulty growing into a statewide campaign. As a result, it had problems unifying the state efforts and could not grow large enough to do any meaningful voter identification. The wording used on the ballot was also confusing, and seemed "benign" and legalistic; even the voters who fully supported the campaign were uncertain how to vote.[9]

At the November 1992 Task Force–sponsored Creating Change conference, a conference that attracts thousands of activists from across the country, Oregon campaign manager Peggy Norman issued a warning to attendees: "Don't think even for a minute that because we won in Oregon that we did it right and because they lost in Colorado they did it wrong."[10] However, throughout the conference the Colorado campaign's strategy and actions were picked apart in session after session for examples of what not to do. Criticism of the campaign oftentimes came from Colorado activists themselves. One Colorado campaign worker characterized the problem with the campaign as a strategy problem: "It wasn't so much about money, it was about strategy. It was so complacent. It was a closeted strategy. It de-gayed the whole issue. It was a strategy that we deliberately chose."[11] The Oregon campaign quickly became the model campaign; lessons learned in Colorado were characterized as negative, and any possibly positive lessons learned were lost.

Subsequent use of the No on 9 campaign as a model focused on the prominence of tactics in explaining the campaign's victory. According to one No on 9 campaign leader, the Oregon and Colorado campaigns were not comparable because Oregon had "an easier ballot measure to fight" thanks to the extreme nature of the initiative.[12] Alternative explanations for No on 9's success, such as the outpouring of national involvement and financial support in the last four months, were neglected; almost all the credit for success was attributed to the tactics used in Oregon. Because the trend was to celebrate the Oregon campaign and its tactics, subsequent campaigns ignored disputes that had, at times, paralyzed the campaign. The dominance of the Oregon model was buoyed even further by victories in unexpected places. A win in Idaho in 1994 in a campaign that modeled its tactics on the No on 9 campaign reassured LGBT activists that Oregon campaign tactics could work in conservative states as well.[13]

Even leaders from victorious and unsuccessful campaigns were treated differently. Many No on 9 campaign leaders went on to work for national organizations and achieved visibility within the LGBT media. One Oregon campaign activist described feeling like a movement "celebrity" and said that many Oregon leaders were treated like "giant killers" because of their success against the Right. In contrast, Colorado activist Sue Anderson described the "cannibalism" of leaders in Colorado after the defeat, as leaders were attacked for their decision-making and leadership styles.

This interpretation of Oregon's victory and Colorado's defeat led to the development of dominant tactics and a model campaign plan. When the Religious Right dramatically escalated its use of ballot measures after 1992, LGBT leaders were able to identify which tactics worked in Oregon, demonstrating the interplay between victories and countermovement mobilization. For the first time, there was a "model campaign," a campaign plan of best practices and winning tactics, that could be used to defeat the anti-gay Right. National organization support became critical for spreading these model campaign tactics all over the country.

The Model Campaign

This model campaign based on No on 9 was more sophisticated than earlier campaigns; it was larger, better funded, centrally organized, well-disciplined, and systematic in its approach to finding supportive voters. A handbook about ballot measure campaigns by the Lesbian Avengers, a direct-action group, refers to them critically as "mainstream campaigns" and traces their origins to the 1992 election year.[14] National field-workers initially called this "the Oregon model" of campaigns, modeled after the 1992 Oregon campaign and its strong field program.

Forming a model campaign started with a small group of knowledgeable, politically savvy activists with connections in the larger LGBT community. The group probably included paid staff of the local LGBT organizations. Generally, this smaller committee then trained and recruited volunteers, hired a campaign manager (and ideally a few support staff members), worked with national organizations to train more involved volunteers on issues like media speaking and voter identification, pulled in enough money through fund-raising to put a poll in the field to determine the best campaign messages, and sorted the individuals on the committee into clear campaign roles such as treasurer and volunteer coordinator. The steering committee then ideally proceeded to work with the campaign manager to run the campaign, creating a campaign message, holding press conferences, getting endorsements from political and religious allies, creating commercials and print advertising, creating and distributing yard signs, fund-raising, and coordinating large number of volunteers in phone banking and door-to-door canvassing in order to identify voters. The defining feature of these campaigns was their overriding focus on getting at least 50 percent of the vote (plus one more voter) on election day. This model campaign illustrated the *ideal* campaign; many campaigns were unable to engage in *all* these tactics. The success of individual campaigns at fund-raising often determined which tactics a campaign could use. Without enough funds, for instance, the campaign could not create television political ads or hire a volunteer coordinator.

Even so, the Oregon model spread remarkably quickly. In 1993, just months after the success in Oregon, activists anticipating statewide initiatives (many of which never materialized) prepared plans that mirrored the Oregon campaign. When the Missouri "Show Me Equality" organizers found themselves in the throes of internal squabbling over how the campaign should be run, they developed a plan that depended on "standard political expertise and the history of similar campaigns to design and mount a winning campaign. We will rely on professional consultants, pollsters and field workers to help us determine the best message and tactics with which we can convince the required number of voters to oppose this initiative in November."[15] The two most important parts of the model campaign were changes in voter contact and messaging, along with the size and scale of campaigns.

Voter Contact

The biggest change the Oregon model brought to campaign tactics was the systematic use of voter identification. Many campaign consultants describe voter ID and systematic voter contact as *the* biggest change in LGBT campaign work overall. The power of voter identification came from its success in No on 9. The No on 9 campaign trained activists across the state, tested phone scripts, and ultimately identified 138,000 voters. Voter identification became a key focus because organizers realized that the key to winning campaigns was a simple matter of numbers: the campaign with the most supportive voters will win. Accordingly, the easiest way to win is to ensure that you have enough supportive voters to constitute a majority, and make sure those voters show up on election day. Voter contact and identification were a critical part of the model campaign. Many campaign plans during this time period lauded the necessity of an "aggressive grassroots campaign of one-on-one voter contact."[16]

Such an aggressive campaign included identifying the number of supporters and designing the campaign to reach and motivate only those individuals who voted on a regular basis (frequently called "chronic voters"). As one campaign leader explained, "Signs don't vote. Mailings don't vote. Even people don't vote. Voters vote." Voter contact strategy typically started with a list of registered voters, ideally a list that was sorted by demographics, such as party or marital status. If a campaign did not have such a detailed list and/or was short on time, managers would narrow their focus to specific precincts or counties that were known as being Democratic, or more liberal. With a list of registered voters, staff could contact potentially supportive voters, to establish their base, their network of funders, and regular volunteers to run the campaign. Later, the list made it possible to contact other potential supporters. Through phone banking and door-to-door canvassing, volunteers then contacted and identified strong and "soft" supporters, along with potentially persuadable voters (PVs). This process expended no effort to engage voters who were strongly opposed to LGBT rights. The model campaign process was to identify those strongly opposed in the first voter contact, subsequently to engage with them little and plan no future contact. However, identified supporters and persuadable voters were contacted with direct-mail material and follow-up phone calls to remind them to vote on election day. On election day, volunteers sat with a list of supportive voters, checking them off as they voted and, as poll closing times approached, calling any voters who had not yet cast their vote.

Voter identification required growing the number of volunteers who worked on campaigns, and developing more "people power." In order to identify all these voters, campaigns had to recruit large numbers of volunteers, looking to progressive heterosexual support as well as LGBT community members. As campaign manager Nicole LeFavour noted, members of the Idaho campaign in 1994 "had to do something on a scale that I don't think the progressive community in Idaho had ever done before."[17] The 1990s campaigns also relied on the growth of computing technology and the growing availability of affordable personal computers that could be used to track large numbers of identified voters.

Messaging

Campaigns systematically contacted targeted voters, delivering a message about the content of the ballot measure and the consequences of its passage. According to Pacy Markman, a campaign consultant on LGBT ballot measure campaigns, campaigns needed to do two things to deliver their message: first, in addition to support from professional pollsters and a media consultant, they needed "a campaign manager who has real power," who would "fend off the well-meaning suggestions for media advertising that everyone and his brother and sister will offer";[18] second, they needed a focused message as they were working within the constraints of the electoral system, in which voters have a limited attention span and campaigns have a limited amount of money. During this period, more campaigns used professional polls to develop their message, and, consequently, messaging became more professional and savvy at framing the opposition. Their messaging became more disciplined—the campaign staff and volunteers repeated the same message over and over again—and, with a smaller number of people making most of the decisions, messaging became more organized and centralized.

As with earlier campaigns, the LGBT movement continued to debate how visible LGBT lives should be within the campaign message, and whether the message should serve a long-term goal (such as education) or a short-term goal (such as winning), or both. As professional pollsters and media consultants developed the language for each successive wave of legal-restrictive initiatives, they found that most effective messaging focused on unintended consequences of legal-restrictive initiatives (i.e., altering the Constitution or union contracts), fear of government intervention, and disdain for the Religious Right as a movement of outsiders or extremists. For example, when the LGBT community in Maine fought a stealth legal-restrictive initiative in 1995, a professional poll done by Celinda Lake suggested that the message should oppose the initiative by pointing out that "it is written by Maine outsiders who don't know what is best for the state and who don't care about the consequences because they will leave the state once the battle is over. We need to show to Mainers that we are inside Maine through and through and that we have the best interests of the state at heart."[19] Similar messaging was used in Idaho and Oregon. It seldom focused on gay or lesbian visibility, because polling suggested that that approach would not sway voters in a tight election. As Pacy Markman noted, "Our research showed what you would expect— that no thirty-second commercial could undo 30 or more years of learned homophobia."[20] Ironically, professional polling often resulted in less LGBT visibility in campaign messaging.

At a time when LGBT visibility was increasing, and increasingly seen as important, the model campaign's approach to messaging flew in the face of queer, direct-action sensibilities. Messaging was expensive, especially in statewide campaigns, and many activists lamented the loss of funds to messages that could have been used to further LGBT visibility, in addition to increasing voter numbers. Idaho activist Bob Dunn expressed his concerns about money spent on campaigns and dominant tactics even after the defeat of Idaho Proposition 1, a replica of Oregon Ballot Measure 9. Dunn lamented that "many arts, education and other worthwhile groups had to do without our donations due to this campaign. A gay and lesbian community center could have been built. We could have also done a lot of educating about gays and lesbians."[21] National field-workers also criticized Idaho's messaging as potentially harmful to the long-term goals of the movement: a focus on "big government intrusion" could backfire and harm efforts to pass a statewide LGBT rights bill. Lack of lesbian and gay visibility may lead to gay and lesbian community members having less ownership in the campaign.[22] Other national field-workers encouraged local campaigns to use professional polling but to develop messaging that addressed the real issue of the campaign: "gay rights." Even within the campaign against Ballot Measure 9, messaging about how the initiative was a threat to all citizens created "considerable behind the scenes turmoil within the gay and lesbian communities over the perceived invisibility of gay and lesbian people in the campaign and its messages."[23] Direct-action activists such as Christina McKnight of the Lesbian Avengers were critical of the campaigns for allowing the Religious Right to monopolize the messaging about LGBT life, because "whenever the Christian right is the only group talking about us, we are in trouble."[24]

Model campaign messaging responded to neither the Religious Right claims about gay and lesbian life nor the use of racialized special rights language. That approach damaged efforts at coalition building (see chapter 6). Finding a pithy, narrow message to counter special rights language was difficult, as evidenced by the campaign against Amendment 2. As one campaign organizer stated, "there is no one good phrase or slogan to counter 'special rights.' It takes fifteen minutes of real discussion to undo the damage that phrase does."[25]

What did improve with the increased use of professional polling was better campaign messaging about the opposition. Through professional polls and work by organizations such as People for the American Way, local campaigns conducted more opposition research than they had in the past to help them understand their local Religious Right. As a result, Oregon messaging in the 1992 and 1994 campaigns effectively demonstrated the extremism of the OCA, the group proposing the LGBT initiative. With professional polling, campaigns started to experiment with language such as "the far Right" to describe the Religious Right, language that resonated with voters. In Idaho, activists were able to position the Right as outsiders coming over from Oregon. At times, LGBT campaigns' opposition messaging went too far. During Cincinnati Issue 3, a local legal-restrictive initiative, campaign workers developed a series of political ads that compared the opposition to Nazis, an approach that was criticized nationally as contributing to their loss.

These four key elements—improved voter contact, the development of effective messaging, successful fund-raising, and an increase in professional campaign staff—were the primary thrust of the model campaign, a model that would dominate LGBT campaigns for the next two decades. Coupled with the continuing use of pre-ballot legal challenges and ballot box avoidance techniques, this model campaign plan approach has been credited with several statewide victories between 1992 and 1996, including in Maine, Idaho, and Oregon. The lack or misuse of these widely acknowledged successful tactics was a recurring explanation for failed campaigns. While failed campaigns received support and sympathy from national organizations and local activists, they received criticism as well, particularly in the area of political messaging. In addition to the focus on these model campaign tactics, activists continued innovating with new ways of fighting legal-restrictive initiatives.

Postelection Challenges

Complementary to the development of model campaign tactics were new tactics to prevent current or future legal-restrictive initiatives. These new tactics did not conflict with model campaign tactics and included post-ballot legal challenges to invalidate initiatives like Amendment 2 that had passed at the ballot box. There were also attempts at both boycotts and "buycotts" (a reverse boycott in which supportive businesses are rewarded with clientele) to discourage the Right from sponsoring initiatives and to warn future voters of the consequences of approving anti-gay ballot measures. Although post-ballot legal challenges were overwhelmingly supported within the movement, boycotts and "buycotts" were more controversial. The 1990s saw LGBT organizations experimenting with their effectiveness, but for the most part, boycotts and "buycotts" were not used after this time period.

These new tactics exploited the weaknesses of legal-restrictive initiatives, including their questionable constitutionality and evident unfairness. Once referendums were passed, the LGBT movement had few grounds through which to challenge them legally; however, there had been successful post-ballot legal challenges of initiatives in Oregon in 1988 and Concord in 1991.[26] LGBT legal advocates had some success in getting ballot measures dismissed post-ballot because of voting irregularities. Yet often when ballot measures were thrown out because of irregularities, as in Tampa and Junction City, Oregon, it just resulted in another ballot measure. However, three legal-restrictive initiatives—Colorado Amendment 2, Cincinnati Issue 3, and Alachua Charter Amendment 1—were challenged post-ballot, and two of these challenges resulted in findings that were a marked success for the movement.[27] When Colorado Amendment 2 was overturned in the Supreme Court case *Romer v. Evans,* it was the biggest legal victory for the LGBT movement to date. In their book *Strangers to the Law,* Lisa Keen and Suzanne Goldberg document the complexity of the court case. The Supreme Court struck down Amendment 2 as unconstitutional on the grounds that it makes lesbian and gay individuals strangers to the law, along with allowing voters across the state to eliminate local city ordinances. The immediate consequence of *Romer v. Evans* was that the anti-gay Right canceled ballot initiative petitions circulating in Oregon and Idaho for the 1996 ballot.[28] The long-term consequences were that statewide legal-restrictive initiatives were prohibited, discouraging the Right's use of this strategy and demonstrating that even the LGBT movement, the smaller movement, could succeed in diverting the Right's tactics.

The second attempt at altering the Right's tactics post-ballot with boycotts and "buycotts" were not as successful. The passage of Colorado Amendment 2 was the most significant defeat for the LGBT movement to date, because it eliminated not only existing protections but also the potential for future legislation. The defeat sent shock waves across the movement nationally. Colorado community leader Sue Anderson recalled that the morning after Colorado Amendment 2's passage, there were 110 messages on her answering machine from all over the country. At the Task Force's Creating Change conference shortly after the election, Anderson was present when organizers from across the country strategized on how best to respond to the amendment's passage:

> I remember sitting in the floor of a hotel somewhere in Detroit
> or Dallas or wherever we were that year. We were all strategizing

and Urvashi [Vaid] was there and talking about having something like a Mississippi Freedom Summer thing in Colorado and just having people flood the state with organizing. And we had this hour-long conversation strategizing. Meanwhile, on the steps of the Capitol, a group of activists who weren't really involved in the campaign were calling for a boycott. I came out of the meeting and got phone messages about the boycott, and had to go right back to the drawing board.[29]

The boycott emerged out of a group aptly called Boycott Colorado and was unconnected to the campaign to fight Amendment 2. Indeed, several leaders expressed feeling "boxed into a corner" by the demands of the boycott, including the demand that the boycott not be lifted until statewide nondiscrimination protections were passed. The inspiration for the boycott came from a series of boycotts led by other movements in the early 1990s, including the boycott of Arizona for not recognizing Martin Luther King Jr. day as a holiday and Miami for not welcoming antiapartheid leader Nelson Mandela. Both the LGBT movement and the anti-gay Right had attempted business boycotts as well. The Arizona and Miami boycotts had been invoked during campaign messaging during this time period, particularly in the Oregon Ballot Measure 9 messaging that targeted business leaders.[30] Although the boycott ostensibly slowed down tourism in Colorado during the ski season, many LGBT activists argued that it disproportionately harmed gay and lesbian business owners and low-income hospitality workers.[31] It was seen as successful, however, in costing Colorado more than $40 million in income. That is a trivial amount in a state with such a large tourism industry, but the boycott was also seen as having harmed Colorado's reputation. A shorter boycott was led by queer activists in Cincinnati after the passage of Issue 3, and an unsuccessful "buycott" was held in Tampa after the passage of a referendum, both in 1993.[32]

These innovations did not conflict with model campaign tactics and provided options for LGBT communities to continue fighting anti-gay ballot measures long after their passage. However, the boycott as a tactic was controversial in Colorado and elsewhere, and its efficacy was debated. These tactics did not receive as much institutional support as model campaign tactics. Although Lambda Legal assisted with post-ballot legal challenges and there was great organizational investment in the *Romer v. Evans* Supreme Court case, most movement resources went toward teaching LGBT activists how to run campaigns.

Creating a Movement Infrastructure for Ballot Measures

In 1993, Dave Fleischer was a newly hired campaign trainer for the Gay and Lesbian Victory Fund (GLVF). One of his first actions was to accompany two Task Force staff members to Lewiston, Maine, to see the ballot measure campaign there. Fleischer was a white gay man who had been involved in electoral campaigns all throughout New York State, working with many minority candidates. Working with minority candidates gave him "some insight into how to help people from communities that are usually shut out figure out a different model for how you run for office. Because when you just mimic what a favored individual does or what a favored group does, it usually isn't very successful."[33] Fleischer learned a great deal about LGBT ballot measures on his trip to Lewiston:

> That one-day trip was really instructive for me. I had paid attention to anti-gay ballot measures, but I guess I didn't appreciate how much trouble we were in locally. What really struck me in Lewiston was . . . that our side was essentially not responding in a way that was going to have any impact on the electoral outcome. What we were doing was well intended but really small . . . It was really apparent in even spending a day there . . . that they didn't have very many people involved, so they hardly had anyone volunteering to do anything. They had hardly any people donating any money. They had very little people power and very little money, which is why nothing they were doing was going to be very effective. And so I felt good about going up there, in the sense that I learned something.[34]

Fleischer went on to become one of the most influential campaign trainers in LGBT history, teaching thousands of activists how to fight anti-gay ballot measures. In 1993, as he was beginning to form strategies for including ballot measures in his campaign trainings for GLVF, other national organization staff members were considering how they could best assist local campaigns during this intense period of Religious Right activism.

The early to mid-1990s was a period of accelerated Religious Right activity that shook up existing LGBT organizations and added to the growing infrastructure to support ballot measures campaigns. One of the biggest shifts was the development of resources and allocation of staff in national organizations to help local campaigns fight ballot measures, along with the development of statewide organizations that grew out of campaigns. National organizations began to focus on ballot measures, supporting and spreading model campaign tactics and hiring and training staff members whose job was to assist campaigns.

National organizations — specifically, the Task Force, GLVF, and HRCF — played a role in spreading Oregon model campaign tactics across the country. In the face of Religious Right attacks, some of national organization energy was channeled into assisting local campaigns.[35] Funding and staff resources were diverted away from existing programs to local campaigns and field programs.

However, the roles national organizations played in supporting campaigns differed from organization to organization. The Task Force, which specialized in grassroots organizing and organizational team building, established a Fight the Right program in 1993 to work on organizational development and fieldwork support for campaigns. It hired Scot Nakagawa, who had worked on the No on 9 campaign, as a field-worker. The Task Force Fight the Right was technically less funded and more community-focused than HRCF, which Task Force field staff described as "the 50 percent + 1" group. In 1993 alone, Fight the Right field staff conducted twelve workshops in eleven states, along with presentations at three conferences.[36] Nakagawa remembers that when Task Force field-workers led a workshop for Fight the Right at Creating Change in 1993, there was so much interest in the program that "there wasn't a ballroom that could contain all the people who wanted to participate."[37] The Gay and Lesbian Victory Fund, which focused on supporting openly lesbian and gay candidates during elections, started including ballot campaign leaders in their trainings on how to run political campaigns, which emphasized the importance of fund-raising and volunteer recruitment. Fleischer and GLVF colleagues trained campaign leaders from all ten of the states that were facing anti-gay initiatives in February 1994. They also conducted many other trainings that were ultimately used to develop the Power Summit training now used by the Task Force.[38] And HRCF, which had strengths in fund-raising and media coverage, gave start-up funds to hire managers for local campaigns, including the 1994 campaigns in Oregon, Idaho, and Maine.[39] HRCF's goals included going to ballot initiative states to "provide technical support, on-site research, implement houseparty fundraising programs, trainings, conduct constituency outreach and participate in a comprehensive Get Out the Vote program."[40] Part of the HRCF campaign was national coordination and the creation of "products that will be of use to every campaign such as media spots, message development and opposition research."[41] HRCF planned to spend almost $1 million on its new ballot measure campaign program, Americans Against Discrimination. Much of HRCF's support to local campaigns was visible only to campaign staff and steering committees in an attempt not to "threaten the local control of the campaign or give the appearance or opportunity for headlines about 'national gay right activists' descending on their state."[42] Other organizations helped as well. Lambda Legal Defense and the ACLU launched pre- and post-ballot legal challenges, and People for the American Way conducted background research on the Religious Right.[43]

LGBT activists across the country were not sure what surprises would be in store for them in 1993 and 1994. After the passage of Amendment 2 in Colorado, Religious Right activists across the country collected petitions for their own statewide initiatives, sending the LGBT movement into a state of panic. After 1992, campaigns across the country adopted the Oregon model of voter identification, disciplined political messaging, pre-ballot legal challenges, and direct action to prevent petition collection. The Oregon campaign's emphasis on professionalism, including using paid staff and professional polling to develop messaging and voter identification strategies, reflected trends that had already existed, but after the Oregon campaign's success in 1992, those trends became dominant campaign tactics.

The most dramatic evidence of the shift toward the use of the Oregon model can be seen in the Task Force Fight the Right literature, a training guide widely used by LGBT activists in organizing against local referendums or initiatives in the mid-1990s. The 1992 Fight the Right kit, which was written before the vote on Oregon Ballot Measure 9, emphasizes four main tactics: registering gay and lesbian people to vote, media activism, pressuring presidential candidates, and organizing demonstrations and other direct-action events. Most of the material in the kit came from noncampaign-related organizations, such as the AIDS Action Council.[44] However, in 1993

Fight the Right staff members revised their kit, filling it with advice from the Oregon No on 9 campaign and emphasizing three key tactics: voter identification, canvassing, and GOTV.[45] Almost all articles within the 130-page guide were written by Oregon activists, and the guide was ultimately distributed to more than ten thousand activists in 1993 and 1994. Future guides for activists reflected this emphasis on Oregon campaign tactics with little variation. The No on 9 victory clearly influenced the advice given in the Fight the Right kit. And the distribution of the Fight the Right kit demonstrates the role of national organizations in documenting and advocating for the use of dominant tactics.

This development of resources for campaign activists often came at tremendous cost to organizational resources. After the Fight the Right campaign in 1993 and 1994, the Task Force was drained financially; the field staff was drained emotionally and burned out. Gay historian and former Task Force board member John D'Emilio called Fight the Right a failure:

> [Fight the Right made the Task Force] thoroughly reactive, completely dependent on what one's political opponents did rather than on what queer communities wanted or needed. It offered few tangible achievements that the organization could claim for itself or deliver to its constituency. It made many of the organization's partners angry as commitments to preexisting work, such as the antiviolence project or the campus project, were dropped. Finally, it created within the organization a sense of embattlement, of being besieged by enemies, of daily being on the verge of Armageddon.[46]

In particular, D'Emilio criticizes the way programs like Fight the Right turned the focus of national organizations into a defensive rather than an offensive posture, eliminating educational programs like antiviolence programming in favor of defeating anti-gay ballot measures. Queer activists nationally were critical of the narrow focus of Fight the Right and the way the organization's tactics were predetermined and inflexible. For example, journalist and activist Donna Minkowitz was publicly critical of the Task Force's presentation on campaign tactics at the 1993 March on Washington: "I wish the Task Force's Fight the Right project had used the presence of a million queers in D.C. last weekend to build a movement, not to blindfold and gag it."[47]

Nationally, there was also dissent about the role of national organizations' involvement in local campaigns (covered in greater detail in chapter 5). After a GLVF training for organizers of campaigns in potential battleground states in 1994, organizers jointly penned a letter to the Task Force and the HRCF that presented several demands, including a unified, coordinated campaign plan between national organizations and changes in fund-raising. These organizers expressed concern that national organizations were reacting to Colorado Amendment 2 and various initiative threats with a heightened sense of urgency by focusing on national fundraising. Organizers demanded that the Task Force and HRCF instead direct more of the available funds to local campaigns.[48]

Statewide Organizations

The spread of model campaign tactics was also facilitated by the creation of statewide organizations in many battleground states that were targeted by the Religious Right and the growth of social networks between activists in different states. Activists founded statewide organizations to support both state and local level ballot measures; these organizations were most likely to develop in battleground states after each round of new initiatives.[49]

Oregon and Washington developed the strongest statewide organizations during the 1990s. Oregon's Basic Rights grew out of campaign organizations developed in 1992 and 1994, when the state faced its third initiative. No infrastructure grew out of the 1988 campaign. After the 1988 Oregon campaign, activists "threw everything important in a few boxes, gave the furniture away, swept the floor and left," leaving little trace of their approach to campaign organizing beyond the personal memories of individuals involved in the campaign. According to longtime LGBT campaign consultant Thalia Zepatos, after the 1992 campaign they had "real knowledge these weren't individual efforts and they were going to happen again and again."[50] What Oregon activists realized was the importance of creating a social movement organization that could be a launching pad, if necessary, for upcoming campaigns; and in between, campaigns could conduct voter identification efforts and education efforts. Further north, Washington State LGBT activists conducted a campaign that successfully prevented a series of statewide initiatives from reaching the ballot box. The campaign was organized in part by Washington Citizens for Fairness/

Hands Off Washington, a political organizing committee founded in 1992. Although it was short-lived, Washington Citizens for Fairness trained a future generation of political leaders in that state.

The development of statewide organizations made it easier for campaign tactics to be shared through networks between state leaders. For example, activists in both Maine and Idaho consulted directly with Oregon activists when they were experiencing statewide initiatives.[51] Statewide organizations also engaged in foundational work for campaigns between elections. For example, they grew their voter identification lists after the campaign and used the list to get LGBT or pro-gay candidates elected, thus facilitating the passage of pro-LGBT legislation. This use of voter identification could facilitate coalitions with other progressive social movements. For example, in Idaho in 1994, LGBT campaign activists teamed up with the Idaho pro-choice campaign to create voter identification lists that were later used to support a minimum-wage initiative. This extended use of voter identification continued into the next wave of LGBT initiatives in the early 2000s, as is discussed in chapter 5. Most important, these organizations provided "continuity and historical memory." According to Dave Fleischer, "Where we don't learn, where our community has the equivalent of Alzheimer's disease, is because there isn't a local institution."[52]

This developing movement infrastructure was critical for the support and dissemination of model campaign tactics. Local activists did not just read about model tactics in an LGBT newspaper but also heard about them at national conferences, in trainings on how to run campaigns, during phone calls with field-workers, and from other campaign leaders. The model tactics supported by the No on 9 campaign were becoming increasingly popular.

Challenging Model Campaigns

Although the Oregon model became the dominant and expected model by which to run a campaign, buy-in was not universal; there were many disagreements about the Oregon approach. Many activists criticized model campaign tactics as being too mainstream, too dogmatic, and too focused on a "one size fits all" approach that denied the diversity of experiences and attitudes within communities. Others suggested that reliance on this campaign style was harming the movement. Resistance to the model campaign approach was one of the factors that led to formation of splinter groups that broke off from several main campaigns, including campaigns in Oregon and Alachua County, Florida, to pursue a different set of tactics. Other campaigns held together, but with a great deal of dissension over use of the model campaign tactics. One such campaign, Show Me Equality, which was formed to fight the attempted Missouri initiative, experienced infighting about whether to follow the Oregon model or a set of campaign tactics that emphasized public education or direct action.[53] Although dissension is not always harmful, it can be seriously debilitating to campaigns, consuming a great deal of the limited time campaigns have, as activists reconcile their disagreements.

The most sustained and visible challenges to model campaign tactics came from two sources: organizations that used direct action as their main tactic and rural campaigns. Although neither of these challenges ultimately altered model campaign tactics, they did raise questions about their effectiveness. And both challenges reflected larger issues in the movement, either disputes between mainstream and direct-action activism or differences in the lived experiences of urban versus rural gays.

Lesbian Avengers and Bigot Busters

Direct action was a thorn in the side of those campaigns that focused on professionalism and used fieldwork to target moderate voters. This tension mirrored debates that were raging in the 1990s about direct action versus mainstream politics in the larger movement. Campaigns were pulled in two directions—preplanned hierarchical professionalism or spontaneous, nonhierarchical protest and guerrilla theater. Model campaign tactics effectively limited direct-action protest during a period in which direct-action groups such as Queer Nation and ACT UP were visible and active.

Debates raged about how "mainstream" the movement should be. Political pundit Andrew Sullivan and movement leader Urvashi Vaid debated the advantages and disadvantages of mainstream politics in their books *Virtually Normal* and *Virtual Equality*.[54] Vaid acknowledged that while mainstream tools such as legislative strategizing have led to movement gains, they have not remedied the underlying cause of anti-gay legislation, homophobia.[55] She argued that "we consciously chose legal reform, political access, visibility, and legitimation over the long-term goals of cultural acceptance, social transformation, understanding and liberation."[56]

Many activists disagreed not just with the types of issues and tactics selected by the increasingly mainstream movement but also with how LGBT organizations were being run. Integral to this debate of the mainstreaming of the movement was a criticism of how the movement and its campaigns were beginning to mirror the corporate world, as LGBT events became funded by corporations and corporate business models were used to run SMOs. Scholars such as Jane Ward have been critical of the ways that the LGBT movement depends on corporate models of how to run the movement.[57] This professionalism was at the heart of what direct-action activists found so problematic.

Mainstream, professional (and "respectable") activism was quick to distance itself from direct action. Attitudes about direct action within the movement at this time are documented by Deborah Gould in her book *Moving Politics,* which analyzed the growth and decline of ACT UP. Although there was space within the LGBT movement in the late 1980s for the direct-action tactics of groups like ACT UP, by 1992 even Urvashi Vaid declared that there was a consensus that direct action was dead.[58] Gould writes that, "in addition to being construed as dangerous and threatening, ACT UP was often portrayed, contradictorily, as simply ridiculous or silly, and most frequently as uninformed, overwrought, unreasonable, irrational and childish."[59] She argues that these were not merely responses to tactical differences but also reflected an emotional distancing by LGBT individuals from direct-action tactics and the gay men and lesbians who took part in them.

This ambivalence toward direct action extended to campaigns, specifically, the work of such direct-action techniques and organizations as Bigot Busting and the Lesbian Avengers. Bigot Busting, the tactic of using direct-action counterpetitioning that had been innovated in earlier LGBT campaigns, came under fire during the fight against Ballot Measure 9 in Oregon. In that campaign, a local pro-life activist sued nineteen groups and individuals associated with the campaign, accusing them of racketeering and "conspiring among themselves and with others to disrupt, harass, and otherwise harm persons who exercise their constitutional rights and the democratic process in opposition to their special rights agenda."[60] This

suit targeted the practice of Bigot Busting, the direct-confrontation activities of counterpetitioning, although it also named many individuals
and companies (including a grocery store that sued for the right to prevent petitioning on store grounds) unrelated to the direct-action groups.
Partly in response to the lawsuit, mainstream groups quickly distanced
themselves from direct-action groups such as Bigot Busters, No on Hate,
and Radical Women. Although the lawsuit was dismissed, it created lasting divisions. Rather than the direct confrontation of petition signers
and collectors in counterpetitioning, Decline to Sign campaigns — which
educated voters about the potential direct democracy measure through direct mailings, press releases, and bumper stickers — became more popular.
Counterpetitioning that did persist also used some of the model campaign
tactics, such as disciplined messaging and ranking of voters.[61]

Although Bigot Busting was problematic for many mainstream activists, even more contentious was the use of guerrilla theater, rallies, satirical flyers, and protests by direct-action groups.[62] Although these groups
included ACT UP and Radical Women, the actions of Lesbian Avengers
was the source of most discussion and dissent among campaign activists.
Lesbian Avengers was a direct-action organization formed in New York
City in 1992. For a few years, it ran the Lesbian Avengers Civil Rights Organizing Project (LACROP), which fought anti-gay ballot measures across
the country. LACROP activists from New York City and other cities were
involved in Lewiston, Maine (1993), Idaho (1994), and Oregon (1994)
campaigns. LACROP's activities focused on media visibility and mobilizing the LGBT community, particularly the lesbian community. Its activists also took action to counter anti-gay activity with LGBT visibility. For
example, they planned a "happy homosexual" rally outside an anti-gay
church a week before the election in Idaho.[63]

In both Idaho and Lewiston, LACROP and the mainstream campaign
were critical of each other. LACROP criticized the mainstream campaign
for its closeted, invisible strategy and for limiting community input into decision making. In line with queer activism that stressed multi-issue politics
and visibility of marginalized groups, LACROP also focused on fighting
racism and classism; it argued that the Religious Right was mobilizing poor,
rural, communities of color, and that "traditional campaign groups . . . have
virtually ignored low-income and rural regions and communities of color
based on the assumption that these communities are not valuable voting

blocs, they're too small, too dispersed, too homophobic, or they're probably not registered or willing to register to vote, anyway."[64] It was also critical of disciplined, singular messages and the ways that "highly centralized, volunteerist campaigns . . . ask that we put off our long-term goals of strengthening our community in favor of the short-term objective of winning the vote."[65] LACROP activists found fault with both the Oregon-based model tactics used by mainstream campaigns and the way the campaigns were organized.

In return, both local and national campaign activists were critical of the Lesbian Avengers. One national field-worker criticized the group for using a "white," "urban ghetto strategy" that was vanguardist, inappropriate, and ineffective, in that it came from New York City with "no idea what the texture of life in these [small-town] communities is like."[66] The most common criticism was that direct actions like the "happy homosexual" protest had the potential to generate bad publicity for the campaign or negate campaign messages.[67] Mainstream campaigns also feared that the Lesbian Avengers' strategy played into the hands of the opposition. According to Tina Fetner, the Religious Right "took these acts of guerrilla theatre out of context, stripped them of their satirical content, and presented them to their constituents as the genuine agenda of the lesbian and gay movement as a whole."[68]

Mainstream campaigns reacted by locking out direct-action tactics and activists, forcing them to organize independently from the main campaign. Many mainstream activists considered model campaign tactics, which included professionalism and moderation, to be irreconcilable with queer activism. The tensions around visibility, professionalism, and grassroots organizing that arose during the 1990s between LGBT groups continues to this day. Even when there are no tensions between advocates of guerrilla theater and advocates of lawn signs, organizations have to deal with tension around whether or not campaigns should be democratic, grassroots-oriented, and education-focused.

Rural Organizing

The challenges to model campaign tactics were not always direct and pointed. A pervasive question was whether or not one set of tactics could effectively serve all campaigns, regardless of location, size of population.

or culture. Ironically, the challenges to these tactics often came from the same place from which they originated: Oregon — specifically, small-town Oregon. The majority of campaigns during this period were in small towns and counties in Oregon, where the OCA was using campaigns to build a base in preparation for another statewide initiative in 1994. These small-town campaigns were twice as likely to fail as campaigns elsewhere.

Arlene Stein, in *The Stranger Next Door,* documents the difficulty of organizing a campaign in one rural town in Oregon, where there was little LGBT visibility, no LGBT organizations, and few vocal heterosexual allies.

Using model campaign tactics in these small communities was often problematic. Such campaigns generally had no funds for a professional staff, no LGBT community infrastructure on the ground, and had to contend with a greater fear of coming out and LGBT visibility. According to one rural organizer in Oregon, "trying to translate [the campaign model] to campaign places in small communities is a daunting proposition!"[69] The campaigns were often run based merely on a few mailings to voters and some letters to the editor. Rural organizer Gary Smith argued that focused "sound bite" messages were ineffective in smaller communities, where "more complex messages, repeated more often in more forms and forums are needed."[70]

Some small-town communities did create campaigns using model campaign tactics. For example, Keizer, a town on the edge of the Salem metro area, ran a campaign that used print media and contacted 23 percent of the voters by phone. The campaign also sent out GOTV postcards to all self-identified "No" voters.[71] The Marion County campaign, which was considered to be an important county as it represented a demographic microcosm of the state, used targeted mail pieces and door-to-door canvassing in the most favorable precincts. The Marion County campaign canvassed 15 percent of the voters but ended up with contradictory results. Ironically, a post-campaign analysis revealed that undecided and opposed voters "actually voted heavily in favor of the measure; it appears that within the context of the total campaign strategy, the phone poll effort actually benefitted the sponsors of the measure."[72] This post-campaign analysis concluded that "there is substantial evidence that campaigns waged by... pro-gay rights forces had little effect on the outcome, especially in Marion County."[73]

These campaigns struggled with a limited local movement infrastructure, although a statewide infrastructure was built during this period. In the absence of an LGBT community, rural campaigns had to build organizations out of the larger progressive community. Many of these campaigns grew out of human dignity groups (HDGs) that focused on a broader response to the right-wing attacks in Oregon. Two statewide organizations emerged as well, the Save Our Communities Political Action Committee (SOC PAC) and the Rural Organizing Project (ROP). SOC PAC was a statewide campaign to help coordinate and support local battles. Its work included two initiatives: a "Refuse to Sign the Son of 9" campaign, which included keeping sixteen out of thirty attempted initiatives in rural Oregon in 1993 off the ballot, and pre-ballot legal challenges in Troutdale, Umatilla, and Polk counties that defined legal-restrictive initiatives as "requiring discrimination."[74] Many local HDGs gave SOC PAC's efforts more praise than the 1992 No on 9 campaign; however, some activists complained that SOC PAC leaders were fixated on too few tactics, such as phone banking. In contrast to SOC PAC, ROP emerged out of the 1992 campaign and was created by Marcy Westerling, who had worked in her local community's HDG during the campaign. She described ROP as different from a campaign. Instead of a campaign, she envisioned it as a long-term support network for rural grassroots progressive organizing. Unlike campaigns, which focus money and resources on larger communities, Westerling described ROP as focusing on smaller and more rural communities, because "these are the folks that have too often been ignored. They are also doing work that is geared toward the long-term — creating understanding as opposed to getting that 50 [percent] plus 1 in an election."[75]

Such rural organizing led to tactical innovation that was sometimes successful. When Junction City organizers faced two elections, in the first, they tried GOTV and voter ID tactics. In the second, they tried something new — raising awareness through building housing for poor residents. Although they lost by only a handful of votes in the first election, they lost by 150 votes in the second. According to Westerling, "these are the tough lessons we're learning. We cannot assume that people will make the connection between our good works projects and knowing to vote no on an anti-gay rights measure."[76] Other alternative tactics included an Anne Frank exhibit that traveled around rural Oregon, a tactic that received a lot of attention: it is estimated that approximately half of each community saw the exhibit.[77]

Although model campaign tactics were gaining prominence, there was no consensus within the LGBT movement as to either their ideological purity or their political effectiveness. The disputes around the model campaign were intimately connected to larger debates about the role of direct action, urbanity, and "mainstreaming" within the movement. It is also evidence that even though these campaign tactics grew in popularity, they never were completely supported by all activists within the complex, ideologically diverse LGBT movement.

Making Campaigns, Making a Movement

Between 1992 and 1996, as the model campaign approach developed, campaigns and social movements supported each other in terms of building movement infrastructure. National organizations and the growth of the larger movement provided support to campaigns. Statewide campaigns grew into permanent organizations, and the mass mobilization required by volunteer-based model campaigns helped the movement grow. These changes to broaden the movement's base and bring in diverse approaches were critical for the development of model campaign tactics during this time.

This period was marked by the development of dominant tactics, as national organization support and study of victories and defeats converged with the escalation of Religious Right activity. Of necessity, the escalation of Religious Right anti-gay activism dramatically changed the way that LGBT activists fought ballot measure campaigns. The escalation of Religious Right activity and the draconian nature of legal-restrictive initiatives brought a great deal of attention to the unexpected victory of the campaign to fight Ballot Measure 9. The result was that the campaign tactics Oregon campaigners used to successfully defeat Ballot Measure 9 became a set of "model" campaign tactics, widely disseminated and utilized in subsequent campaigns. Similar to other movement–countermovement dynamics, the rapid innovation of the Religious Right created "urgent needs for tactical responses and, hence, structural changes" to "shake up organizational inertia" in the LGBT movement.[78] And LGBT activists and organizations were indeed shaken up. The infrastructure created by national organizations to support local campaigns was a direct response to the sudden growth of state-level initiatives sponsored by the Religious Right. Victories involving the use of these tactics reinforced the effectiveness of and emphasis on certain campaign tactics. With the escalation of the anti-gay Right, the LGBT movement was actually pushed to institutionalize tactics.

What the next two time periods in the evolution of LGBT campaign approaches reveal is that the fieldwork programs developed by national organizations only grew in strength and support of dominant tactics. These tactics became dominant owing to their persistent and increasing use by LGBT campaigns across the country.

Yet, even in this early period we can see the seeds of contradiction between ballot measure campaigns and social movements. Attempts to accommodate direct action and queer activism within mainstream campaigns met with resistance, because dominant tactics could not accommodate direct-action protest. Rural campaigns also challenged those tactics. As we will see in chapter 6, this period was also marked by tensions within the social movement, as campaigns negated some of the previously achieved gains for racial inclusion in the larger movement.

CHAPTER 4

A WINNING STREAK
TEACHING CAMPAIGN TACTICS, BUILDING STATEWIDE ORGANIZATIONS, AND SPREADING VICTORIES

> We can win these campaigns only if we shift strategies in two critical ways. First, we must realize that campaigns are won by votes, not media advertising. The labor-intensive process of voter identification, constituency organizing, and public education are how we will win. Second, we must be well trained in our work. There is no better trainer in our movement than our new senior fellow, Dave Fleischer.
>
> Urvashi Vaid, Task Force press release, January 25, 1999

ON THE HEELS of the *Romer v. Evans* Supreme Court victory in 1996, the LGBT movement entered its first and only winning streak at the ballot box. During this time, it won the majority of direct legislation battles, and between 2001 and 2003, it won all local referendums and initiatives. These victories included the retention of an LGBT rights ordinance in Miami Dade County in 2002 — a symbolic victory and evidence of the movement's growing potency. This winning streak was coupled with other victories, such as rising lesbian and gay visibility in the media and mainstream, the passage of state hate-crimes legislation after the 1998 murder of Matthew Shepard, and the increasing number of state legislatures passing nondiscrimination legislation.[1]

Why was the LGBT movement suddenly victorious? In this chapter, I argue that this winning streak cannot be disconnected from the widespread adoption of model campaign tactics. Between 1997 and 2003, more campaigns than ever before used campaign tactics such as voter identification, the large-scale use of volunteers, and narrow messaging. Although not all campaigns that used model tactics won, all winning campaigns used model tactics. Studying social movement success such as winning a ballot measure can be difficult. To explain success, social movement theorists tend to either focus on internal factors (things within the control of the movement such as tactics and organizational structure) or external factors (things outside the control of the social movement such as historical timing and political opportunities).[2] The limited scholarly analysis of anti-gay ballot measure success focuses on external factors such as voter fatigue, election timing, and voter composition, with little attention paid to the campaigns themselves.[3] In this chapter, I emphasize the importance of this widespread adoption of model campaign tactics for understanding victories during this time period. Other factors, such as whether or not the campaign was in a battleground state or was fighting a same-sex marriage ban initiative, do matter. However, the analysis of victories and defeats in this chapter, particularly the case study of Michigan, suggests that without this widespread adoption of campaign tactics, the victories would not have happened.

This widespread adoption of campaign tactics was supported by a growing movement infrastructure within national and state LGBT organizations. These infrastructure changes included growing institutional strength within the LGBT movement and increased effectiveness of campaign trainings run by national organizations. The strength of movement infrastructure and support within the infrastructure for dominant tactics may be critical to the widespread adoption of any tactic within a social movement.

Although this growing infrastructure was a source of strength, at times it hampered the spread of model campaign tactics. Even with the widespread adoption of model campaign tactics, not every campaign adopted them, of course. In conjunction with the previously discussed challenges to campaign tactics through direct action and queer activism, dominant tactics were challenged when some campaigns accepted both help from national organizations and dominant tactics. At times this challenge was a result of conflicts between the identity of local and national organizations. Local grassroots organizations rejected the tactics promoted by professional "outsiders" who were uninvolved in their community. Model campaign tactics were also challenged by Religious Right innovations, such as the increasing use of statewide initiatives and same-sex marriage bans.

Winning in Battleground States

The movement did not win everywhere. Both the frequency of victories and the use of dominant tactics depended on whether or not a state was a

State	Number on Ballot	Number won by LGBT Movement
Michigan	7	5
Maine	5	3
Florida	4	4
Washington	2	2
Oregon	1	1
Colorado	1	0
California	1	0
Non-battleground States	9	0

Figure 5. Direct legislation sponsored by the Religious Right, by state, 1997–2003.

battleground state. As Figure 5 demonstrates, most of these victories were in battleground states such as Michigan, Maine, and Florida, where the local LGBT community had accumulated campaign knowledge and experience. There were some important defeats in battleground states as well. Three of the most significant defeats were statewide losses for a referendum on Maine nondiscrimination legislation twice (in 1998 and 2000) and the passage of the Knight Initiative in California, which banned same-sex marriage. However, battleground states fared better than non-battleground states such as Hawaii and Nebraska, where the LGBT community faced its first anti-gay ballot measure ever, typically a same-sex marriage ban.

In this chapter, I analyze Michigan as a case study to demonstrate the use of campaign tactics in battleground states. Michigan was both the state most under attack by the Religious Right during this time period and the state with the most victories. In Michigan, LGBT activists used the campaign trainings sponsored by national organizations, a new state-wide organization, strong leadership, cautionary models of defeats, and social networks between activists to build several victorious campaigns. Michigan as a case study demonstrates how activists with few resources and little experience fighting ballot measures ultimately prevailed using model campaign tactics.

Battleground Michigan

Unlike other battleground states, before 1996 Michigan was relatively un-touched by the anti-gay ballot measures sweeping the nation; the local

Religious Right had attempted a few ballot measures, but none made it onto the ballot. There were plenty of opportunities for anti-gay referendums. Between 1972 and 1995, nine Michigan cities passed nondiscrimination ordinances, but only the Religious Right in Grand Rapids unsuccessfully collected petitions for a referendum. There was also an attempted state-wide legal-restrictive initiative that mobilized the LGBT community. In March 1993, George Matousek, a Bay County fish farmer, under the auspices of the Michigan Family Values Committee, filed a legal-restrictive initiative with the board of elections.[4] LGBT community members created the statewide Michigan Campaign for Human Dignity (MCHD).[5] Although gay activists described Matousek as a "a lone gun, with no known political base or organization," MCHD activists took his threats seriously and prepared for a ballot measure that never materialized by attending HRCF and Task Force campaign trainings. The first Religious Right–sponsored ballot measure was in 1996 when the Lansing LGBT community faced two simultaneous referendums on a newly passed nondiscrimination ordinance, losing both.

This state of affairs quickly changed after the Lansing defeat. As Figure 6 demonstrates, between 1997 and 2003, the Michigan LGBT community faced seven ballot measures in quick succession, along with several attempted initiatives in 2001. In 1998, a referendum in Ypsilanti garnered national attention from the Religious Right, after which Michigan became the target of the Michigan branch of the American Family Association (AFA) and its leader Gary Glen. This attention led to a wave of ballot measures in 2001 and 2002, including a revival of the legal-restrictive initiative, and attempted initiatives all across the state.[6] Several cities, such as Ypsilanti and Kalamazoo, faced multiple ballot measures.

Michigan was a remarkable success story and a critical part of the 2001 and 2002 winning streak for the LGBT movement. Michigan victories also demonstrate the effectiveness of model campaign tactics in local campaigns. Many external factors that may account for victories—a silent and disorganized opposition, strong public support for LGBT rights, and LGBT organization and visibility—do not adequately explain these victories. With a strong Religious Right and lukewarm public opinion toward LGBT rights, Michigan activists lost in cities with strong LGBT organizations and gay or lesbian city council members and won in cities with little LGBT organization and visibility. As the next three sections demonstrate, the success of Michigan campaigns can be attributed to the growth of strong LGBT

City	Type of City	Year	Type	Win or Loss?
Ypsilanti	Working class	1998	Referendum	Win
Ferndale	Detroit suburb	1999	Referendum	Loss
Royal Oak	Detroit suburb	2001	Referendum	Loss
Huntington Woods	Detroit suburb	2001	Referendum	Win
Kalamazoo	Working class	2001	Legal-restrictive	Win
Traverse City	Northern tourist	2001	Legal-restrictive	Win
Ypsilanti	Working class	2002	Legal-restrictive	Win

Figure 6. Michigan referendums and initiatives, 1997–2003.

campaign leadership and statewide organizations that were committed to campaign tactics. These local resources were supported by growing social networks between Michigan campaigns and national organizations, which included campaign trainings by the Task Force. According to many activists, campaign tactics were adopted in many cities thanks to the cautionary tale of cities "where we should have won but didn't." The next three sections juxtapose these examples of Michigan campaigns with national analysis of the adoption of model campaign tactics, dissent from tactics, and the development of a social movement infrastructure.

Creating Model Campaigns

Although many scholars study the spread of tactics, we know little about how tactics become widely accepted — indeed, expected — within a social movement. More campaigns used model campaign tactics in this time period than in any previous time period. These tactics were spread through trainings on how to run campaigns, social networks between campaign activists in different cities and states, and national and statewide organizations. When LGBT community members were putting together a campaign, they could access all these resources to create their campaign plan. Campaign tactics such as voter identification had reached a critical mass of both use and acceptance. This accumulation of knowledge, combined with the clear effectiveness of these tactics during the LGBT winning streak, contributed to their widespread adoption.

In this section, I first demonstrate the adoption of model campaign tactics by the 1998 Ypsilanti referendum campaign. In Ypsilanti, campaign workers without any previous ballot measure experience created a large-scale professional campaign that employed model tactics. After illustrating the adoption of model campaign tactics through the Ypsilanti case study, I examine the role of national campaign trainings as one of the most effective ways of spreading model campaign tactics.

A Model Campaign

The first victory in Michigan was also the first time voter identification had been used in a campaign, in the 1998 Ypsilanti referendum campaign. Ypsilanti was an unlikely place for a ballot box win. A small city outside of Ann Arbor, Ypsilanti boasted the commuter university of Eastern Michigan University (EMU) and a town–gown divide between white professionals and a large African American working-class community. The nondiscrimination ordinance was controversial; it was a response to a local LGBT student organization's attempting to get raffle tickets for an antihate rally reproduced at a local printing shop, Standard Printing. When the shop owners, Carole and Loren Hansen, refused to print the tickets because of "objectionable moral content," the city council ordered a newly formed Human Relations Commission to mediate the dispute, which resulted in weeks of contentious, packed hearings. After the Christian Coalition's *Religious Rights Watch* newsletter reported on the hearings, letters opposing LGBT rights laws arrived in the mayor's mailbox daily from all over the country. After the commission decided a nondiscrimination ordinance was unnecessary, the city council ignored its recommendation and unanimously passed an inclusive nondiscrimination ordinance that included protections for sexual orientation and gender identity, along with categories such as race and sex, on December 16, 1997.[7]

Shortly after the ordinance was passed, the local Religious Right campaign, Citizens Opposing Special Treatment (COST), began gathering two sets of petitions: a referendum to overturn the ordinance and a legal-restrictive initiative modeled after Cincinnati's Issue 3 to amend the town charter. The local LGBT community had begun meeting during the Human Relations Commission hearings earlier that summer and created the Ypsilanti Campaign for Equality (YCFE), a group primarily composed of middle-aged professional lesbians and gay men who lived in Ypsilanti and Ann Arbor.[8]

Although YCFE was less hierarchical than most campaigns and did not hire a campaign manager, it rapidly adopted many model campaign tactics. It tried to avoid the ballot box through a successful lawsuit to challenge the charter amendment and a Decline to Sign campaign, which included six thousand pamphlets to voters educating them about the petition drive and the nondiscrimination ordinance. When the referendum qualified for the ballot, YCFE activists engaged in large-scale fund-raising using house parties and other events, as well as individual solicitations for money. The YCFE field program included voter identification through phone banking and door-to-door canvassing, and training volunteers to identify supporters and undecided voters. Shortly before the election, YCFE engaged in GOTV activities to rally supporters. Recording who was voting on election day in all precincts allowed YCFE volunteers to call voters who had not gone to the polls yet that day. YCFE activists attributed their majority win in all precincts to this record keeping, as one precinct was won by a narrow margin created by last-minute transporting to the polls of supportive voters who had forgotten to vote. These tactics were adopted with dissent among activists, and they were used in conjunction with other tactics such as racial coalition building. However, activists were heavily influenced by the widespread adoption of model tactics by other campaigns and by support from national organizations.

YCFE tactics were developed through organized leadership, including the early election of cochairs Beth Bashert and Paul Heaton, along with social networks with both national organizations and other campaign organizations. Bashert, a white butch lesbian, described her networking with other campaigns, particularly in Maine and Oregon, where voter identification had been successful, along with Cincinnati and Lansing. She said that at the beginning of the campaign "we didn't know what to do to win, and I got on the phone and I started calling around the country . . . It was shortly after they lost in Maine, and I called the Task Force. And they hooked me up with folks in Maine, and they hooked me up with folks in Oregon." Bashert described talking to other campaign leaders in Oregon and Maine, along with field-workers at the Task Force and HRC, for hours throughout the campaign. These leaders and field-workers guided her through the process of identifying supportive voters by developing a phone-banking script, calling voters to identify potential supporters, and getting supporters out on election day.[9] YCFE was also assisted by Gay, Lesbian, and Straight Teachers

Network (GLSTN), Lambda Legal, and campaign activists in Lansing and Cincinnati. Cochair Heaton, a white gay man with experience in local city council campaigns, attended a Task Force training to get information on tactics late in the campaign. He suggested that "if we hadn't taken that training from the Task Force, I don't know that we would have been as successful."[10]

Ypsilanti won in a special election on May 5, 1998, 56 percent to 44 percent, one of the largest margins achieved against an anti-gay referendum at that time, gaining national attention. Heaton wrote a special column for the national LGBT newsmagazine the *Advocate* in which he argued that the Ypsilanti win was a result of extensive direct voter contact through voter mailings, door-to-door canvassing, and phone banking.[11] In this column, he presented a model campaign, following the examples of Oregon and Maine and the advice of the Task Force and Lambda Legal. The success of Ypsilanti was known throughout Michigan, as other Michigan cities tried to pass local gay rights laws and Michigan became the target of the American Family Association (AFA).

Training Activists

This short case study of Ypsilanti effectively demonstrates how a group of campaign workers went from lack of knowledge about campaign tactics to running a model campaign in a short time period. YCFE leaders adopted model campaign tactics through working with national organizations, attending trainings, and hearing the same advice when they spoke to campaign activists in such states as Maine and Oregon. Spreading tactics through social networks and institutions is a well-studied and common approach.[12] I examine here an additional contribution to the widespread adoption of model tactics: the intentional tactical training of activists by special programs. These trainings taught activists the skills they needed to implement model campaign tactics, along with providing a clear stamp of approval on such tactics from key movement players. Campaign trainings were also able to integrate modifications and extensions of campaign tactics as activists learned from victories and defeats.

One of the biggest developments in this time period, and one that YCFE was able to use, was that the training of activists on how to use model campaign tactics improved. The Task Force remained heavily involved in local campaigns, building a strong field program from 1999 to 2003 as it recruited Dave Fleischer from GLVF and constantly improved its regional training of campaign activists. The fieldwork support staff at the Task Force grew from a small team to eleven paid field-workers under Fleischer. From 1997 to 2001, Fleischer and his team offered small-scale campaign trainings through first the GLVF and then the Task Force. A Hawaii 1998 campaign field staff member summarized for her fellow activists the 1997 GLVF training she attended:

> We need 50% of the ballot cast plus 1. To assure that we have that number, we do voter ID; we TALK TO the voters person-ally and tally those on our side. We get organized; we plan. We raise $. We don't rely on media to pitch our cause. We win the campaign voter by voter. We start NOW.[13]

This and later trainings emphasized a specific type of voter identification, which included identifying "the voters most likely to support us and focus[ing] on them. We don't want to waste time on Mormon districts or on voters . . . who aren't likely to vote NO . . . We can use existing polling and voter lists to help us."[14]

The GLVF and Task Force training was developed into the Power Sum-mit, an elaborate campaign training that was launched by Fleischer and his team in 2001. The Power Summit training took place in an easily ac-cessible city in a contested state that could train both local activists and activists from nearby states. In 2003 alone, the Power Summit team held trainings in Ohio Valley, California, Oregon, and New Mexico, training at least two hundred local activists who would become campaign managers, volunteer coordinators, and spokespeople for local campaigns. Often these trainings took place well in advance of an anticipated ballot initiative.

One of the major changes with the Power Summit was the develop-ment of hands-on training in such campaign basics as voter identification and fund-raising. According to Power Summit trainer Thalia Zepatos, this hands-on component made the training more effective and activists more likely to implement the tactics at home:

> At one point the big flash was that no matter how much we *talk* to people about voter ID and going door to door, they're never going to do it unless we help them experience it for the first time. So,

every Saturday morning at every Power Summit we're going to go canvassing, folks. We had to push people through their intense fear of talking about LGBT issues at the door. And that really became a transformative piece. If you've done it once and you see that you can talk to people and engage them and either bring them around or, at the worst, they're not going to do something nasty... People are more likely to go home and engage in voter ID at home.[15]

As Power Summit trainers added more hands-on components, such as practicing door-to-door canvassing and fund-raising, the Power Summit became not just as a way to train campaign activists but to launch campaigns. The training was frequently the first meeting of campaign leadership in the targeted state. Statewide campaigns could be launched in a weekend as activists left the training with a list of donors, volunteers, and supportive voters in hand. For example, the August 2003 New Mexico Power Summit was in anticipation of a referendum on a newly passed statewide LGBT rights bill. At the end of the weekend, the thirty-five participants raised $51,400 for the campaign during their fund-raising practice, a sum that was then doubled dollar for dollar by the Task Force.[16]

There were some criticisms that by starting campaigns during the training, the training served as a gatekeeping mechanism for campaign leadership.[17] However, many activists attributed the widespread adoption of tactics and victories during this time to the Task Force trainings and the campaign tactics it supported. A post-campaign analysis of the Miami Dade County win emphasized the importance of disciplined messaging and voter identification.[18] Tacoma, Washington, activists had lost two referendums at the ballot box in the previous fifteen years. The 2002 Tacoma campaign manager attributed their astonishing 58–42 victory to Task Force involvement: "the Task Force is able to bring the skills out, teach them to local folks, and when they leave, the community is so much stronger than it ever was before."[19]

As tactics became more widespread and integrated into multiple layers of the social movement infrastructure, when campaigns were being formed activists learned about model campaign tactics from multiple sources. This support of model campaign tactics by national organizations, campaign trainings, and experienced organizers who had worked on campaigns all across the country was integral to the adoption of model campaign tactics in Ypsilanti in 1998. The widespread adoption of these tactics was also propelled by the development of hands-on campaign trainings that taught activists how to engage in campaign tactics. Overall, these trainings were critical in spreading such tactics as voter identification and effective media messaging, and helped local activists build the organizational capabilities they needed to run a campaign.

Identities and Tensions

Not all activists attended a training or successfully implemented these model campaign tactics. An unexamined mystery in the study of social movements is why popular, seemingly effective tactics are adopted by some groups and not others. Scholar Francesca Polletta has suggested that "to account for movement groups' strategic decisions, scholars must pay attention to the cultural beliefs that make some tactics options attractive or unattractive regardless of how effective these options are likely to be."[20] As Polletta suggests, the explanation is not merely a matter of effectiveness, but also of cultural beliefs. According to scholar James Jasper, groups have "tactical tastes" that may be a developed "cultural sensibility" within the group rather than something neutral based on efficacy and rationality.[21]

To fully understand this fact we need to consider more seriously the role of organizational identity in the selection of tactics. Each social movement organization has its own identity, a model that includes the structure of relationships within the organization and the "sets of scripts for action culturally associated with that type of organization."[22] Activists may reject a tactic because it conflicts with their group's organizational identity.[23] For example, queer activists may prefer a kiss-in over visiting their legislature. In addition, when tactics are being spread within a social movement, we need to consider the organizational identity of campaigns, along with the relationship between that organization and others.

At the heart of ballot issue campaigns is the relationship between national and local politics. Studying these campaigns can tell us a lot about the relationship among different levels within a social movement, particularly the connections among national, state, and local organizations. Most studies of social movements are either national studies or local case studies, with few multilevel studies.[24] Campaign activists fostered different relationships with various national organizations, depending on the organizational identity of each national group, and the spread of tactics was affected by these relationships. These relationships also affected other interactions between organizations, including the funding of campaigns and campaign staff workers. This section illustrates the rejection of model campaign tactics by examining the campaign in Ferndale, Michigan, which did not adopt model tactics, as well as analyzing tensions about money and other types of assistance between national and local organizations.

Rejecting Dominant Tactics

Despite the widespread adoption of model campaign tactics, not all campaigns, in Michigan or elsewhere, adopted them. Less than a year after Ypsilanti's victory, activists in the neighboring city of Ferndale consciously rejected those tactics. This rejection was partly motivated by an organizational identity focused on making the campaign a local, grassroots effort that rejected outside help, particularly from national organizations. In the end, the Ferndale referendum passed narrowly, eliminating the existing nondiscrimination law.

Ferndale was an unexpected place to lose a referendum. A suburb directly north of Detroit in Oakland County, it was known as an LGBT-friendly city in the late 1990s. The small city boasted a downtown area with several gay-owned or gay-oriented businesses, an out gay councilman, Craig Covey, and the Detroit LGBT community center. Local activists had unsuccessfully attempted to pass a nondiscrimination ordinance in the past. In the early 1990s, after the Ferndale city council ignored a proposed nondiscrimination ordinance, gay resident Rudy Serra collected petitions for an initiative that failed at the ballot box. However, in 1998, the Ferndale city council passed a nondiscrimination ordinance that included protections for sexual orientation.[25] Ferndale residents collected enough petitions to send the ordinance to the ballot box during the February 1999 Republican primary election. Local LGBT community members formed the campaign organization Keep Our Human Rights (KOHR).

One reason campaigns may engage in alternative tactics is lack of knowledge about model campaign tactics. However, Ferndale's KOHR leaders had access to national and local advice on such tactics. KOHR members attended a Task Force campaign training sponsored by the newly created statewide organization, Michigan Equality. They also met with Beth Bashert from YCFE to learn how the Ypsilanti campaign was successful. One white gay KOHR activist recalled that Bashert was "politically really smart, and she understood what it took politically to pass an ordinance like that," yet he lamented that KOHR "took hardly any of her advice."

Remarkably, although KOHR leaders had access to national and local advice, they adopted few, if any, of the dominant campaign tactics. Although the rejection of successful campaign tactics might reflect a lack of political savvy, Ferndale activists described their action as a resistance to both outsiders and outside advice. It reflected both their own organizational identity and the relationship among other organizations within and outside the movement. Their selection of alternative tactics had political costs, but it also kept their organizational identity intact. KOHR did not use voter identification or disciplined messaging about discrimination against gays. Instead, it focused on a community approach that emphasized education and the importance of human rights, rarely mentioned the word *gay,* and focused on connections with the community. By rejecting dominant campaign tactics, Ferndale activists positioned themselves as grassroots, nonhierarchical, locally focused, and noble, even in their loss. In interviews and campaign literature, KOHR activists constantly emphasized the local, grassroots nature of their campaign. Many described this focus on the community, on neighbors, and on keeping the dispute within Ferndale as a way for the group to be "noble." This nobility included refusing outside assistance from the larger LGBT community, including monetary assistance and advice from national organizations. KOHR activists contrasted this organizational identity with other LGBT ballot measure campaigns and the Religious Right, which were described as professional campaigns that used "outsider" advice and resources and included the 1991 Ferndale initiative campaign, the 1998 Ypsilanti referendum campaign, and the Ferndale Religious Right. In 1991, the initiative campaign had brought in speakers from groups such as the National Organization for Women's affiliate in Detroit and union workers to speak in support of the ordinance. At city council hearings, Ferndale residents lambasted these speakers and the initiative campaign as "outsiders" attempting to change Ferndale life.[26] In addition, the 1999 Ferndale Religious Right campaign was primarily composed of individuals from outside of Ferndale, including Gary Glen. One white gay activist remembered that, early in KOHR's formation, "I brought up that we should make certain it is handled within the city. People pushing for the repeal were from outside the city, and you can't gripe about it if you are too." The contrast between a campaign that utilizes outsiders and a noble, grassroots campaign included eschewing professionalism. Some KOHR members compared their campaign with the more professional YCFE campaign. For example, one lesbian asserted that "we did it from Ferndale and with Ferndale people, as opposed to the successful Ypsilanti, who put paid staff in place." YCFE did not use a paid campaign manager in the 1998 campaign, and YCFE members also identified their campaign as a grassroots endeavor. This comparison, however inaccurate, allowed KOHR members to craft an identity for their campaign as grassroots and noble.

The Ferndale referendum lost by a narrow margin; the defeat devastated the Michigan LGBT community. The failures of the Ferndale campaign were amplified when Royal Oak activists lost their campaign less than eighteen months later. Royal Oak was another LGBT-friendly Oakland County city that faced a referendum on its recently passed nondiscrimination ordinance.[27] Both campaigns were described by national and local activists as two places where "we should have won but didn't."

Post-campaign analyses of Ferndale and Royal Oak emphasized that lack of voter identification and poor messaging contributed to both defeats. Voter identification, absent in Ferndale and only scantily used in Royal Oak, was blamed for the poor turnout in both elections, as Ferndale lost by fewer than 250 votes and Royal Oak lost 2 to 1 with only a 25 percent voter turnout. One YCFE activist criticized the Royal Oak campaign for not "valuing the field." A lesbian KOHR member recalled sitting down with other campaign workers after the election and realizing that they knew collectively at least two hundred pro-LGBT voters who did not turn out. Poor, evasive messaging in both campaigns also made the voters vulnerable to last-minute Religious Right attacks. During this time period, campaign trainings heavily encouraged campaigns to use straightforward messaging about the perils of "discrimination against gays" rather than avoiding the subject of sexual orientation. Both Royal Oak and Ferndale messaging stressed the way the contested ordinance covered a range of different "human rights" rather than addressing the issue of LGBT rights. Many activists described it as a closeted approach to political messaging, which was controversial at a time in which gay and lesbian visibility was an important component of campaign tactics.

This criticism of both campaigns came from statewide and national activists. In both Ferndale and Royal Oak, the Religious Right dropped literature on voters' doorsteps the morning of the election. In Ferndale, the flyer emphasized the threat to children, coupled with sexualized pictures of gay men. In Royal Oak, the opposition left a flyer that pictured two men (one black, one white) holding hands, a flyer that one activist referred to as a "two for the price of one, racism and homophobia."[28] A Michigan Equality activist stated that after the literature drop, "we looked like liars. We hadn't done our prep work with the voters. We didn't have a base of support there. And we lost in Ferndale where we could have won by a landslide . . . All white, high level of college-educated voters in there, high level of gay community." Local activists claimed that this evasive messaging was the result of internalized homophobia within the KOHR campaign — that activists were afraid of talking openly and honestly about LGBT life. These critiques were echoed by national activists. Shortly after the election, Dave Fleischer wrote a public criticism of the Royal Oak campaign in the Michigan LGBT newspaper *Between the Lines*. Fleischer criticized Royal Oak's approach as "self-defeating" and a cautionary tale for future campaigns. He accused the Royal Oak campaign of ignoring the racism of the Religious Right and minimizing use of the word *gay*. Instead, he suggested that "when we speak our truth clearly — when we use the 'g' word upfront, without shame or timidity, particularly when we talk person-to-person with our neighbors — we're no longer total strangers."[29] He argued that half the vote was lost on evasive messaging and the other half of the vote was lost on a lack of face-to-face campaigning with voters, or of voter identification.

Ferndale rejected model campaign tactics because of the organizational identity of the KOHR campaign as grassroots and local, not nationally connected and professional. Model campaign tactics came from the outside, spread by national organizations and local campaign leadership, and thus were in conflict with the grassroots nature of the campaign. Cultural beliefs about the value of insider knowledge and dangers of outsiders motivated the dismissal of dominant tactics. Although both national and local social movement organizations were ostensibly working within the same social movement with similar goals, local activists often viewed themselves as having a deeper understanding of their own community and the needs of their campaign. They felt that having a campaign overrun by national activists would make them inauthentic or illegitimate, decreasing the power of their campaign. This conflict between organizational identities manifested in several other ways within the LGBT movement, as national or statewide organizations cultivated relationships with local campaigns through monetary and staff support.

Sources of Dispute: Field-workers and Money

The campaign trainings were perhaps the least controversial way that national organizations supported local campaigns. Other ways that national and local organizations connected was through fieldwork help and monetary assistance. Both fieldwork and money were vehicles through which national organizations promoted the use of model campaign tactics. Both types of support also created conflict between national and local organizations.

National organizations did not just consult over the phone or in training workshops but also directed young, freshly trained activists to local campaigns and contributed field staff on a temporary basis. Sometimes these field staff contributions were extraordinary, as was the case with the concerted contributions of Task Force field staff in Miami–Dade, Florida, in 2002. Compared to earlier time periods, field-workers tended to come earlier in the campaign and stay for longer, at times working as staff within the campaign. For example, Task Force–trained field-workers were hired as campaign managers in Michigan, and HRC was heavily involved in Hawaii's 1998 same-sex marriage campaign. Field-workers were often welcomed with open arms, as staff members who could work full-time in an otherwise volunteer campaign. A national organization could easily double the number of paid staff on a local campaign by sending two field-workers to assist the campaign.

Unlike the trainings, providing support with field-workers led to more tension between local campaigns and national organizations around the issue of local autonomy, and field-workers at times were perceived as the embodiment of national organizations. Activists described feeling resentful of "when the Task Force came charging in," yet they were also appreciative of outside resources. Even in the successful Kalamazoo campaign of 2002, campaign activists described being conflicted about help from the Task Force and statewide organizations like Michigan Equality. One organizer from the campaign suggested that Task Force field-worker Dave Fleischer was "heavy-handed" and "had no interest in supporting local organizers . . . [they wanted] to bring in professional organizers because they thought we didn't know anything."[30] There were additional resentments over the type of experts engaged, including the use of heterosexual campaign managers and political consultants. Field-workers who came into the campaign in the final weeks could both contribute a last-minute boost of energy and inadvertently displace existing staff.

An additional bone of contention between national and local organizations was money. Ballot issue campaigns need lots of money up until election day. Most studies of social movements ignore the issue of money or funding in favor of studying strategies, identities, or movement growth/decline. Yet money and fund-raising are central to understating ballot issue campaigns, for campaign activists are working against the clock to raise funds for a controversial issue. Many model campaign tactics, such as focus-group polling, disciplined messaging sent out to a large media market, and phone banks, add up financially. Indeed, the majority of campaign budgets are spent on message development and delivery.

Money was an ongoing source of tension between national and local organizations. Local campaigns often expected national organizations to financially support them. And indeed, national organizations did contribute money to local campaigns, often to fund expenses early in the campaign, such as the hiring of a campaign manager or polling for message development. Both HRC and the Task Force became more financially supportive of campaigns and of preemptive public education and voter identification in the early stages of the campaign. How this money was allocated and who received it contributed to tension between local and national organizations, particularly between local activists and the HRC, the largest and most well-funded LGBT organization.

There was ambivalence within the HRC field team about how much and when HRC should contribute money to local campaigns. Throughout this time period, HRC reshaped its focus on helping campaigns to emphasize its assistance to critical, test-case initiatives. The more important the campaign (e.g., Hawaii and Miami Dade), the larger the campaign (e.g., statewide versus local), and the more likely the campaign was to use dominant tactics (e.g., most Oregon campaigns), the greater chance that HRC would contribute funds. For example, in Hawaii in 1998, HRC spent more than thirty thousand dollars to fight just the legislative battle on the constitutional amendment. In 2000, when four states — Nevada, Nebraska, Oregon, and Maine — faced an initiative, HRC disproportionately supported Maine by donating more than thirty thousand dollars to the campaign and several staff members. HRC national field director Seth Kilbourn says the organization budgeted its resources for Maine based on the favorable polling data. "It indicated we'd win," he says. "There was no opposition campaign, and Maine was a key state for Gore, so that's where we put our resources."[31] When HRC did fund local campaigns, it was frequently through the growing number of statewide organizations. In 2001 and 2002, HRC implemented an Equality Fund grant program for statewide organizations that gave more than a hundred thousand dollars in grant money in 2001 alone. These funds were often used for campaign purposes, such as a five thousand–dollar grant in 2002 to the statewide organization Equality Florida to help the local campaign SAVE Dade in Miami–Dade.[32] These funds, particularly early money in campaigns to support polling for message development or buying voter lists, were critical in supporting model campaign tactics.

However, national organizations depended on local fund-raising to support a federal agenda and did not always want to sink money into failing campaigns. At times this fund-raising resulted in a reciprocal relationship between national organizations and local campaigns, but more often it produced tension over money and fund-raising practices. Sometimes these fund-raising efforts were not as friendly, or funding was attached to use of voter identification lists. In Kalamazoo, a predominately white working-class Michigan city, there was tension over local funders and whether or not the Task Force could use voter identification lists for its own fund-raising purposes. One Kalamazoo activist said this sharing was problematic, because so many gay and lesbian residents were closeted and did not want to receive unsolicited mailings and phone calls.[33] For this activist, national organizations were "outsiders," coastal and "out," misunderstood closeted gay life, and thus were disrespectful of gay fund-raising to closeted gays and lesbians.

These interactions fostered tension between national organizations and local campaigns, problematizing national–local relations. With HRC, this organizational identity was crafted through the use of money. Many activists and movement documents describe bitterness toward HRC, which they describe as too "selfish" to share its funds. This perception varied depending on the history of HRC funding in a given community. In states where HRC had been financially supportive, such as Idaho, it maintained good relationships with local campaign organizations. In other places, there were lasting tensions. For example, early in the campaign, YCFE steering committee members had approached HRC for twenty-five thousand dollars in funding to help with voter identification, but the request was denied. Later, many YCFE members described being angry that HRC had issued a press release about the Ypsilanti victory without actually assisting the campaign. YCFE campaign workers even wrote HRC an angry letter asserting that "you shouldn't have bragged about it if you didn't help." HRC did give cochairs Bashert and Heaton leadership awards for their involvement in the campaign, but there was lasting anger.

As this section demonstrates, the spread of model campaign tactics was intimately tied to organizational identity of both campaigns and national organizations. Local campaign activists rejected model campaign tactics at times out of concern about outsiders invading and disrupting the grassroots identity of their campaign. Tactics became associated with certain organizations, and these organizational identities led to disputes between national organizations and local campaigns.

Building an Organizational Movement

Despite the difficulty and ambivalence of national–local relationships, the LGBT movement grew a stronger movement infrastructure at this time period on the national, state, and local levels. National organizations became more central to the movement, statewide organizations grew stronger, and local organizations became more stable. This growing infrastructure was true both in Michigan and nationally. As it grew larger and stronger, it also grew more supportive of the widespread adoption of campaign tactics.

The growth of this movement infrastructure supported the necessary scale and size of campaigns required for the use of tactics such as voter identification. According to campaign trainer Dave Fleischer, the reason "we started winning at the local level on these nondiscrimination ballot measures is that we finally started campaigning . . . The single biggest difference, more than techniques, is whether you're campaigning at all. And whether you're doing it on a scale where you can get the results you need."[34] Fleischer describes these model campaign tactics as "campaigning" but suggests that scale and size are important. Campaigns grew larger, as more volunteers were recruited into the LGBT movement, reinforcing the growth of this movement infrastructure.

In this section, I will analyze how the development of a stronger state-wide infrastructure in Michigan supported local campaign victories. Then, I demonstrate that the growing strength of organizations was evident nationally as well, as a movement of organizations transformed into an "organizational movement."

Michigan Equality and the 2001/2002 Victories

The defeats in Ferndale and Royal Oak became cautionary tales that provided legitimacy for campaign tactics in future Michigan campaigns. The rejection of campaign tactics in Ferndale also provided impetus to create the statewide organization Michigan Equality, to counter the escalation of Religious Right activity in the state. As national organizations and Michigan Equality spread campaign tactics across the state, Ferndale and Royal Oak became cautionary tales on the dangers of ignoring the field and not engaging in voter identification. Michigan Equality founder Beth Bashert called Ferndale and Royal Oak "two really big examples of what not to do to be able to show people."[35]

Michigan Equality grew directly out of the Ypsilanti 1998 campaign, founded by out butch lesbian Beth Bashert.[36] In 1999 she developed a plan and recruited board members from both the Ypsilanti and Lansing campaigns. Michigan Equality founders differentiated themselves from the other existing statewide organization, the Triangle Foundation, which they consistently described as a "community center" focused primarily on legislative work rather than ballot box politics. The new statewide organization was founded using Basic Rights Oregon and Equality Florida as role models. The initial focus of Michigan Equality was the creation of a master list of LGBT-supportive Michigan voters. This list "will never become obsolete as a political weapon, will always grow stronger, and will make our political presence in the state undeniable and effective."[37]

As LGBT activists were mobilizing into Michigan Equality, Glen led the AFA in a flurry of petition gathering for referendums and legal-restrictive charter amendments all across the state in an attempt to bombard the

LGBT community with several ballot measures in the November 2001 election. Glen and his fellow activists targeted cities that had ordinances that were passed quietly in the 1980s and early 1990s, along with cities that were considering passing a nondiscrimination ordinance.[38] Former YCFE members were shocked when they discovered at the annual Ypsilanti Elvis Festival that professional petition collectors were gathering signatures for a legal-restrictive initiative, which was placed on the 2002 ballot.[39] In 2001 and 2002, there were four ballot measures on the ballot across the state, including one referendum in Huntington Woods and three legal-restrictive charter amendments in Kalamazoo, Traverse City, and Ypsilanti.[40]

Thanks to the efforts of Michigan Equality and Triangle Foundation in coordinating campaigns, a Task Force training in Michigan, start-up funding provided by HRC, and the energy and vigor of local activists, Michigan activists defeated four anti-gay referendums and initiatives in 2001 and 2002. This series of stunning wins effectively stymied the use of legal-restrictive charter amendments in Michigan and altered the tactics of the local Religious Right. Both national and statewide organizations were supportive of the campaigns that arose to fight this round of ballot measures. Activists in all cities conducted phone banks and door-to-door canvassing in order to get enough supportive voters to the polls. In Traverse City, a small tourist town in northern Michigan, the campaign was headed by Paul Heaton, who had helped lead the first Ypsilanti ordinance campaign to victory.

The defeats in Ferndale and Royal Oak bolstered and legitimized voter identification and GOTV tactics. In Huntington Woods, another Oakland County suburb, a campaign leader suggested that not anti-gay attitudes but a lack of GOTV led to the Royal Oak defeat, because of the low turnout in the election.[41] Voter identification and GOTV were affirmed again when Kalamazoo, a medium-sized working-class city with a small LGBT community, defeated an anti-gay initiative. With help in fund-raising from Michigan Equality and national organizations, Kalamazoo Against Discrimination (KAD) hired a campaign manager, a volunteer coordinator, and an office manager. KAD identified five thousand pro-LGBT voters, close to its goal of eight thousand chronic registered voters.[42] In the November election, of the eleven thousand registered voters who turned out to vote, 54 percent voted against the anti-gay charter amendment. According to one political analyst, "A closer look at the results shows that KAD won the race by turning out voters in three key neighborhoods, all three turned down the anti-gay measure by a margin of nearly 3 to 1."[43]

Michigan's final victory in 2002, in Ypsilanti, where the legal-restrictive initiative was defeated, came in the same year as the defeat of Miami–Dade County's referendum, a feather in the hat of the LGBT movement, a signal of a winning streak like no other to this point in time. This winning streak has continued in local elections in Michigan, as Ferndale and Kalamazoo activists beat back referendums on their newly passed non-discrimination ordinances in 2006 and 2009, respectively. Michigan has not been as successful in its singular statewide campaign, a 2004 same-sex marriage super-DOMA initiative, and a 2008 referendum in the Detroit suburb of Hamtramck.

Michigan illustrates the importance of statewide and national organization involvement, along with the convincing nature of cautionary tales of "places that we should have won but didn't." In Michigan, support from both statewide and national organizations, and development of a national movement infrastructure, were critical in the series of victories during this period.

Growing Organizations

Both national and statewide organizations grew during this time, becoming more professional and larger. Both types of organizations grew as the social movement terrain was shifting around issues like HIV/AIDS, transgender inclusion, movement visibility, and the tensions between mainstream and radical protest. Lesbian and gay life was becoming more and more visible in the mainstream media, facilitated by Ellen DeGeneres's coming out on her television show in 1997. After the advent of protease inhibitors in 1996, which dramatically changed the life of individuals with HIV/AIDS, the LGBT movement faced a waning interest in social movement activism.[44] At the same time, the movement faced tensions about transgender and bisexual inclusion, as both groups pushed for inclusion and visibility within LGBT organizations. There were also growing disputes about how mainstream or assimilationist the movement should be, particularly in its support of the new issue of same-sex marriage. Amin Ghaziani suggests that before the turn of the century the LGBT movement shifted from a movement in which organizations played an occasional role to an "organizational movement" in which heavily institutionalized, politically mainstream organizations ran the movement.[45] This "organizational movement" was contested, particularly in the controversial 2000 Millennium March on Washington, as many activists argued that the movement was too hierarchical and commercial.[46] During this time period, HRC, the Task Force, and statewide organizational growth were critical to the development of an infrastructure to support campaigns.

HRC, which by 1996 had grown into the largest and most prominent LGBT organization, worked primarily on the federal level to pass legislation. HRC re-created its image in the late 1990s, changing its mission statement to include activities such as lobbying congressional representatives and public education along with changing its name from the Human Rights Campaign Fund to just the Human Rights Campaign. This change was accompanied by a new Web site and the logo of a yellow equal sign on a dark blue background.[47] Despite this image overhaul, HRC was also under fire in the late 1990s for issues around mainstream politics and diversity. For example, it was heavily criticized for supporting New York Republican Senator Al D'Amato, not supporting transgender inclusion in the federal Employment Non-Discrimination Act (ENDA), and for being elitist.[48] Because of HRC's federal focus, it struggled with an organizational identity that was often perceived as opportunistic, as it needed the financial and political support of local communities to do federal work. HRC worked during this time to make more connections with statewide organizations through its Action Network program.[49] HRC leaders negotiated the organization's role in local ballot measures, with ambivalence about the group's role in local campaigns and its heavy involvement in initiatives in 1996.[50] HRC also recruited Donna Red Wing and other former Oregon activists for its field program after 1997.[51]

The Task Force was floundering at the end of 1995, financially drained from fighting both HIV/AIDS and the Religious Right, experiencing organizational disillusionment after a series of short-lived directors, and in dire financial straits. However, after 1996 it saw a period of growth, as a new policy institute grew under the leadership of former Task Force director Urvashi Vaid. The policy institute was a wedding of organization leaders, activists, academics, and religious leaders to develop social movement strategy.[52] As more Religious Right activism focused on the statewide level, Task

Force leaders began to focus on statewide organizing and statewide support, deepening an organizational identity of the Task Force as a grassroots-focused organization. The Task Force spearheaded the organization of statewide organizations into a federation in 1997, now called the Equality Federation, which still meets on a regular basis and shares resources.[53] This organization at the statewide level included the March 1999 "Equality Begins at Home" tour, which included more than 250 actions in one week in all fifty states, the District of Columbia, and Puerto Rico.[54] Leaders and staff also committed the Task Force to diversity, a conscious inclusion of bisexual, transgender, and minority issues. This commitment included the addition of bisexual and transgender to the Task Force mission statement in 1997; activists also increasingly referred to NGLTF as The Task Force, which downplayed the exclusive use of "gay" and "lesbian" in the name. Organizationally, the Task Force "filled a different niche: it was the oldest and most prominent national *grassroots* organization self-consciously dedicated to the movement's diversity — especially at the local levels."[55]

Statewide organizations also continued to grow during this period, as activists learned to transition from campaigns to permanent organizations and vice versa. As the Religious Right increasingly focused on statewide campaigns, the existence of a statewide organization in many states became critical. Even if the existing statewide organization could not legally participate in a ballot measure campaign, it could be used as a meeting place and help to recruit volunteers and provide campaign leadership. More statewide organizations arose in response to either state initiatives or a series of local anti-gay direct-democracy measures. In Colorado, Oregon, Maine, Washington, and Michigan, these statewide organizations kept close connections with national organizations, often facilitating local training of activists, field support, organizing state-level campaigns, and operating as repositories for local knowledge about campaigns. It was not always easy for groups to transition from statewide organizations into campaigns, and many early statewide organizations lasted only a few years. Young statewide organizations experienced financial problems, activist burnout, and hard feelings from the campaign, and at times competition from other statewide groups. According to one HRC field-worker, the newly created Basic Rights Oregon was struggling during this period as it tried to craft a mission and goals independent of campaigns, and it was struggling financially.[56] For the growing number of statewide organizations, the

Equality Federation became a place to share the newest wave of Religious Right tactics. For example, in July 1997 statewide leaders discussed at a retreat topics such as attempts to craft language to recriminalize sodomy in California and Colorado, difficulties of organizing on a statewide level, and bringing together different communities.[57]

Other organizations rose to prominence during this period, including regional organizations and new national organizations. The push for same-sex marriage in Massachusetts was assisted by the Gay and Lesbian Advocates and Defenders (GLAD), a New England legal-rights organization that was founded in 1978 and had been involved in providing legal help to Massachusetts and Maine activists dealing with attempted referendums and initiatives. Evan Wolfson, former Lambda staff member who was involved in the Hawaii Supreme Court case for same-sex marriage, founded the first national organization to focus on same-sex marriage, the Freedom to Marry Coalition (FTMC), in 2003. General progressive organizations, such as the Western States Center and Ballot Initiative Strategy Center, also worked to connect progressive ballot measure campaigns with each other. Many LGBT organizations, such as GLVF, HRC, and Basic Rights Oregon, joined the Ballot Initiative Strategy Center and were able to connect with other activists, such as pro-choice activists, who were experiencing similar ballot measures.

These growing organizations created a supportive infrastructure for local campaigns that trained activists, provided them with field-workers, and gave them financial support. Without this organizational strength, model campaign tactics might not have been adopted by so many campaigns. Although the spread of these tactics was complicated at times by organizational identities and relationships between national and local organizations, model campaign tactics were supported at multiple levels throughout the movement.

New Campaign Tactics

As part of this widespread adoption of model campaign tactics, there was resolution within the LGBT movement over the necessity of ballot box avoidance, including the avoidance of LGBT-sponsored initiatives. In addition to the growing consensus over the necessity of ballot box avoidance, activists both nationally and locally began to use voter identification in movement building. Voter identification was harnessed to longer-term movement projects such as working with legislators and passing legislation.

Ballot Box Avoidance

Ballot box avoidance became stronger during this period as a key to maintaining legislative victories. Although activists were becoming better at fighting ballot measures, it was still preferable to avoid the ballot box entirely. This ballot box avoidance included a more consistent use of pre-ballot legal challenges and reservations about ballot measures sponsored by LGBT organizations.

More campaigns dodged and challenged attempted referendums and initiatives during this time than at any other previous time. These ballot measures were avoided because of efforts by local LGBT activists, not inept organizing on the Right. These included challenging petition signatures, Decline to Sign campaigns, and pre-ballot legal challenges. For example, to prevent the 1998 referendum in Maine, the campaign filed a lawsuit in Superior Court claiming that state election officials should not have authorized the referendum because more than fifteen thousand petition signatures were invalid, which was verified by volunteers working around the clock to check signatures. Pre-ballot legal challenges became so common that in 2002 alone there were three well-advertised legal challenges based on procedural violations in the collection of petitions. These well-advertised cases included a lawsuit in Ypsilanti over the use of professional petitioners and deceiving petition signers; the Miami–Dade case in which several petition collectors were arrested on fraud charges; and controversy over bait-and-switch attempts by petition collectors when gathering petitions to eliminate same-sex marriage in Massachusetts. These challenges at times delayed or eliminated the ballot measure and, at the very least, provided free media coverage that marred the image of the local Religious Right early in the campaign.

The other significant change during this period was the avoidance of LGBT-sponsored initiatives. Although popular earlier on, the use of LGBT-supported initiatives declined after 1997 when a Washington LGBT rights initiative failed at the ballot box, 40–60. Washington activists had long fought off attempted statewide initiatives in their state through legal efforts and Decline to Sign campaigns. After a wave of attempted state-wide initiatives targeting gay adoption and civil rights in 1996, Hands Off Washington, an organization formed to fight these measures, sponsored its own initiative to create nondiscrimination legislation inclusive of both sexual orientation and gender identity. National leaders viewed the Washington initiative as risky and unsupported by the local LGBT community; HRC organizers suggested that "undertaking a thumbs up vote on our civil rights is a dangerous and very expensive gamble that, if it loses, will set a bad precedent for the future, inside and outside of the state."[58]

Activists in other states closely watched Washington's efforts, tempted by the possibility of a proactive use of direct democracy. Florida activists had already considered the potential of "winning on our terms" rather than fighting defensively against Religious Right–sponsored initiatives. According to Florida activists, "the most obvious argument for a pro-active approach is that all the blood, sweat, tears, anguish and money we pour into the campaign could actually get us something: the legal right to be free from discrimination, and freedom as well from continued skirmishes with [Religious Right] zealots over these basic issues."[59] When Oregon activists considered sponsoring their own initiative, field-workers in national organizations actively dissuaded key activists from supporting the initiative. Oregon's continual statewide victories made it a symbolic state for national organizations. Local activists who had been involved in the three Oregon statewide campaigns dissuaded others from this approach, suggesting that it might delay progress of the Oregon Employment Non-Discrimination Act (ENDA). One former campaign activist suggested this potential outcome:

> We run the risk of having the failure used against us for at least the next five to ten years. Our true hope of passing ENDA lies within the legislature. If an ENDA initiative fails, our legislative progress will be set back ... Those legislators who were moderately supportive of it in 1997 and those who might be lukewarm in supporting it in later years will have the excuse of saying "the voters have spoken."[60]

These concerns were echoed by HRC and Task Force field-workers, who rushed to Oregon to dissuade the potential effort. HRC field-workers argued that "a referendum on the rights of gay and lesbian Oregonians, while a noble idea, is not a politically astute one . . . we cannot be assured of a win. It is not even a fair possibility."[61]

After Washington's failure, no other statewide organizations sponsored a gay rights initiative in which they had to collect petitions until Maine in 2011. In 2000, two other ballot measure attempts were supported by LGBT activists. In California, renegade activists Thomas and John Henning attempted to counter the 2000 same-sex marriage Knight Initiative with a petition to put an initiative on the ballot to make same-sex marriage legal. Activists working to fight the Knight Initiative lambasted them as diverting money, resources, and media attention from the campaign and nothing came of the petitions.[62] In 2000, when Maine LGBT activists secured statewide nondiscrimination protection, it was contingent on the legislation getting voter approval at the ballot box. In the wake of the 1998 defeat, many Maine activists criticized the decision to push forward so soon on a second ballot measure.

Campaign Tactics beyond Campaigns

In Dave Fleischer's treatise on voter identification, he asserts that one way voter identification builds movement power is that at the end of a campaign "we end up with a list of anti-racist, gay and pro-gay progressives to use in every project, from lobbying to pass legislation to raising money. We are also maximally prepared for the next election — and there is always another election that will matter to our community."[63] As voter identification became more widespread, activists began to see the value of voter identification both long before a campaign started and long after it ended. National organizations and statewide organizations began to support voter identification both as a preemptive effort to anticipate future campaigns and as a way of using campaign work in future electoral campaigns. Fleischer and staff began emphasizing in their trainings that voter identification could help legislative campaigns after the ballot measure campaigns were over.[64] There was a growing awareness of the need to start campaigns early and to use the groundwork of voter identification for other political goals.

Until 1997, there had been some attempts to continue to use campaign resources after the election. Sometimes either HRC or the Task Force and local campaigns were able to engage in reciprocal fund-raising, in which the organizations shared membership lists for fund-raising purposes. For example, in 1996, Idaho campaign activists wanted to create a statewide progressive voter file to support both LGBT and other progressive campaigns. HRC donated five thousand dollars to the voter file in exchange for being able to use the list for fund-raising purposes.[65] As HRC became more involved in legislator elections, it brokered deals with campaigns such as Idaho's No on 1 campaign in 1996 to fund voter identification in exchange for the use of voter identification lists for fund-raising for legislators. In 1996, HRC successfully used Oregon voter identification lists from the 1994 Oregon campaign to work on senatorial campaigns.[66] For Senator Ron Wyden's campaign, it used seven hundred volunteers to make ten thousand ID calls and thirty-seven thousand GOTV calls, helping Wyden to victory. Members of Basic Rights Oregon also served as campaign consultants for Wyden, using their ballot measure campaign skills in the electoral arena.[67]

Activists also realized that voter identification could serve the movement even after the votes were counted. In HRC's internal evaluation of its field program in 2004, a listed weakness was the lack of HRC involvement with state-level organizations, suggesting that "voter file and GOTV efforts can build the new political machine for the future of HRC." In 2003, many national and statewide activists knew that the writing was on the wall for a series of initiatives about same-sex marriage in the 2004 election. Some statewide organizations began to initiate voter identification projects in anticipation of these campaigns, hoping to identify supportive voters ahead of time. The Task Force gave out five hundred thousand dollars in Community Impact Fund grants in 2003, all of which went to statewide or strong regional organizations in potential initiative states that would fund the expansion of the volunteer base of the organization and the identification of supportive voters.[68]

The growing political savvy of the LGBT movement allowed activists to be supportive of non-LGBT ballot measure campaigns and work more effectively in electoral campaigns. For example, HRC and Equality Colorado became involved in the Parental Rights Amendment in 1997 and connected the Colorado campaign with pro-gay campaign consultants.[69] Stephanie Anderson, campaign manager for Ypsilanti in 2002, after capitalizing on her Task Force campaign trainings, went on to train Dean for America organizers in 2003 using the same techniques.[70] The Task Force assisted with door-to-door canvassing and voter identification for the campaign to defeat California Proposition 54, the Racial Privacy Initiative. And the Maine Rural Network, which was established to do outreach in rural communities after the 1998 Maine referendum, helped organize against referendums addressing abortion and civil rights in 2000.

As more ballot measure campaigns used voter identification, activists throughout the LGBT movement became more likely to harness voter ID for movement projects. This use of voter identification was one of the ways that campaigns began to support the larger LGBT movement, creating opportunities for building a pro-LGBT voter constituency, working in coalition with other progressive movements, and supporting pro-LGBT legislators. This resounding success of voter identification in many local ballot measure campaigns stood in stark contrast to the statewide campaigns, where it was difficult to effectively use model campaign tactics, and to same-sex marriage ban campaigns, where even the most diligent use of model tactics resulted in defeat.

Places of Struggle

Even during the largest winning streak the LGBT movement had ever experienced at the ballot box, it did not win everywhere. Indeed, the tactical innovations of the Religious Right — the push for more statewide and same-sex marriage initiatives — challenged LGBT activists across the country. The LGBT movement fought more statewide initiatives in this six-year time frame than in the preceding twenty years. Out of fifty-three attempted ballot measures during this time period, seventeen were proposed on the statewide level. Although dominant tactics were becoming widely supported, the scale and size of a campaign required to use tactics like voter ID were difficult for statewide campaigns. In addition, same-sex marriage was so contested that statewide campaigns in states unfamiliar with ballot measure campaigns were doomed to failure. This section addresses why both statewide campaigns and same-sex marriage initiatives were especially difficult to organize.

Going Statewide

Although the LGBT movement became savvy at winning local ballot measures at this time, winning more than 76 percent of local ballot measures, it failed at statewide initiatives. Compared to 1974–96, when the LGBT movement lost only one statewide anti-gay ballot measure, between 1997 and 2003 it lost all but one statewide ballot measure, including the Washington initiative described earlier, two referendums in Maine, and same-sex marriage campaigns from Hawaii to Arkansas.[71] The one statewide victory was the defeat of an initiative to prohibit the promotion of homosexuality in schools in Oregon, a state with a history of winning statewide initiatives.

According to one campaign manual, "winning at the statewide level was difficult under the best of times," and the scale of organizing required for statewide ballot measure campaigns was overwhelming. This included a statewide communications network, fund-raising, paid staff, media buys in many markets, and a huge volunteer recruitment effort.[72] Statewide initiatives could both grow statewide organizations or communication networks and create lasting movement divisiveness. Maine activists experienced the divisiveness that could come from statewide campaign work, a divisiveness which often centered on whether or not to use model campaign tactics.

Maine was the site of multiple defeats. Activists successfully defeated a stealth legal-restrictive initiative in 1995, but lost two referendums in a row in 1998 and 2000. Organizing on the statewide level for three ballot measures in less than a decade was very difficult for Maine activists, and each defeat led to divisiveness. To analyze Maine, I draw heavily from Kimberly Simmons's dissertation on all three Maine campaigns, in which she was involved and during which she interviewed campaign activists extensively.

The problems in Maine began in the aftermath of the 1998 campaign, which built on the victories and campaign structure of Maine Won't Discriminate (MWD), the 1995 initiative campaign, and implemented a short campaign that focused on GOTV of already-persuaded voters. A February 1998 vote brought unforeseen challenges, including a short campaign time period and a severe ice storm in early February that distracted the media and caused the campaign to lose momentum.[73] Although the polls predicted that MWD would win at the ballot box, it narrowly lost 49–51. After the unexpected defeat, LGBT community members across Maine criticized MWD and its leaders, including for hierarchical and exclusive leadership styles. According to journalist Sam Smith, the main criticisms were as follows:

Critics argued that MWD had ignored the rural areas of the state; the organization had been too Portland-centric and had lost the election because of it. That was the most fundamental criticism of the organization, but it wasn't the only one: MWD had started too late; it hadn't raised enough cash; the cash it raised wasn't maximized; it diluted itself on favorable polls; it never embraced the gay and lesbian community; it never attacked the opposition on its empty (but maddeningly potent) "special rights" rhetoric. By the time its evisceration was completed, MWD had lost a great deal of credibility.[74]

This kind of infighting and finger-pointing was common after defeats, especially narrow defeats. One national political consultant referred to the criticism of campaign leaders after the election as "cannibalism," because the movement "ate" its own leaders.

When Maine faced a 2000 ballot measure, the new campaign Yes on 6 or Maine Coalition for Equal Rights (MCER) did not use any resources or leaders from previous MWD campaigns. MCER focused on consensus building and inclusivity, with less focus on model campaign tactics such as voter identification. Political pundits suggested that the MCER campaign failed because of its lack of centralized leadership, which left local rural groups floundering, volunteer fatigue from the previous campaign, lack of support from the community, and lack of fund-raising.[75]

Both Maine campaigns demonstrate the difficulties of statewide campaigns, including mobilizing disparate field offices in rural areas, contending with legitimacy issues, continuity between campaigns, and disputes about campaign tactics. The greatest complication is that statewide campaigns need to form more hierarchical and professional campaigns in order to manage such a large infrastructure. Although hierarchical decision making is considered unproblematic within many other social movements, in the LGBT movement it is frequently criticized as an exclusive structure that privileges homonormativity within the larger movement.[76] During post-campaign cannibalism in 1998, MWD leaders were accused of — among many other things — using the campaign to further their own political careers. In Maine, one of the 1998 executive committee members commented that "you cannot run a successful statewide political campaign without a central decision-making body who ultimately says, 'this is the ad, this is the message, this is how the money is going to be spent.'"[77]

This hierarchical leadership becomes most problematic in urban–rural relations within statewide campaigns. Most states are predominately composed of rural counties, so, during any statewide campaign, activists have to negotiate dynamics between campaign headquarters, which are located in an urban center, and rural campaign field offices. Most campaign tactics such as voter identification rely on the development of tactics by a central headquarters, which are then disseminated to rural field offices. For example, using model campaign tactics such as disciplined messaging requires that everyone within a statewide campaign use the same message consistently, so messaging is developed by headquarters. Activists in rural field offices often chafe under the instructions of headquarters, arguing that different messaging or tactics should be used in rural areas. This disagreement was an issue in later Maine campaigns because of the development of more autonomous rural organizations that were mobilized into being field offices. In 1995, any existing rural organization in Maine was an MWD chapter. When Maine faced its third campaign in 2000, most rural areas had their own preexisting organizations, which created complications with disciplining message. Ironically, the growth of a movement infrastructure made the campaign more difficult. One rural Maine activist commented: "we worked independently on the campaign, and we would use their literature and stuff but we made our own decisions on how to organize and didn't use their message either."[78]

In 2000, activists focused on a more inclusive campaign. In the push to create a new campaign, MCER used few leaders from either the 1995 or the 1998 campaign, and institutional memory was lost. No reliable voter identification list was maintained between campaigns, requiring each campaign to identify voters from scratch. One political pundit suggested that the push for inclusivity went too far, suggesting that MCER was "focusing so strongly on not duplicating the faults of MWD's '98 campaign—and developing a very touchy-feely, all-inclusive campaign that attempted to mirror the gay and lesbian community itself—the group lost sight of what MWD did right."[79] For Maine, both 1998 and 2000 were brutal lessons in the complexities of running statewide campaigns. Although model campaign tactics were used in 1998 (and then criticized), they were abandoned in favor of a more inclusive, less hierarchical campaign in 2000 that left many activists dissatisfied as well.

Maine provides us with more insight as to why statewide campaigns were so difficult for LGBT activists, as they negotiated issues such as decision-making styles and urban–rural relationships. However, these statewide campaigns mainly demonstrated the difficulty of applying model campaign tactics on a large scale; they did not necessarily challenge the logic of model campaign tactics. Few political analysts or LGBT leaders at the end of these campaigns suggested that model campaign tactics were ineffective. However, to add insult to injury, these statewide initiatives were increasingly focused on the difficult topic of same-sex marriage.

Challenged by Same-Sex Marriage

Same-sex marriage initiatives were a losing gamble from the start for the LGBT movement. With the exception of Alaska and Hawaii, the first two initiatives in 1998, these initiatives eliminated a right that did not exist, making them difficult to defend. Same-sex marriage was unpopular with voters. Of the seven same-sex marriage bans during this time, only 31 percent of voters on average voted to defeat the bans. And, with the exception of the California Knight Initiative, these initiatives took place in states that were not battleground states. LGBT communities in Alaska, Hawaii, Nebraska, Arkansas, and Nevada had to mobilize slim statewide resources and inexperienced volunteers to run a statewide campaign.[80] Although the LGBT movement was victorious in other types of campaign, including local referendums on domestic partnerships, these early same-sex marriage bans lost by the largest margins since the first wave of referendums in 1978.

For LGBT organizers, the elation of the first winning streak the movement had experienced was tempered by losses across the country on same-sex marriage. HRC was most heavily involved in the 1998 campaign in Hawaii (and to some extent Alaska). National organization fieldworkers considered a victory in Hawaii to be the equivalent of a victory in Colorado in 1992, the potential prevention of an initiative that would spur on the Religious Right and provide it with a new way of thwarting LGBT rights.[81] Hawaii became a battleground for mainland forces and organizations from both the LGBT movement and the Religious Right fighting it out over same-sex marriage. After an initial evaluation of Hawaii, HRC became heavily involved.[82] The HRC field program anticipated spending more than a million dollars on the Hawaii campaign, sent staff to work with the campaign, conducted polling, and directly hired its own campaign manager to run the campaign, Protect Our Constitution/HRC.[83] This campaign manager was trained in Washington, D.C., "to become fully invested in HRC. S/he must be our player."[84] HRC and GLVF trained Alaska activists in two separate campaign trainings.[85] The Hawaii campaign used a number of familiar tactics, including filing campaign law violations against the opposition, the Hawaii Christian Coalition.

Although all eyes were on the Religious Right's tactical innovation in Hawaii, less attention was paid two years later to a tactical innovation in Nebraska, the emergence of the first super-DOMA. The Nebraska constitutional amendment expanded the statewide ban on same-sex marriage to a ban on any rights "like marriage." Nebraska revealed the Religious Right's new tactic: targeting conservative states that were unlikely to pass same-sex marriage. As activist Michael Gordon noted, Nebraska is "incredibly rural, incredibly red, incredibly conservative," and the same-sex marriage initiative seemed to come out of nowhere.[86] Yet, Nebraska activists described a general lack of concern about their initiative from national organizations. One activist noted that HRC field-workers kept telling the Nebraska campaign, "It's Nebraska. It's conservative. This language won't fly anywhere else."[87] Yet Nebraska activists, acutely aware they were fighting a losing battle, still engaged in many model campaign tactics such as door-to-door canvassing in Omaha, where areas with high saturation of canvassing voted against the initiative.

It was clear from these early campaigns that initiatives about same-sex marriage would be tough to fight. Same-sex marriage was not well supported in the general public, and there was dissent within the LGBT movement about mainstreaming and the support for marriage.[88] These early campaigns faced problems with developing messaging about same-sex marriage. Early polling indicated that if campaign messaging focused on marriage it would fail, a concern that was reiterated over and over in campaign documents in Hawaii and other states (I discuss this issue further in chapter 5). For example, No on Knight campaign messaging focused on the initiative's being not about just marriage but "an attempt by Pete Knight and his allies to use marriage as a wedge issue to further a broad, extreme right-wing agenda for California." The main message of the campaign was: "It's divisive. It's intrusive. It's unfair," with an emphasis that the initiative was also unnecessary. The focus-group–tested message was part of a "50%+1 vote targeted strategy" to win.[89]

There were signs in 2002 and 2003 that there was a coming storm of same-sex marriage initiatives, and that same-sex marriage was the new big fight. The *Newsweek* cover on July 7, 2003, asked: "Is Gay Marriage Next?" HRC and many other activists, including the newly formed Freedom to Marry Coalition, were involved in combating the Federal Marriage Amendment on the national level, which entailed developing a series of messages about the dangers of amending the Constitution. An anti-gay group worked to attempt to amend the Massachusetts constitution by citizen initiative to prevent same-sex marriages, which involved mobilizing against it. The legislature stopped the initiative in its tracks. With Massachusetts's legalization of same-sex marriage looming on the horizon, there were signs in 2003 that the presidential election in 2004 were going to be a good year for the Religious Right.

Learning How to Win (and Lose)

This time period is one of the most critical (and unexamined) moments in the fight of the LGBT movement against anti-gay ballot measures. After a long period of losing against the Religious Right, suddenly the movement was winning local referendums and initiatives. These victories cannot be understood without analyzing the growing movement infrastructure, trainings, and widespread adoption of model campaign tactics. What made these campaign tactics dominant is that they persisted past the initial support for them during the flurry of Religious Right escalation in the mid-1990s. National organizations developed more sophisticated ways of disseminating campaign tactics and working with local campaign activists, and a spate of victories in 2001 and 2002 reinforced the effectiveness of these tactics. Both ballot measure campaigns and the larger social movement grew in size and scale. In Michigan and elsewhere, the widespread adoption of model campaign tactics led to a series of unprecedented victories.

Not all campaigns adopted model campaign tactics, however. Within the study of tactical adoption, it is just as important to understand why widespread tactics are not adopted by all organizations. KOHR in Ferndale, for example, dismissed tactics such as voter identification and narrow campaign messaging, along with professionalism and outside advice, as inconsistent with its organizational identity. Other campaigns struggled with relationships between national and local organizations while dealing with funding or field-worker issues. This analysis suggests that the relationships between social movement organizations need to be placed at the center of our understandings of how tactics spread within a social movement, building on the existing literature that connects tactical diffusion and organizational connections.[90]

Even campaigns that did adopt campaign tactics did not necessarily succeed. These dominant tactics did, however, need some modification as the Religious Right began to use statewide same-sex marriage initiatives on a large scale. It was difficult for campaigns to adopt tactics on the statewide level, and they did not work effectively against same-sex marriage bans. Ideologically, these difficulties did not challenge model campaign tactics.

During this period, the growing size and scale of the LGBT movement supported the development of large campaigns that could engage in model campaign tactics. The development of more people power and organizational power helped propel ballot measure campaigns to victory. A tremendous amount of social movement resources, including money and the employment of staff members from national organizations, went to supporting local campaigns. In turn, ballot measure campaigns helped to develop technologies such as voter identification that supported movement projects.

CHAPTER 5

LOSING AT SAME-SEX MARRIAGE
RETHINKING BALLOT MEASURE TACTICS

> The campaign for same-sex marriage has been an unmitigated disaster. Never in the history of organized queerdom have we seen defeats of this magnitude. The battle to win marriage equality through the courts has done something that no other campaign or issue in our movement has done: it has created a vast body of new antigay law.
>
> John D'Emilio, "The Marriage Fight Is Setting Us Back"

IN A CRUEL TWIST OF FATE, just as the LGBT movement was celebrating a series of victories between 2000 and 2002, it experienced the agony of defeat in the November 2004 general election. In this one election, more statewide anti-gay ballot measures were on states' ballots and passed than in any previous election. The trend of losing ground in state elections continued for five years, as marriage bans were passed in many states or as constitutional amendments and marriage gains were retracted in California and Maine at the ballot box. These losses led LGBT organizations to reconsider campaign tactics, specifically the way campaign tactics serve the larger movement.

As the excerpt at the start of this chapter demonstrates, same-sex marriage is seen as both the most important goal of the movement and the most controversial. More time, energy, and money have been spent pursuing same-sex marriage rights than any other issue. Yet it is also one of the most controversial issues within the LGBT community. Many LGBT and queer activists criticize the institution of marriage as being too mainstream, patriarchal, and assimilationist. Historian John D'Emilio suggests that marriage equality has "confuse[d] ordinarily intelligent queers by purveying the line that full dignity, full respect, and full citizenship will come only when gays and lesbians have achieved unobstructed access to marriage."[1] In July 2006, a group of prominent LGBT activists and policy makers issued a statement titled "Beyond Same-Sex Marriage: A New Strategic Vision for All Our Families and Relationships" that argued that the movement needs to protect all family configurations, not just married ones.[2] Year by year, consensus around these issues has grown within the LGBT movement, but there is still some dissent.

Although the movement suffered losses at the ballot box between 2004 and 2009, there were also many victories, including an increase in the number of states recognizing same-sex marriage or civil unions, the passage of a federal hate-crimes bill, and progress on rescinding the military ban on homosexuality. But at the ballot box there was a series of failures. Many same-sex marriage bans passed as state constitutional amendments, making them difficult to change. They passed both in some of the strongest battleground states (e.g., Oregon and Michigan) and in states where LGBT campaigns were fighting anti-gay ballot measures for the first time (e.g., Montana and North Dakota). Fighting these ballot box initiatives cost LGBT organizations millions of dollars—and resulted in little in the way of tangible benefits.

In the years before 2002, the Oregon model campaign tactics were the acknowledged approach to LGBT campaigns, but as LGBT groups lost fight after fight to legalize same-sex marriage, those tactics were called into question. The Religious Right brought a great deal of innovation to the campaign tactics used in these ballot box initiatives. Prior to 2002, reliance on the Oregon model campaign tactics was so strong that losing campaigns were inclined to attribute losses to reasons other than campaign tactics. But in the face of such losses, and in the face of the Right's innovative campaign tactics, LGBT campaigns were forced to reevaluate the effectiveness of the Oregon model. This chapter echoes scholar Holly McCammon's findings that defeats lead to a reconsideration of tactics and tactical shifts.[3]

The tactical shift in LGBT campaign approaches was minor, however, owing to the widespread adoption of campaign tactics. Part of this tactical shift was the reconsideration of the relationship between campaigns, particularly failed campaigns, and the larger movement. As marriage bans passed in many states, movement leaders questioned whether campaigns that face inevitable loss should engage in tactics that further long-term social movement goals rather than engaging in tactics focused on achieving short-term wins. This reconsideration of the relationship between social movement goals and campaigns evolved out of the decades-long tensions between and within LGBT organizations about visibility and messaging, and from questions about the efficacy of polling. In addition to the reconsideration of messaging, campaigns fought from 2004 to 2009 focused more on movement building and organization building to help develop movement infrastructure.

Losing and Winning

From California to Maine, from North Dakota to Texas, the LGBT movement has lost same-sex marriage bans at the ballot box. Many of these ballot measures were super-DOMAs, which write into the state constitution not just a ban on same-sex marriage but also anything "like marriage," such as domestic partnerships. The LGBT community in Colorado, Alaska, and Washington also confronted ballot measures to eliminate or prevent domestic partnerships. The escalation in use of marriage bans by the anti-gay Right made this time period, from 2004 to 2009, one of the most difficult ones for the movement. Of the thirty-eight referendums and initiatives on the ballot during those years, the LGBT movement won only eight. Six of those eight were local referendums, reflecting the continuing efficacy of the LGBT movement in winning referendums. Two victories were statewide ballot measures: an initiative to pass a super-DOMA in Arizona and a referendum on domestic partnerships in Washington.

Even with thirty defeats, this decade has brought signs of progress. In 2000, same-sex marriage was completely illegal throughout the United States. At the close of 2010, it was legal in six states, and seven states gave same-sex couples broad relationship recognition with laws recognizing civil unions.[4] Evan Wolfson called 2009 "the winningest year ever" for same-sex marriage rights.[5]

The LGBT movement also held on to legislative and judicial gains in Massachusetts, Iowa, and Washington, D.C. LGBT organizations targeted Massachusetts and Iowa for legalizing same-sex marriage because it is difficult to get constitutional amendments passed and on the ballot in those states. After the legalization of same-sex marriage in Massachusetts, the organization Mass Equality worked for years to keep a constitutional amendment banning same-sex marriage off the ballot. According to one Mass Equality organizer, it only kept marriage off the ballot through "millions of dollars, that's the short answer... the long answer is that we engaged very strategically in the political process, both in lobbying and in elections." In a four-year campaign, the group narrowly avoided getting the marriage ban on the ballot twice. At the start of 2011, there were continuing efforts to get same-sex marriage on the ballot in Iowa.

Even at the ballot box, there have been signs, however small, of progress. Between 1998 and 2009, in more than a decade of voting on same-sex marriage, voters were increasingly supportive of same-sex marriage and domestic partnerships in statewide votes. As demonstrated by Figure 7, voters have gone from 31 percent to 46 percent in support of marriage and domestic partnerships in a decade. Public opinion has changed within individual states as well. In California, between the 2000 Knight Initiative and 2008 Proposition 8, voters went from 39 percent to 47.7 percent opposition to a ban on same-sex marriage. Marriage activists such as Evan Wolfson have considered this increase in support a sign that ballot measures will start winning more often. In addition, there have been a few victories (Arizona, Washington), "near" victories (Maine, South Dakota), and policy victories (Alaska) to buoy the spirits of LGBT activists.

This marginal progress caused campaign organizers to reexamine campaign tactics. The lessons learned during the 2004–9 campaigns were many, as marriage ban campaigns across the country were so varied. Organizers also learned much from the astonishing defeats in Maine and California, where marriage bans eliminated existing same-sex marriage. The few victories and "near victories" were analyzed closely for evidence of successful tactics; but, unlike the 1992–98 period, when campaign activists based

Time Period	N	Mean	Standard Deviation	Lowest Percent	Highest Percent
1992–2002	7	31%	4.3	25% (Arkansas)	39% (California)
2004–2005	14	29.1%	7.9	14% (Mississippi)	43% (Oregon)
2006–2007	11	38.1%	12.3	19% (Alabama)	51.8% (Arizona)
2008–2009	5	46%	5.6	37.9% (Florida)	53.15% (Washington)

Figure 7. Average percentages voting to oppose marriage bans or elimination of domestic partnership benefits, statewide votes only, 1998–2009.

their tactics on the winning Oregon campaign, organizers of these campaigns looked to the dramatic defeats in Maine and California as the basis for rethinking campaign tactics.

Statewide Campaigns in the Heartland

Most marriage ban campaigns during this period were waged outside of the battleground states. Indeed, LGBT community members in states such as Kentucky and Tennessee faced ballot measures for the first time. The marriage ban campaigns helped heartland states develop more of an infrastructure and gave them valuable experience; but the campaigns also led to dissension, as many activists were upset that so much attention and resources were diverted to same-sex marriage. In general, these heartland defeats had little impact on existing campaign tactics, as these campaigns were unable to effectively use most model campaign tactics.

Because each of the thirty-five states where campaigns were fought was unique, it is difficult to gauge the effectiveness of the campaign tactics used. There was a dramatic disparity from state to state in the strength of the movement infrastructure, in public opinion, and in the financial resources available to fight these ballot measures. As Figure 7 attests, there is quite a difference in the characteristics of a ballot measure campaign between Alabama and Arizona. Indeed, a few states, such as Mississippi, did not mount a ballot measure campaign at all. Other states, as in North Dakota and Montana, worked with a shoestring budget of less than $150,000. Lack of funds led to creative innovations; when the South Dakota campaign raised last-minute funds, volunteers taped a radio ad by sitting on the campaign office floor under a pile of coats, and using the campaign director's cousin for the voice talent.[6] Many of these state campaigns had weak movement infrastructures, with few LGBT organizations generally and statewide political organizations specifically. However, a few states, such as Arizona, Virginia, and Wisconsin, ran large-scale campaigns, mobilizing significant local resources to raise millions of dollars.

Fund-raising challenges in the crowded election cycles in 2004 and 2008 brought additional complications. During these election cycles, national organizations and local donors alike had to make decisions about which campaigns were most important and most likely to succeed. In 2004, the HRC and the Task Force targeted Oregon as the state most likely to win its campaign, based on its long history of victories, and chose to support Oregon's fight against Ballot Measure 36. According to one HRC field staff member, making decisions about funding was like "doing triage. That was a difficult process to go through." But Oregon was targeted, because HRC and the Task Force had "a lot of faith in the campaign, the statewide organization and the people running it — they had a winning strategy." Collectively, the two national organizations contributed more than $640,000 to the Oregon campaign. The Task Force also assigned two veteran field staff members to work on the campaign full-time, and sent a last-minute surge of field staff to Oregon to support in the final weeks of the campaign.[7]

The competition for financial resources was even more intense in 2008. Although there were only four anti-gay ballot measures in the 2008 election, the No on 8 campaign in California got the lion's share of national attention and resources. With California receiving so much funding and support, activists in Florida, Arizona, and Arkansas described how difficult it was to fund-raise for their own campaigns. So overwhelming was the support for California's campaign that one Arizona fund-raiser stated that even Arizona residents were donating to the No on 8 campaign rather than to their home state. In this competition for fund-raising, heartland states inevitably got the short shrift.

Lack of funds had a significant impact on the heartland campaigns' ability to succeed. Without funding, they found it difficult — or impossible — to implement dominant tactics, such as professional messaging and voter identification. Some activists were skeptical of the Task Force emphasis on voter contact, although many campaigns in states such as South Dakota and Montana used voter ID in their most liberal areas with success. A Missouri campaign staff member noted that the voter contact was an "enormous, enormous undertaking" for the campaign's resources to support, and he was "not sure the model has been proven effective on such a large scale."[8] The heartland campaigns were skeptical that tactics developed in more liberal states would work in their more conservative political environments. This ambivalence was complicated by interactions with some national campaign trainers, who were at times dismissive of the size and scale of existing political activities in these states. However, many campaign managers from heartland campaigns lauded national LGBT organizations for organizing and funding national trainings for all the marriage ban campaigns in 2004, and providing mentoring and possibilities for social networking.

An additional resource in short supply was enthusiasm for same-sex marriage campaigning. Many heartland states did not have same-sex marriage on their agenda and instead had been pushing for passing employment nondiscrimination legislation or hate-crimes bills. Doug Gray, a political consultant, commented that when he worked on the Missouri campaign in 2004, marriage as an issue "was thrown upon us . . . We weren't asking for marriage in 2004 . . . This isn't a fight in a battle that we brought on."[9] It was also demoralizing to fight campaigns that activists felt had no chance of succeeding, fighting a campaign "no one thought had a chance," according to many activists. These issues made it hard to rally enthusiasm for marriage ban campaigns.

However, most activists noted that a positive outcome of the ballot measure campaign was that it built local movement infrastructure and unified the community. In the face of impending defeat, campaigns could shift their focus to movement building rather than campaign running. One organizer from Kentucky noted that although there was "a slim to none chance to win," organizers used the campaign "to build long-term power." For many states, such as Louisiana, it was the first time the LGBT community had organized a project statewide. Activists learned how to access larger media markets, and the process helped them create social networks across states. Campaigns in Alaska, Idaho, South Dakota, and Tennessee, though unsuccessful, emerged with statewide organizations.

Many of these defeats had no impact on other campaigns' reliance on the standard campaign tactics. Analysts blamed defeats in Alabama and Missouri, for example, on the local electorate and movement infrastructure, rather than a result of the campaigns' tactics. They did, however, raise questions about the relationship between these ballot measure campaigns and the larger social movement. In campaigns doomed to failure, activists considered whether long-term community building was a more effective use of time and resources than typical campaign tactics, as analyzed later in this chapter. Defeats in battleground states such as Oregon and Wisconsin raised questions about the efficacy of existing tactics to fight marriage ban ballot measures.

Learning from Victories and "Near Victories"

Even within this series of defeats there were some glimmers of hope, some lessons to be learned. Although many organizers thought that Oregon's 2004 campaign would result in its being the first state to defeat a marriage ban, victory against marriage bans did not come until 2006. In 2006, there was both a victory and a "near victory." A campaign in Arizona defeated a super-DOMA, and a campaign in South Dakota came close to defeating a marriage ban after 48 percent of voters opposed the ban. In addition, Washington activists successfully defended their domestic partnership benefits, which proffered all the rights of marriage to same-sex couples, in a referendum in 2009. These campaigns dramatically differed from each other in size, funding, and approach, giving mixed messages about how to defeat marriage bans and other relationship recognition ballot measures. These campaigns did not completely challenge dominant tactics but suggested that tactical flexibility could be critical. The lesson learned was that each state can have its own "path to victory." According to Jon Hoadley, director of the South Dakota campaign, his near victory reminds us "that campaigns are both an art and a science. We have the science piece down but we need to be flexible and take opportunities as they come. We need to be able to pivot at the end of the campaign when opportunities arise." Many LGBT organizers focused on lessons learned about messaging in all three campaigns over the impact of other factors.

In Arizona, post-campaign analysis focused almost exclusively on messaging. After the surprising victory, an article in the *Advocate* asked: Do activists "want to get straight people to vote against an antigay ballot initiative? Make it all about them."[10] For their spokespeople, the Arizona campaign used an older heterosexual couple who were registered as domestic partners and would lose their benefits if the super-DOMA succeeded. Campaign leaders suggested that this messaging, although unpopular in the LGBT community, was not misleading; it expressed the truth about the super-DOMA, as most unmarried couples are heterosexual. The messaging was developed and supported by professional polling throughout the entire campaign. Krysten Sinema, chair of Arizona Together, suggested that the Arizona campaign was successful because "we were disciplined and we shared our message over and over again. We polled like crazy. That's how we won."[11] The group's organizing motto was "Research. Truth. Discipline."[12]

South Dakota campaign leader Jon Hoadley also advocated the importance of developing the "right message for the right audience and delivering that message to them."[13] The campaign in South Dakota was tiny compared to that in Arizona, and in accordance with Hoadley's beliefs, used many unorthodox tactics. For example, faced with limited funds, the campaign used print and radio ads rather than television, including political ads in small-town weekly circulars such as the *Pennysaver*. The messages also used humor, which was unusual in political messaging and thus got a lot of attention. For example, the messaging mocked the term "quasimarital" in the initiative language, calling it a "made-up word." Similar to the controversial messaging in Arizona, the campaign did not try to persuade voters on same-sex marriage. One of its messages suggested that "Whether you vote no or yes, gay people still can't get married in South Dakota."

In Washington, the referendum campaign faced an extremely short campaign time period, less than six weeks, which forced innovation. Rather than running a statewide campaign, the campaign focused its resources on the western third of the state, which is more populated, more progressive, less religious, and includes a disproportionate number of same-sex couples.[14] In addition, rather than conducting a voter identification campaign, the Washington campaign engaged in voter modeling, in which it used demographic information from a voter file to divide voters into potential and strong supporters in order to target messaging accordingly. The campaign used this information to focus its GOTV activities. According to advocacy director of Equal Rights Washington, Joshua Friedes, voter modeling "saves money, eliminates the need for traditional voter ID, and allows you to target your messages and messengers."[15]

Analysis of these campaigns ignored such factors as advance campaign work, poorly organized opposition, and the subject of the ballot measure. For example, according to Arizona Together campaign worker Cynthia Leigh Lewis, campaign organizers began to organize two years before the ballot measure, and conducted polling and focus group work in early 2005. That advance work was, she believes, a major factor in the campaign's success. However, that was not the case in 2008, when they "threw the campaign together."[16] In South Dakota, local politics is insular, the campaign did racial coalition building with the Native American community, and the opposition was poorly organized and had few coherent messages.[17] Washington was voting on domestic partnerships, not same-sex marriage.

The use in these campaigns of various new tactics to fight similar battles challenged model campaign tactics by suggesting that tactical flexibility might be more critical than previously expected. One HRC worker, after discussing the Arizona victory, suggested that there had been too much "cookie-cutter, it-worked-there-so-it'll-work-here" with ballot measures, when each community and state was unique, and needed tactics that addressed its particular needs.

The Defeat of Marriage in California and Maine

Although defeats in the heartland and victories using new tactics challenged existing ways of running ballot measure campaigns, the most dramatic challenge to the status quo was the passage of marriage bans in California and Maine, where the marriage bans eliminated existing same-sex marriage rights. The high level of national investment in both the California and Maine campaigns led to national-level scrutiny of both campaigns as well, and activists analyzed both defeats closely for tactical lessons.

In 2008, when the LGBT community fought against Proposition 8, which was going to eliminate existing same-sex marriage rights in California, California was seen as a bellwether state. As San Francisco mayor Gavin Newsom commented after the legalization of same-sex marriage by the California judiciary, "As goes California, so goes the rest of the nation."[18] Evan Wolfson of the Freedom to Marry Coalition stated that "Holding California is an outright win . . . [whereas with typical marriage bans] we will not have advanced—but simply beaten back an attack."[19] The campaign in Maine was significant in that it was the first time that a legislature had passed same-sex marriage and had it challenged at the ballot box. These two campaigns were also the two biggest ballot measure efforts to date by the LGBT movement.

No on Prop 8 mobilized almost fifty thousand volunteers and raised more than $38 million, more than all the campaigns against marriage bans thus far.[20] Polling showed the campaign consistently ahead, which initially made it difficult to rally enthusiasm. Campaign support increased once the opposition began airing ads on TV.[21] And in early October the campaign leadership divulged to LGBT media directors that polling and fund-raising were behind.[22] One campaign leader noted that "We basically did better than any other marriage campaign has ever done, but that's not good enough."[23] Despite the large scale of the campaign, there was concern that the campaign was not big enough and that saturation had not been achieved. According to one campaign staff member, the biggest challenge in the California campaign was "we just didn't have enough money to hire enough field people early enough to reach all the places we wanted to reach."

After LGBT supporters lost the campaign, protests erupted all over the country and there was much analysis of what had gone awry. There was significant media coverage of the Mormon church's involvement in the campaign.[24] As might be expected after a dramatic and unexpected defeat, the LGBT national community criticized the campaign and its leadership. Much of the criticism focused on the campaign's use of closeted messaging, the insular nature of the campaign leadership, and poor racial coalition building. Critics suggested that the campaign was on the defensive and let the opposition define the message. According to Steve Smith, who managed the No on 8 campaign, "To win you have to define the issue, and we didn't do that."[25] One campaign consultant uninvolved in the campaign noted that No on Prop 8 was "run very poorly. We all know that it was a poorly run campaign. The money was there but they didn't know how to keep everyone on message."

LGBT activists criticized the campaign leadership for failing to reach consensus and to get community buy-in. It was difficult to keep everyone on the same page, according to one field-worker:

> I think the most challenging moment . . . 10 days before election day the upper echelons of campaign management, without much consulting of the statewide leadership, decided to pull the plug on continuing to do voter id and GOTV. That was the most awful moment . . . We fought it tooth and nail but that was the orders . . . It was horrible . . . it was absolutely horrible to explain it to the staff and all the volunteers who were planning to come

out and work in the final week . . . Strategy changing that close to the election was really fucking dramatic.

Other campaign workers described it as a "campaign made up of consultants," which reduced accountability. Another element of the campaign that the LGBT community criticized harshly was the lack of racial coalition building, an issue that is discussed in more detail in the next chapter.

These lessons learned were passed on to Maine. According to Equality Maine director Betsy Smith, "we were lucky California went first."[26] Because Maine won same-sex marriage through the legislature and Maine had a long history of ballot measures, LGBT organizers had anticipated that their victory would be challenged by a ballot measure. Once they won through the legislature, they immediately launched a public education campaign. It was a large campaign, raising $5.2 million with more than 24,000 small to mid-level donors, and with 65 paid staff (plus 25 donated staff from partner organizations and 20 full-time volunteer staff), and more than 8,000 volunteers.[27] Early polling suggested that no messages the campaign had developed would persuade voters. Anticipating a 53 percent turnout rate, rather than running a campaign to persuade voters, Maine's large field program ran a turnout campaign that focused on identifying and keeping supportive voters. At the start of the campaign, it had identified 25 percent of the voters and by the end of the election it got enough supporters to the ballot box to win any other election that had been held in the history of Maine, but that was not enough for a victory in this case.

Campaign leaders and political analysts blamed the high turnout in the election for the Maine loss much more than campaign failings. The turnout was 60 percent, the largest turnout in a Maine election ever. But the campaign used what was a "good strategy at the time," based on the information that it had. Betsy Smith stressed that "we did a lot of right things in this campaign, including leaving a feeling of inevitability about marriage in Maine."[28] For example, a growing percentage of Maine voters expressed support for same-sex marriage; in 2008, 40 percent supported gay marriage, and in 2009 that increased to 49 percent.

What were the lessons learned from both campaigns? One campaign worker from No on 8 said that the thing the movement learned the most was "humility." The biggest challenge came from reexamining critical parts of model campaign tactics, including messaging and voter identification.

Rethinking Campaign Tactics

These two defeats, particularly Proposition 8, led LGBT campaigners to reexamine how best to fight marriage bans. In particular, they have rethought the model campaign approach to messaging and voter identification, with concerns about movement building and efficacy. In the face of sustained defeats, there has been a push in the direction that even ballot measure campaigns that do not win should further social movement goals (specifically marriage equality) and build social movement power through mobilizing more activists or building social movement organizations. The losses also led to a systematic examination of model tactics to determine whether they are effective. The alterations discussed by organizations are not wholesale revisions of campaign tactics but rather a reconsideration of the ways that ballot measure campaigns can serve the larger movement. Cynthia Leigh Lewis, from the Arizona campaign, suggests that these losses were a "wake-up call to make the [LGBT] community relevant again."[29]

Ironically, part of this tactical alteration is reconsidering the role of polling in campaign work. As Hoadley described earlier, campaigning is both an art and a science. The "science" element was embraced as part of the development of tactics but is now regarded by many organizers and leaders with increasing skepticism. In interviews, many campaign consultants and leaders expressed the view that, in their experience, in marriage ban campaigns "polling lies," particularly in the larger campaigns such as Maine, California, and Oregon, in which polling predicted a win on election day. Following the losses in California and Maine, organizers also began to question the practice of using polling as a basis for message development, as the end result was that polling provides suggestions that are contrary to movement goals, such as avoiding the topic of same-sex marriage in order to win votes. Although the lost campaigns led organizers to be skeptical of polling, the current consensus is that one-on-one conversations do support grassroots organizing and movement building—the power of "changing hearts and minds."

Build, Win, Build

In this time period, national organizations like HRC and the Task Force continued to provide support to local and statewide campaigns, but the

Task Force now places increased emphasis on movement building. Interviews with Task Force field staff suggest that the organization has reconsidered the relationship between ballot measure campaigns and the broader social movement, particularly with respect to the way campaigns can build movement infrastructure. The Task Force field program uses the motto "Build, win, build" to model the growth of the movement through campaigning and grassroots organizing.

HRC and the Task Force also continue to provide early money for ballot measure campaigns and staff support, along with supporting other types of campaigns. Support for local campaigns has expanded to offer coordination of small, local campaigns and use national resources to address local needs. For example, in 2005, the Task Force was heavily involved in the Topeka, Kansas, battle to defeat an anti-gay ordinance. Instead of training local activists to do both phone banking and door-to-door canvassing, the Task Force reduced the pressure on the local campaign by coordinating volunteer phone banks in New York, Kentucky, Washington, D.C., and Tacoma, Washington, to call undecided voters, allowing the Topeka campaign to focus on door-to-door canvassing. This organizing, called the Volunteer for Equality program, has been used in several local referendums, including Gainesville and Montgomery County.

Although some activists are reconsidering the model campaign tactics that first became popular in the campaigns of the 1990s, national organization trainings have continued to promote the same dominant tactics. The 2006 Midwest Power Summit on same-sex marriage initiatives stressed the same fund-raising, voter identification techniques, and messaging tactics as did earlier trainings, and featured several organizers from the original 1992 Oregon campaigns. The Task Force encouraged the use of these traditional tactics, but with two caveats: concerns about voter identification and the content of disciplined messaging. LGBT campaign trainers at the Power Summit described voter identification as a tactic that relies on a strong base of identifiable supportive voters and a flexible percentage of undecided voters. The Task Force and HRC view voter identification as a tactic appropriate to campaigns for LGBT rights laws, because those campaigns usually have a high percentage of undecided voters. But Task Force organizers have seen that, historically, votes on same-sex marriage have a different voter base, with most voters being overwhelmingly against same-sex marriage, with very few undecided voters. This demographic makes

voter identification tactics less effective. That said, several states that anticipated same-sex marriage initiatives, including California in 2006, engaged
in preemptive voter identification before petitions were circulated for a
ballot initiative. Later in this section I will address the reconsideration of
political messaging about same-sex marriage.

During the 2004–9 period, Task Force trainings and fieldwork began
to focus on the development of social movement infrastructure through
grassroots organizing during ballot measure campaigns. Dave Fleischer,
who was the head of the Task Force organizing and training department
until 2006, commented: "If you're going to be a leader in one of these
fights, you take on the responsibility to run a campaign that's going to
think seriously both about the short-term goal of winning and the long-
term goal of strengthening our community."[30] One Task Force field-worker
noted that in organizing ballot measure campaigns, both winning and
building community are important. This field-worker emphasized that
the Task Force has shown that "even though we do marriage campaigns
and don't win, we still build scale and community." According to another
field-worker, Task Force organizers are working to answer the question of
"How can we grow more leaders nationwide?" and "How can we build
infrastructure within organizations so that when campaigns come along
and go they actually strengthen the infrastructure?" As part of building
movement infrastructure, Task Force organizers want to lessen "the tension between long-term building power and short-term building power."
When pressed for examples, both field staff members interviewed stressed
the importance of large-scale volunteer involvement and volunteer trainings. Those approaches empower local community members with tools on
electoral organizing, rather than running a campaign with national-level
organizers who disappear once the campaign ends.

The attempt to lessen the tension between the local and national organizers seems to be working; many Task Force field-workers have noted
the smoother relationships between field-workers and campaign workers.
One Task Force field-worker said that when staff goes to work supporting a
campaign, "we take off our Task Force hat and put on our campaign hat . . .
it's 100% working on the campaign." This approach works well on campaigns that rely on dominant tactics. However, in interviews, some local
campaign leaders described the Task Force staff members as "movement
people" rather than "campaign people," differentiating between individuals

interested in long-term and short-term organizing. For example, in the Michigan marriage ban campaign in 2006, when Task Force staff members pushed too hard for clear messaging on same-sex marriage, manager Ethan Roeder sent them home. In 2006, when Task Force and Arizona organizers disagreed on messaging issues, the Task Force refused to fund the Arizona campaign.

The pressure on campaigns to look beyond winning to create more movement infrastructure and to serve movement goals resulted in a change in model tactics. Central to the success of strengthening infrastructure and movement goals was the approach to messaging. Both the development and delivery of messaging have been a critical part of the change in tactics used in LGBT campaigns.

Persuading Voters on Marriage

At the Task Force's Midwest Power Summit training in spring 2006, the spotlight was on marriage; almost all attendees were facing imminent marriage bans in their home states. In the sessions on messaging, trainers played television ads used during the 2004 campaigns. One showed two African American women speaking honestly and openly about their love for each other. Another asserted that "denying marriage to committed couples is discrimination," echoing the messaging used about discrimination for referendums.[31] Many ads suggested that meddling with the constitution was dangerous, a common message in the 2004 campaigns; in Missouri, the ad suggested that the proposed marriage ban "isn't about gay marriage; that's already banned in Missouri. It's about putting unequal treatment in Missouri's constitution, permanently."[32] At the close of the session, the trainers admitted that they were not certain which messaging worked and which did not; no one present was certain, either. Trainers did, however, encourage the campaign workers present to focus on messages that move "hearts and minds," messages that were emotional and that represented same-sex relationships.

Messaging is one of the most important issues for contemporary campaigns, because effective messaging must be crafted specifically for the unique needs of the campaign and meet three criteria: it must be new and fresh, responsive to the opposition, and persuasive to opposing voters. First, the clear, concise messaging developed for referendums about the perils of discrimination against gays is not easily or effectively applied to marriage ban campaigns; many voters do not see inability to marry as an issue of "discrimination." Thus, LGBT organizers have been searching for messaging that is short, concise, and effectively addresses same-sex marriage. Many LGBT organizers and activists have sought to make this messaging effective not just within the state waging the campaign, but also for the larger goals of the social movement, including the support of same-sex marriage and nondiscrimination protection.

In particular, these organizers and activists are questioning the "traditional" model campaign approach to messaging used in early marriage ban campaigns. One thing many LGBT campaign trainers and activists agree on is that traditional campaign language about discrimination and equality, and attempts at evasive messaging (e.g., reframing the debate as a constitutional one rather than a marriage one), are ineffective — not just for the larger movement, but for campaigns. Fleischer explains that this "reframing of the debate" uses a messaging technique borrowed from Democratic Party politics. It "markets" the campaign, erroneously presenting it as being about constitutional issues or heterosexual couples. He suggests that "it's a poor model for us that instead of talking honestly about what the issue is that we're going to pretend that we're going to succeed at talking about something else and we're going to fool voters into thinking it's about something else."[33] Yet, with this evasion, as the media covers the ballot measure as a same-sex marriage issue, the LGBT campaign's avoiding "trying to say anything but gay and anything but gay marriage . . . isn't fooling anybody."[34] In early 2009, Fleischer suggests that in the movement "we still haven't run a campaign that fully acknowledges what the issue is." Many activists described this evasive messaging as harmful to the movement goals of same-sex marriage. In interviews, some statewide campaign leaders stated that in retrospect they think less evasive messaging would have been more effective, not just in terms of sustaining the organization but in the success of the campaign itself. One campaign leader noted, "We spent a quarter of a million dollars on a big ad buy [about the constitution] and still lost with 30 percent of the vote. In the months following the campaign I really thought about the benefits of a gay-positive ad, that the community would have been better off."

In addition to the concerns about evasive messaging, LGBT campaign activists are rethinking how to counteract the opposition's messaging around children and curriculum issues. The opposition has been effective at messaging that recruits supporters for the Religious Right and that makes evasive LGBT campaign messaging particularly ineffective. In a post-campaign poll by David Binder Research, the Yes on 8 ad that voters remembered most was the *King and King* ad, described in chapter 2, that claimed children would be taught about same-sex marriage in schools. Eighteen percent of the voters remembered the ad, although only 9 percent of voters polled claimed that was the main reason they supported the ballot measure.[35] The biggest concern for LGBT organizers is that this messaging targets soft supporters and undecided voters, who may be supportive of LGBT rights but are also concerned about children and school curriculum issues. Although Religious Right activists have been using messages about children and schools for decades, the small margin required to win in states like Maine and California has made messaging about children a key issue for LGBT campaigns. These arguments about kids are potent, suggesting that first graders may be taught about gay sex and forced to read LGBT-positive books. Scholar Patrick McCreery argues that the conservative argument about children and marriage "has at its heart an anxiety that children should learn proper gender roles."[36]

Many HRC and Task Force field-workers said they are unsure how they can best respond to these messages. One suggested that the biggest lesson from Prop 8 is that "We haven't found a way to really combat the opposition's messaging . . . It's not that voters are afraid of gay people. I think voters are afraid their kids will become gay. It's not really homophobia, more like heterosexism. It's not a fear of gay people, it's that they believe being straight is better." Particularly in liberal states, Religious Right messaging was able to build on heterosexist sentiments, which encourage voters to like their LGBT friends or neighbors but have reservations about same-sex marriage or their children growing up to be gay or lesbian. According to one HRC staff member, the biggest lesson from California and Maine campaigns was that "we have to stop pretending that kids don't exist and kids aren't going to hear about same-sex marriage. We try to avoid children like the plague, but we need to be proactive about bringing up kids."

The messaging has to be persuasive, turning "soft" opponents into supporters, as there are not enough voters who support same-sex marriage at the start of a campaign. This emphasis on persuasion targets opponents. That approach is dramatically different from the tactics emphasized in most previous ballot measures, where the focus was on a traditional turnout campaign in which supporters are identified and encouraged to vote. A persuasion campaign poses different messaging challenges. Campaigns waged in 2004–9 found that, with few genuinely undecided voters and strong Religious Right messaging about marriage, it was difficult to persuade soft opponents during the short campaign period. Since the dramatic defeats in 2004, both national and statewide organizations have engaged in extensive research on effective, persuasive political messaging on same-sex marriage initiatives. In many ways, the needs and issues in same-sex marriage campaigns are different from those of referendum campaigns or legal-restrictive initiatives. In same-sex marriage campaigns there are fewer genuinely undecided voters, and those voters vote overwhelmingly against LGBT rights on election day. Campaigns have also recognized smaller messaging challenges, such as the need to develop messaging more convincing to men, especially young men who are parents.

Some activists are skeptical that the intensity of a campaign is not conducive to persuading undecided voters on a complex issue like same-sex marriage. According to one analysis of persuasion in California, "Moving people on the issue of same-sex marriage is a *cultural* endeavor much more than a *political* endeavor. The meaning of marriage runs deep in people's psyches."[37] In response to concerns about persuasion, some organizers are pushing to start a "campaign before the campaign," preempting campaign work with years of persuasive public education, with large media buys, and through one-on-one discussions. The Equality California (EQCA) campaign, Let Freedom Ring, is an excellent example of this approach to preemptive public education. Two years before same-sex marriage went onto the ballot again in California, EQCA launched the Let Freedom Ring campaign. According to EQCA staff member Seth Kilbourne, fund-raising was challenging because it was "difficult to get donors to feel that urgency without an immediate threat."[38] EQCA launched the public education campaign in the summer of 2006, focusing primarily on Santa Barbara County, and it achieved a slight shift in public opinion about same-sex marriage. Many activists point to the rejection of Proposition 8 in Santa Barbara County as evidence that the campaign was successful. Those who initiate ballot measures have the advantage of having time to prepare; as many LGBT activists and organizations consider putting forward an LGBT-sponsored ballot measure for same-sex marriage, they have the opportunity to do several years of public education beforehand.

Experimenting with Fieldwork

As part of this reconsideration of tactics (and specifically messaging), activists went back to the drawing board, engaging in a series of fieldwork experiments both inside and outside of campaigns. After the passage of Proposition 8, a few organizations took advantage of the lull in Religious Right organizing to engage in fieldwork experiments and assess fieldwork effectiveness. These experiments focused on approaches to persuasive messaging.

The first experiment was conducted in 2009 and 2010, spearheaded by the Vote for Equality project in the Los Angeles Gay and Lesbian Center. Realizing that many canvassing scripts were short, to the point, and worked with predetermined questions, Vote for Equality staffers worked with Dave Fleischer (now of the LGBT Mentoring Project) to experiment with other approaches to canvassing scripts around same-sex marriage. This canvassing experiment used longer, more open, and persuasive discussions with voters about the subject. It focused on Los Angeles County neighborhoods, particularly minority communities. The script it used was longer and more flexible than regular scripts, asking a series of open-ended questions about voters' thoughts about marriage, about lesbian and gay friends, and about the effect of same-sex marriage on school curriculum issues. Analysis of volunteers' notes and videotaping of their canvassing conversation allowed field-workers to constantly fine-tune the canvassing script. In 2009, this ongoing experiment resulted in more than sixteen thousand doors being knocked on and more than 5,500 conversations with voters in Northeast, South, and East Los Angeles. The conclusions showed that, through these discussions, around one-quarter of undecided and unsupportive voters reconsidered their stance on same-sex marriage.[39] This experiment served to both improve canvassing methods and get a jump start on the next marriage ballot measure in California. This canvassing model, which has been called "the most sophisticated canvassing model with which we have ever worked," and other lessons learned are being used all across the state by other organizations.[40]

In summer 2009, Basic Rights Oregon conducted an experiment about persuasion to test whether direct-mail or door-to-door canvassing was more effective in persuading voters to support same-sex marriage. The reasoning behind the experiment was that "much of our movement's work is based on instinct steeped in years of experience. But only seldom do we subject our education programs to rigorous evaluation. To conduct this experiment, we suspended our assumptions about what works and doesn't work in convincing voters to embrace marriage equality."[41] The persuasion experiment used three experimental groups (direct mail only, canvassing only, and both mail and canvassing) and a control group (no contact) targeting 19,804 Oregonians in several areas of the state. After a follow-up contact of both experimental and control groups, the experiment demonstrated that all voters who were contacted by mail and/or through canvassing increased their support of same-sex marriage by about 5 percent. Democrats were more likely to be persuaded, but the experiment showed no statistical significance in voters contacted by direct mail and canvassing. That finding questioned the strong support for and long history of door-to-door canvassing in Oregon. What was affirming in the results was that "we can indeed move individuals to support marriage equality."[42]

Neither the Oregon experiment nor the California experiment can account for how voters can be persuaded (or not) during an actual ballot measure campaign, when the opposition is delivering its own messages. However, they do represent a tactical shift in considering how and if existing fieldwork tactics can or should be used to persuade voters on marriage. They also show the value of a "campaign before a campaign," giving organizers ways to get a head start on future campaigns.

Whither the Future?

What does the future hold for LGBT ballot measure campaigns? The close of the first decade of the twenty-first century is a time of both uncertainty and potential. According to Wolfson in 2010, "we have the attention of the American people, individuals writ large, in a way we never have had before in the last 40 years."[43]

Ballot measures are clearly a part of the landscape for the next several years, if not the next decade. Although the bulk of this chapter has been spent analyzing same-sex marriage ballot measures, other kinds of campaigns have been—and will continue to be—waged. Both national and local activists interviewed suggested that the movement is too finely tuned to marriage ballot measures, and is too often turning a blind eye to the urgency of other types of ballot measures. For example, activists who fought the adoption initiative in Arkansas asserted that too little attention has been paid to efforts to ban gay adoptions. Other critical ballot measures have included attempts to rescind the inclusion of gender identity in the nondiscrimination ordinance of Montgomery County, Maryland, which was the first time transgender rights had been exclusively targeted in a ballot measure.

Like *Romer v. Evans,* the use of marriage bans may be limited by the Supreme Court. More likely is that the movement will have to win same-sex marriage at the ballot box, state by state, until there are federal marriage rights for same-sex couples. In a huge shift, these ballot measures may be proposed by the LGBT movement rather than the Religious Right, which may present a challenge to the use of existing LGBT campaign tactics, but also give campaigns the opportunity to begin campaigning earlier, and to know definitively when a campaign is going to take place.

Returning to the Ballot Box?

In the wake of Proposition 8, the question the LGBT community asked most often was "What next?" Not content with losing same-sex marriage rights and facing the potential invalidation of tens of thousands of existing marriages in California, the community pushed for a return to the ballot box. The challenge posed by marriage bans that are passed as constitutional amendments is that they are difficult to reverse. In California, Proposition 8 can only be reversed by a federal court challenge or an LGBT-sponsored constitutional amendment to annul the proposition. The unexpected defeats in Maine and California may lead to a reemphasis on LGBT-sponsored ballot measures on a scale never before seen, as organizations in Maine, California, Oregon, and Michigan consider returning to the ballot box. The challenges of these LGBT-sponsored ballot measures may include voter persuasion, fund-raising, and countermovement challenges. This return to emphasis on ballot measures is a clear shift in tactics toward taking the offensive, which is ironic in that the movement has yet to demonstrate that it can defeat marriage bans.

California LGBT campaigners considered returning to the ballot box in 2010 in the wake of Proposition 8's passage. In the months following the defeat, same-sex marriage seemed to be gaining traction all over the nation in places such as Washington, D.C., Maine, New Jersey, New York, and Vermont. Since the defeat of Proposition 8, state legislatures have passed same-sex marriage bills in Vermont, New Hampshire, and New York. In addition, state legislatures have passed civil union or domestic partnership bills in Illinois, Delaware, Hawaii, Nevada, and Wisconsin. As of 2011, the states of Rhode Island, Maryland, New Mexico, and Illinois also legally recognize same-sex marriages performed in other states.

In addition to this optimism stemming from sudden movement gains, proactive initiatives such as ballot measures have been ideologically popular among LGBT activists because they allow the movement to act offensively against the Right, putting things on the movement's agenda at their own pace and in their own time. This desire to set the terms of the fight has persisted in the push for California's proactive initiative:

> In one year, we have achieved marriage equality in Iowa, Maine, Vermont, New Hampshire, and Washington, DC. These victories were only offset somewhat by the loss of marriage rights in Maine, but our opponents, who operate nationally, relish the chance to roll back all of our gains. If we return marriage rights to the California ballot . . . , we set the ground rules of the campaign, we set the stage, and we force our opponents to confront us here.[44]

By setting "the ground rules," LGBT activists gain control over the timing and nature of the initiative campaign. Some political consultants have argued that controlling the timing and the nature of the initiative gives the movement an advantage because it allows it to wait for an opportune moment. Dave Fleischer notes:

> In most of these ballot measure campaigns on marriage, our community is put in a financially brutal position by our opposition, because they control the timetable. But we control the timetable now. Let's use that advantage, and return to the ballot when we're financially ready.[45]

Activists say that one of the strongest reasons for controlling the timing of a campaign is to capitalize on the role of anger, energy, and momentum.

Deborah Gould in her book *Moving Politics* suggests that emotions are an important but theoretically underexamined part of social movement mobilization. One of the most frequently mentioned reasons for returning to the ballot box was momentum and emotion. Activists planned on surfing the anger and rage of defeat with the close temporal proximity of a 2010 ballot initiative. Repeatedly, in blogs and newspaper accounts, activists reported having something "stolen" or "taken" from them, anger that happily married couples could have their marriages invalidated, and pride in the number of protests nationally against Proposition 8. Many blogs referred to a "backlash" that occurred after Proposition 8 passed. Even some experienced strategists have suggested that the "heart" may be ruling the "head" in the decision to return to the ballot box:

> The 18,000 LGBT couples who experienced the joy of marriage in California cannot be the only ones. Nothing could be more important than securing this right for all who desire it. So . . . sometimes when the head is saying one thing, the heart, and in this case the "gut", could be saying something else.[46]

This "gut" is the impulse that many activists described as motivating the return to the ballot box, especially, as they desired to channel the pent-up anger and rage at Proposition 8's passage into a definitive victory. Statewide organizations in California sponsored a series of town hall meetings in 2009 to discuss whether to return to the ballot box in 2010 or 2012, with a community decision made to return in 2012 or later. As of September 2011, the California LGBT community was facing a potential referendum on California SB 48, the Fair Education Act, which could be on the ballot in 2012, creating a campaign that may roll over into a proactive initiative to relegalize same-sex marriage.

It is clear that LGBT-sponsored ballot measures are part of the future of the movement at the ballot box. According to sources at the Ballot Initiative Strategy Center, in 2010, in both Arizona and Colorado, LGBT individuals filed ballot measures that would grant domestic partnerships and same-sex marriage, respectively.[47] And Maine LGBT organizations launched a concerted effort to place same-sex marriage back on the ballot for the 2012 election.

A Time of Defeats

The disparity between this chapter (a tale of defeats) and the preceding chapter (a tale of victories) is telling. Although the confidence in model campaign tactics grew during the LGBT movement's winning streak, there was a reexamination of these tactics from 2004 to 2009. As marriage ban campaigns struggled to find the right approach to winning same-sex marriage at the ballot box, there was a reconsideration of messaging, voter identification, and the role of research in campaigns. Although victories and defeats provided information on the role of model campaign tactics in these campaigns, they also suggested the need for tactical flexibility.

In addition, the sheer number of losses during this time period encouraged activists both nationally and locally to reconsider the relationship between ballot measure campaigns and social movements. Some campaign tactics, such as messaging, have been reconsidered by activists to better complement movement goals. And there has been a push by national organizations such as the Task Force to build more movement infrastructure out of ballot measure campaigns.

The widespread adoption of campaign tactics was earlier buoyed by victories, but this chapter shows what happens to tactics during a time of widespread defeat. Although these tactics were criticized and slightly altered, the logic of dominant campaign tactics held, even in the face of overwhelming defeats.

CHAPTER 6

SMEARS, TEARS, AND QUEERS
RACE AND TRANSGENDER INCLUSION IN CAMPAIGNS

> The Right has a pretty comprehensive agenda when they use
> issues, but all of us—people of color, gay people, women—only
> react when we are targeted. Our divisions keep us apart, and
> meanwhile they exploit those divisions.
>
> Urvashi Vaid, in John Gallagher, "The Right's New Strategy"

GAINESVILLE, FLORIDA, 2009. Between television shows, a commercial
airs. Several children are frolicking on a carousel in the park. One small girl
with long blonde hair jumps off the carousel and walks into the women's
restroom. A scruffy, unshaven man in a baseball cap and sunglasses follows
her into the bathroom. The commercial warns the viewer that their "door
of opportunity is closing" and to act now by signing a petition to place a
recently passed LGBT rights ordinance on the ballot.[1] What does a man
in the women's bathroom have to do with LGBT rights? This commercial
was aired by a Gainesville Religious Right organization Citizens for Good
Public Policy, which was gathering petitions in response to an amendment
of the local nondiscrimination ordinance to include gender identity. Although sexual orientation had been protected in the nondiscrimination
ordinance since 1998, the inclusion of transgender protections and allow-
ances for public accommodations such as restrooms sent the local Religious
Right into a fury. Citizens for Good Public Policy claimed that the addition
of gender identity would allow pedophiles and rapists into women's bathrooms by claiming they were "really" women.

California, 2008. Immediately after the vote on Proposition 8 in California, political pundits and mainstream newspapers across the country
analyzed the paradox that high turnout by Latino and African American
voters to support Obama might have led Proposition 8 to defeat, because

seven in ten blacks voted in support of a ban on same-sex marriage. Civil rights leaders suggested that the LGBT community had done a poor job of reaching out to the African American community. LGBT community members accused the African American community of being homophobic, and African American community members accused the LGBT campaign of making false parallels between the civil rights and marriage equality movements. Although subsequent analysis showed that religion and age played a greater role than race in the defeat of same-sex marriage in California, the message rang loud and clear that many LGBT and African American community members perceived the No on 8 campaign as ineffective at racial coalition building. LGBT people of color described feeling increasingly marginalized from the movement.

LGBT activists in ballot measure campaigns face many dilemmas about how to handle issues that come up, including transgender smear tactics used by the anti-gay Right and racial coalition building. Within the LGBT movement there are long-standing tensions about the marginalization of community members, and ballot measure campaigns have to work with (and potentially remedy) these tensions. According to a national LGBT leader of color, because of the sudden nature and short time span of LGBT campaigns, racial coalition building is like "trying to fix the boat while it's already sailing."

Yet there is also pressure on ballot measure campaigns to engage in model campaign tactics, which often have little flexibility for distractions. LGBT activists thus have to decide whether or not their campaign messaging can include a response to Religious Right smear tactics about bathrooms. They have to make decisions about how much their campaign should engage in racial coalition building in the local community. These decisions take place within an arena of contention in which the Religious Right effectively uses existing tensions within the LGBT movement to divide and conquer at the ballot box. The consequences of responding poorly include increased marginalization of groups within the larger movement, which may contribute to a legitimacy crisis for the movement.

The model campaign tactics analyzed throughout this book provide few resources for responding to these marginalization issues within the movement. Indeed, the professionalization of campaigns that occurred during the 1990s may make remedying marginalization even more difficult.

These tactics require the development of a professional campaign that adopts an instrumental approach to winning. Campaigns have limited time and resources, so any tactic must clearly and directly contribute to victory on election day. Scholar Jane Ward in her book *Respectably Queer* suggests that the professionalization of the LGBT movement has ironically led to the instrumental uses of diversity within the movement. This means that, among other things, differences are only included when they are clearly beneficial to the organization in question. These "diversity projects are ultimately at odds with social justice efforts when they are aimed toward instrumental outcomes . . . formally celebrating the race, class and gender diversity of 'the queer community' can function to stifle forms of difference that are not easily professionalized, funded, or used for other institutional or financial gains."[2] I argue that these same tendencies exist within campaigns, as marginalization is remedied only when imminently and apparently useful to the success of the ballot measure campaign.

This instrumental use of diversity in campaigns can be harmful to the larger social movement. Granted, movements can be harmed by campaigns in many ways that have been documented throughout this book. Campaigns can strain and divert social movement resources, such as money and time, along with derailing the movement agenda. This chapter focuses on the way that the instrumental use of diversity within campaigns can create a contradictory relationship between social movements and ballot measure campaigns. How does this instrumental use of diversity create a problem for the LGBT movement? Because resolving alienation is the focus of identity politics, alienation or marginalization within the movement is doubly problematic and can lead to a legitimacy crisis for the movement.[3] In this legitimacy crisis, community members may view the movement as not representing the entire community and withdraw funding, support, and volunteer help.

In this chapter, after giving an overview of the role of movement issues within campaigns, I analyze how ballot measure campaigns often employ an instrumental use of diversity when engaging in racial coalition building and transgender inclusion. Using examples of campaigns nationally and focused case studies, I analyze how these marginalization issues may create a contradictory relationship between ballot measure campaigns and social movements.

50 percent + 1 versus Grassroots Organizing

As California activists were fighting Proposition 8, the LGBT community in Arkansas was also facing a ballot measure, the Unmarried Couples Adoption Ban. Randi Romo, a Latina lesbian organizer, remembers actively rejecting model campaign tactics, which were described as the "Arizona model" after the successful 2006 Arizona campaign, during early campaign organizing meetings. She described how the campaign strategy was already decided, and any questions she raised about "inclusion and transparency . . . were completely shut down and not listened to."[4] She was concerned that the campaign plan for racial coalition building included being evasive about LGBT issues, a decision made because polling suggested that African American voters were strong opponents of the initiative as long as LGBT issues were not discussed. Romo considered this approach "disingenuous" because LGBT issues were used in the Religious Right messaging and described it as a case of "white people deciding for people of color what information they could and couldn't have."[5] She eventually joined a splinter campaign, called All Families Matter. One activist in the mainstream campaign was critical of the splinter campaign and Romo's approach. She suggested that the All Families Matter campaign wanted to engage in civil rights movement organizing and coalition building because then the Arkansas LGBT community "would have our purity and it wouldn't matter if we lost." However, the mainstream campaign activist was concerned about how much that "purity" would matter when faced with lesbian or gay individuals unable to adopt children. She questioned whether a "moral victory" was better than an actual victory at the ballot box.

As the preceding chapters have demonstrated, although model campaign tactics gained currency within the movement as the most effective way to win, they were not always popular. Indeed, there were many tensions and disagreements within campaigns over tactics that led to splinter campaigns such as All Families Matter in Arkansas. Many activists described these tensions as a clash between two different types of activists: "movement people" and "campaign people." "Movement people" were typically organizers involved in social justice organizing, direct action, or queer activism who pushed for campaigns to serve the movement and the LGBT community. Other activists described this tension as one between two different political approaches: "transformative" and "50 percent + 1" politics.

Although the rise of model campaign tactics has resulted from the victory of both campaign people and "50 percent + 1" politics within these disputes, it is clear that racial coalition building, infrastructure building, and long-term organizing have also been included in campaign politics.

These tensions within campaigns are mirrored within the broader LGBT movement. There is a long history of tension about whether or not the movement goal should be the radical transformation of society or the liberal inclusion of LGBT subjects in existing laws and institutions. Activists who argue for a radical transformation of society may focus on the queer visibility of marginalized members of the LGBT community or multi-issue politics that addresses broader interests such as poverty, racism, and imperialism. The liberal inclusion of LGBT subjects into existing laws and institutions tends to focus on "single-issue" politics that represents the concerns of a presumed white, middle-class, gender-normative gay subject, addressing issues such as discrimination, same-sex marriage, coming out, and pride.[6]

There was resistance within many campaigns to including the proposed tactics of transformative, movement activists, who might push the campaign to consider broader messaging to address other issues, racial coalition building, and visible inclusion of transgender community members and other marginalized members of the community. Even some activists supportive of model campaign tactics encouraged ballot measure campaigns to examine their decision-making processes. For example, Sue Anderson from the campaign to fight Colorado Amendment 2 noted that "I don't know if it would have made a difference in winning, but would have been better in the aftermath if there had been more attention paid to how relationships played out."[7] Many campaign leaders interviewed expressed concerns that some of these goals, such as broader messaging and attention to process, could derail the campaign and lead to a defeat. One Michigan campaign leader described this push for movement goals as follows:

> The first explosion that happened in the campaign was that much more liberal arms of our community wanted us to be more inclusive and wanted us to also fight for racism and other issues. The trouble is that issue campaigns have to be more single-issue than you can possibly imagine. We can't even talk about gay marriage. We couldn't talk about age. We couldn't talk about Muslims. We

couldn't talk about anything other than discriminating against gay people . . . but political campaigns are designed to do one thing and one thing only. If you try and do more than that, you lose.

This activist suggests that coalition work and addressing multiple issues ultimately detracts from a campaign, because campaigns are "designed to do one thing and one thing only." Going off strategy to talk about race and other issues was connected to fear of losing the campaign, which would have eliminated LGBT rights laws.

These tensions existed in almost every campaign studied, although they became less intense during time periods in which there was widespread adoption of campaign tactics. At the center of these tensions were questions about the relationship between ballot measure campaigns and social movements. To argue that a campaign should be multi-issue was to argue that it should remedy existing issues of marginalization. Race and transgender inclusion were the issues of marginalization that came up most often.

Secondary Marginalization in LGBT Politics

Similar to other movements, there has been conflict within the LGBT movement since the 1970s about inclusivity and representativeness. When campaigns struggle with issues such as racial coalition building and transgender inclusion, they are doing so within a social movement history of marginalization and attempts to remedy that marginalization. Like most identity politics, struggles within the LGBT movement include diverse individuals who may have little in common besides gender identity and/or sexual orientation. Cathy Cohen uses the term "secondary marginalization" to describe marginalization of subgroups within an already marginalized group.[8] This marginalization may include actual exclusion of individuals from movement activities but more often is a subtle form of exclusion in which marginalized group interests are not represented in movement goals. At different times, the LGBT movement has included the secondary marginalization of lesbians, people of color, LGBT individuals with disabilities, leathermen and women, bisexuals, and transgendered community members, among others. Scholar Elizabeth Armstrong describes the development of the LGBT movement as based on the power of "unity through diversity."[9] However, in the early movement this diversity was mainly *"ideological and sexual diversity among white, middle-class men."*[10] When ballot measure campaigns engage in messaging for campaigns, put together a board of directors, or hire a campaign manager, they are either resolving or contributing to this conflict around inclusivity and representativeness. The Religious Right places pressure on campaigns to remedy decades of mistrust and misunderstanding with its use of transgender smear tactics and racialized special rights messaging (as described in chapter 1). With racialized messaging, the anti-gay Right raises questions about whether the African American community supports LGBT rights. Referendums and initiatives can quickly become a vote on either African American homophobia or LGBT racism. The stakes are high. The Religious Right's use of racialized messaging and transgender smear tactics has brought both race and transgender inclusion, which are long-standing issues of marginalization within the LGBT movement, to the top of the list of issues that campaigns have to deal with on a regular basis.

One major source of tension in the LGBT movement is the marginalization of LGBT people of color. Activists such as Urvashi Vaid and Keith Boykin have written scathing critiques of the racism within organizations such as the Task Force and HRC in the 1990s.[11] Academic accounts have emphasized the long history of racial tension and attempts at racial representation in LGBT politics.[12] Some of the issues of marginalization faced by people of color within the LGBT movement include overt and covert racism by fellow activists, single-issue politics that ignores crosscutting political issues, and the assumption within identity politics that sexual orientation is activists' master identity.[13] They also face what Allan Bérubé refers to as the "whitening practices" of LGBT politics, which include *"selling* gay as white to make money, make a profit and gain economic power,"* along with *"mirroring* the whiteness of men who run powerful institutions as a strategy for winning credibility, acceptance and integration."[14] LGBT people of color may face tokenism by fellow activists, as the more instrumental effects of diversity, such as visible representation of minorities within the organization, become more important than transforming the culture of social movement organizations.[15] This long history of racial exclusion in the LGBT movement is reflected in the movement's approach to racial coalition building as largely instrumental. This instrumental approach to racial coalition building places LGBT community members of color in a double bind.

Transgender inclusion is also a long-standing movement issue that comes up in campaigns. The term "transgender" came into common use in the late 1980s as a political term and coalitional identity to describe a range of gender-variant individuals, including transsexuals, transvestites, or those who identify as no gender and/or multiple genders.[16] However, similar to disputes about racial inclusion, disputes about gender variance have existed since the beginning of homophile activism in the 1950s and have persisted since then. Homophile activists in the 1950s excluded gender-variant individuals, particularly transvestites and transsexuals, because of the way they tarnished the gender-normative image of gay men and lesbians.[17] Yet gender-variant individuals were major players in the Stonewall Riots, and the earlier Compton cafeteria riots were led by gender-variant individuals.[18] David Valentine in his ethnography *Imagining Transgender* suggests that the calls for transgender inclusion in the mid-1990s could be contradictory. This contradiction was a product of transgender activists who asserted both their difference from gay and lesbian lives and movements and their desire for inclusion based on analogous discrimination and experiences.[19] Despite this contradiction, the LGBT movement has developed a consensus about "adding the T" to LGBT politics and organizations that both builds on these commonalities and asserts differences between transgender and lesbian/gay life. Although there is less tension about the inclusion of "the T" in the LGBT movement at the beginning of the twenty-first century, many transgender activists still argue that transgender issues are insufficiently included within the movement and marginalized, as evidenced by the tension around transgender inclusion in the federal ENDA bill.[20] Many scholars and activists alike have questioned whether this inclusion is complete or satisfactory. Political scientist Shane Phelan in her book *Sexual Strangers* is skeptical of "LGBT" as a coalitional label and the assertion of real transgender inclusion, because, "as an inclusive label, LGBT enables lesbians and gays to deny charges of exclusion without actually changing their understandings or their lives. B and T are not only at the end of the line of initials; they remain the conceptual and political periphery of the L and G communities."[21] Activist Shannon Minter notes that "some gay leaders also feel resentment and fear that transgender will co-opt or derail the hard-won resources and political power that gay people have worked so long to achieve."[22]

These two issues of secondary marginalization are both a part of campaign politics. The next two sections will analyze the ways that the remedy of this marginalization is hampered by the use of instrumental approaches to diversity within ballot measure campaigns. Using national examples, along with short case studies of the 1998 and 2002 Ypsilanti campaigns, I demonstrate the way that inclusion can be complicated by model campaign tactics.

Race in Campaigns

It is 2006 and at the Task Force Power Summit in Milwaukee the hotel ballroom is filled with large tables. Each table is occupied by a team of ten to fifteen activists engaged in a game about how to win campaigns. Each round is a new month of a short-lived campaign, in which activists must make decisions about where to focus their energy, whether on fund-raising, coalition building, or using free media for political messaging. Task Force trainers sit at the side of the room, giving each table "campaign results" based on their decisions. At the end of the hour-long game, campaigns that focused on a few narrow tactics over and over again won over campaigns that engaged in multiple, scattered tactics. In addition, campaigns that engaged in no racial coalition building had twenty points deducted from their final score. A white gay activist from one of the Pacific Northwest states stands up and tersely comments that his team should not be penalized for not engaging in racial coalition building, as there are few African Americans in his state. He sits down, to affirmative nods from others in the room and at his table.

One of the Task Force trainers pulls out an easel pad of paper and writes down the small margin of voters by which most campaigns win. He notes that even in states with a small African American community, coalition building is important, as African Americans are reliable, progressive voters who vote in local elections. Black voters are important because campaigns are often won by a slim margin and they can make up this critical margin. Even when the white activist shook his head to disagree with the conclusions, the trainer repeated the message to drive it home. *Black voters are important, because they will make you win.*

Ballot measure campaigns both contend with the secondary marginalization of LGBT people of color within the movement and pursue the support of black voters. As the trainer argues, the black vote is important for these campaigns.

Not all racial coalition building is with African Americans. It also happened with Asian groups in San Francisco, Latinos in California, and with Native Americans in South Dakota. However, African Americans have become strategically, if not symbolically, important for racial coalition building. Strategically, African Americans, especially African American women, consistently and disproportionately vote progressively. Thus, black voters may help LGBT campaigns win on election day. Symbolically, the support of African American voters gives the LGBT movement legitimacy as being part of the civil rights movement. In his book *The Minority Rights Revolution,* John Skrentny analyzes the ways in which African Americans' position as the first designated minority group in the United States law meant that new minorities had to demonstrate that their situation was analogous to that of African Americans. The support of the black vote also contradicts the Religious Right assertion that the LGBT movement is usurping the civil rights movement.

Courting the black vote through coalition building is complicated by racism within the LGBT community and homophobia within the African American community.[23] Sometimes resistance could be very visible. For example, in some campaigns, African American Council members who were strong heterosexual allies were publicly reprimanded in their churches. Some LGBT activists have denounced this analysis of African American homophobia as overstated; for example, lesbian of color Barbara Smith notes that LGBT campaign workers ignore the fact that "the right wing is more than 99 percent white."[24]

One of the biggest challenges to racial coalition building is the short-term, instrumental focus of campaigns: racial coalition building is only included when expedient and apparently useful to the campaign victory. Because of these instrumental uses of racial coalition building, LGBT campaign organizers can seem both self-interested and unable to work with others in a mutually beneficial way, as Urvashi Vaid notes in *Virtual Equality.* Yet some racial justice organizers have suggested that LGBT activists need to be aware of the racism they are facing, that "we are a movement against racism because racism is what we are fighting, not because we have to be in order to build coalitions."[25]

When LGBT campaigns begin without an existing local movement infrastructure, they may be engaged in racial coalition building for the first time in their community. But racial coalition building cannot be built overnight. It may include working with local organizations such as the NAACP, soliciting the support of African American or civil rights community leaders, and developing messaging or voter identification programs targeted at the African American community.

All of these attempts at racial coalition building may be challenged by model campaign tactics. For example, developing messaging targeted at a particular community does not necessarily contribute to that community. In addition, the messaging developed for African American voters initially attempted to make parallels between the black experience and the LGBT experience, between the civil rights movement and the LGBT movement, but this messaging marginalized African American voters who disagreed with the analogy owing to differences in immutability (e.g., unchangeable characteristics versus behavior) and type of discrimination experienced.[26] This messaging was also an instrumental use of a community without necessarily giving back to it in any productive way. According to a young white queer man who worked on a local LGBT campaign in the late 1990s, "*Both sides* played the black community, really. *Both sides* went to this extra effort to try to court the African American vote. But neither one really contributed to those communities." This criticism has been most pronounced for the No on 8 campaign in California. After post-campaign criticism of the potential role of black voters in passing Proposition 8, the No on 8 campaign was scrutinized carefully by the LGBT and mainstream media for its racial coalition-building practices. Even the campaign working to return to the California ballot in 2012 has been criticized for misguided racial coalition building. In 2010, Reverend Eric Lee wrote a scathing criticism in the *Huffington Post* of the new efforts to get same-sex marriage onto the ballot in California:

> I'm sad to see it appears they have not learned the lessons from the
> mistakes of the California Proposition 8 campaign for marriage
> equality. The strategy of many LGBT organizations remains to de-
> velop messaging *for* the Black community without actually seeking
> the input of those *in* the Black community who have — at consid-
> erable personal and professional costs — taken a stand for marriage
> equality. That LGBT organizers continue to do this, despite the
> overwhelming research, polling, and basic common sense — which
> tells us if you want to energize Black folks about issues, you have to

actually *engage* and *understand* Black people at the beginning of the work—not just as an afterthought... The same organizations that ran the failed Proposition 8 campaign continue to tell the Black community what the message is, and to continue [to] mistake tokenism with community relationship building.[27]

Others like Reverend Lee differentiate clearly between developing messaging and racial coalition building, arguing that developing messaging may not lead to any engagement or understanding of black voters.

This approach to racial coalition building contributed to the secondary marginalization of LGBT people of color within ballot measure campaigns. In campaigns that used this instrumental approach to racial coalition building, there were many instances of LGBT people of color creating splinter campaigns or becoming disengaged from the campaign. In many cases, this disengagement from the campaigns and the larger LGBT movement continued long after the end of the campaign. Although Oregon in 1992 was considered a model campaign, it was the beginning of a history of tension between LGBT people of color and campaign leadership. During the Oregon Ballot Measure 9 campaign, a splinter group had been created by an African American lesbian.[28]

Anger over the campaign's instrumental, self-interested racial coalition building led to permanent divisions in the community, according to one Oregon organizer:

> The current assault against the gay community is being launched by a right wing empowered by years of development using racism as a flashpoint for organizing—years during which the white gay and lesbian community was, for the most part, silent and even hostile to the interests of people of color. The white community *remains* mostly silent and hostile—even as they attempt to bring us into their anti-right campaigns, they neither deal with our issues nor with our communities. We are repeatedly used and discarded to the extent that the [people of color] leadership of Oregon will no longer take part in the campaigns against anti-gay initiatives. Gay and lesbian people of color leaders have turned down offers of positions on the campaign steering committee, and an agreement has been struck to do separate work while communicating occasionally.[29]

The long history of Religious Right racism and LGBT campaigns' failure at racial coalition building in this case led to a long-standing community division that took years to remedy. As the short case study below will demonstrate, the inability or unwillingness of ballot measure campaigns to address the racialized political messaging of the anti-gay Right was a key part of this tension.

Protesting the Racist Right

Political messaging was a flash point of conflict for secondary marginalization, because messaging represented the LGBT movement. When representations were missing within messaging, those individuals felt excluded. The Religious Right's racialized messaging placed campaign activists in a bind. Model campaign tactics encouraged activists to avoid responding to the opposition's message and to instead be on the "offense" with their own disciplined message. However, many LGBT people of color involved in campaigns wanted the campaign messaging to respond to Religious Right claims about African Americans and homophobia. This disjuncture between what would be best for the campaign and what would be best for racial inclusion within the movement led to dissent. The model campaign described in chapter 4, the 1998 Ypsilanti referendum campaign, followed model campaign tactics but also experienced internal dissent over race and messaging. I use this campaign here as an example of how this dissent occurred in many campaigns, not to focus on Ypsilanti as a site of poor race relations within the LGBT movement. Indeed, the YCFE campaign did a far better job of racial coalition building than many other ballot measure campaigns.

The YCFE campaign had implemented model campaign tactics, but not without internal dissent about whether the campaign should focus on multi-issue, grassroots, transformative organizing. Tensions about grassroots organizing came into sharp relief in the final weeks of the YCFE campaign when the opponents in COST held a rally four days before the vote that targeted the African American community by featuring former football player Reggie White, the Winans Sisters, and Alveda Celeste King, who is the niece of Martin Luther King Jr.[30] This joint appearance was a packaged performance used by Religious Right campaigns in Maine and other locations.[31] According to one lesbian in YCFE, it felt like "a battle between the NAACP and the churches for the black vote." The reason both the NAACP and the black churches were fighting over the black vote was the need for African American support to either defeat or pass the referendum. YCFE leaders and committee members decided to respond to the rally by spending the weekend engaging in voter identification and create media kits to frame the rally as an "anti-gay rally." YCFE also released a letter from Coretta Scott King, Martin Luther King Jr.'s widow, which she had written in support of the Ypsilanti ordinance.

Some African American Ypsilanti and Ann Arbor residents, including one or two who were involved in YCFE, disagreed with this strategy and advocated for an active response to the rally's attempt to mobilize African Americans against the ordinance. The disciplined messaging of "NO discrimination against gays" used by YCFE did not leave a lot of space for responses to racial messaging. One African American lesbian activist who volunteered in YCFE objected to the narrow messaging: "I don't think, you know, people wanted to have some dialogue around how issues of race are a factor in this. They just wanted to stay on message with just that sort of narrow [messaging] . . . For a long-term social change, I don't think that is the way to do it, but the goal was just to win in the short term." This activist describes the tension between short- and long-term change and the ability of YCFE activists to discuss issues of race. Although YCFE's strategy would have led to more voters for the ordinance and its potential success, some African American gay men and lesbians were concerned about the cultural implications of the rally connecting African Americans with homophobia. A group of these activists created an alternative organization, African Americans Against Discrimination, specifically for the rally. They sent letters to the editor, brought in national activist Mandy Carter for meetings, and organized a silent, people-of-color-only protest across from the COST rally.

One African American lesbian who organized the rally suggested that some white YCFE committee members did not support the rally, but she felt like it was politically important to see visible support of the ordinance from African Americans, particularly LGBT people of color:

Because we felt like, the radical Right uses race that way. And, you know, we just felt like it was important for us to have a presence to say "no these are not like, you know, white gay people"... That's the picture that people want to paint. There are just white gay people. [But rather] that we are black folks. We are gay, straight, you know, all across the spectrum and we are supportive of this ordinance and we want to speak out against what people like Reverend Yuille and Reggie White are and what they are doing.

The YCFE objection to the response to the rally was rooted in concerns about keeping a unified narrow strategy that does not respond to the opposition and focuses on instrumental politics that will make a difference on election day. The reason some members opposed a people-of-color-only rally may have also been rooted in their own discomfort with race within the campaign. However, for the African American activist involved in the rally, having a visible African American LGBT presence was important. This visibility was a protest against the white face placed on gay issues by the Religious Right and the creation of divisions between the African American and LGBT communities that was harmful for African American lesbians and gay men in particular.

The rally was successful, drawing powerful media coverage to the silent people-of-color-only protest outside the rally. However, the power of the rally also illustrates the limitations of instrumental politics for addressing long-standing racial tensions within the LGBT movement. The instrumental campaign politics supported by YCFE discouraged activists from directly addressing claims about race and homophobia that the rally represented, and the majority of white individuals involved in YCFE also made protesting difficult. Although the African American–led protest against the rally did not lead to visible long-standing divisions within the Ypsilanti LGBT community, it did demonstrate to some LGBT people of color the limitations of their ability to work within the larger LGBT movement.

The model campaign tactics that made many ballot measure campaigns victorious hampered their ability to remedy issues of racial inclusion and racial coalition building. By focusing on instrumental approaches to diversity, in which diversity is included only when immediately and apparently beneficial to the movement, ballot measure campaigns contradicted efforts within the larger LGBT movement to resolve secondary marginalization.

Transgender Inclusion

In 2003, while working on a prospectus on transgender inclusion in the LGBT movement, a transgender friend repeated to me a rumor that the 2002 Ypsilanti campaign had not allowed transgender volunteers to go door to door advocating for the campaign and instead had only let them do phone work in order to protect the public from transgender visibility. I was familiar with fights over transgender inclusion in the local Michigan Womyn's Music Festival and the ongoing marginalization of transgender individuals in the LGBT movement.[32] Upon investigation, this rumor of systematic exclusion from the Ypsilanti campaign was untrue, a fabrication based on an anonymous e-mail sent by a transgender volunteer. Interviews with transgender volunteers demonstrated that they were treated well by the campaign leadership. However, this rumor motivated me to write a dissertation on transgender inclusion in Michigan LGBT politics. It also brought to the surface the legitimacy crisis created by transgender exclusion in LGBT ballot measure campaigns. For this friend and many other transgender community members, this rumor deepened their sense of being marginalized and unwelcome in the LGBT movement. Hearing about the incident made transgender community members and sympathetic allies less willing to volunteer for the campaign or other community endeavors. This legitimacy crisis was deepened when transgender community members did not feel included in the mission and messaging of the campaign.

Tension about transgender inclusion in campaign messaging is brought into sharp relief by the transgender smear tactics described in chapter 1. Similar to its exploitation of racial tensions in the LGBT movement, the Religious Right uses transgender smear tactics to attack the growing number of local and state nondiscrimination ordinances that include transgender protection, along with using them indiscriminately in other referendums and initiatives. In these smear tactics, transgender individuals become dangerous bogeymen, specters of the threat of gay rights. Scholarly and political attention is focused on the attack on same-sex marriage by the Religious Right; but transgender-inclusive ordinances are also increasingly coming under attack. In the 2009 Gainesville referendum, where the commercial described at the beginning of this chapter received national attention, transgender activist Donna Rose was concerned that "if this works in Gainesville, you'll see similar effects all across the country."[33] Indeed, the year before, Montgomery County, Maryland, LGBT activists narrowly avoided the first referendum solely on transgender protection.[34] The Religious Right can easily use transgender smear tactics to confuse voters who might be misinformed about transgender issues. Although transgender issues are increasingly in the media, from movies such as *TransAmerica* to talk shows about transgender men giving birth, many voters are unaware of what it means to be transgender.

The most common smear tactic has been about transgender women and bathrooms, arguing that transgender women are really men trying to exploit women. These smear tactics were widely used in Michigan and many other campaigns, including the Gainesville commercial described earlier. During the 2002 Ypsilanti legal-restrictive initiative campaign, for example, the anti-gay campaign Citizens Voting Yes for Equal Rights Not Special Rights (hereafter Citizens Voting Yes) sent out a flyer (Figure 8) that featured a picture of a Michigan transwoman taken from local LGBT newspaper *Between the Lines;* the backside of the flyer threatened the voter with scary "men in dresses" who would be granted rights by the "radical new city ordinance" that includes "giving men who claim to be female the special 'right' to use all public facilities reserved for women and girls."[35] The flyer described a dangerous group of men posing as women who would endanger the readers' daughter or granddaughter by sharing a bathroom with them. This gender-identity messaging continued in a separate letter from Citizens Voting Yes about the gender identity portion of the ordinance. Among other statements, the letter suggested that, "Bizarre as it is, these so-called 'transgender' activists insist that if a man *says* he's a woman, the law should recognize and treat him as if he actually *is* a woman. In fact, they're so radical that they say they believe he really *is* a female, just because he says so."[36] Citizens Voting Yes messaging stressed the deceptive nature of being transgender, that it was really a hoax being used to exploit and endanger women. The group's flyers emphasized how radical the ordinance was and how detrimental it would be the rights of women and children. According to one female member of Citizens Voting Yes, Gary Glen pushed the local group to send out the flyer under the premise that "if you give voters a shock by how radical it is how the law is enacted, then they'll be active." Even within Citizens Voting Yes, these smear tactics were controversial; some Citizens Voting Yes members suggested that the transgender flyer was un-Christian or ineffective.

Will you vote YES to protect *your* daughter... *your* granddaughter... from being forced to use the girl's bathroom with men like this?

When this man tried to join a women's health club in Lansing, he was refused. But in Ypsilanti, homosexual activists' deceptive campaign put new language in our city law making it illegal for any school, business, or other public place to "discriminate" based on so-called "gender identity."

Now, under city law, a grown man who claims to be female has the special right to use "any place" usually reserved for women and girls.

If you agree it's wrong to give cross-dressing men the special right to violate the privacy rights of others, especially women and children, please vote YES on the YPSILANTI CITY CHARTER AMENDMENT to remove this dangerous language from our city civil rights law.

YES **PRIVACY RIGHTS FOR WOMEN AND CHILDREN** Ypsilanti City Charter Amendment ✔

Photo by *Between the Lines*, a Detroit homosexual newspaper, accompanying a March 6, 2002 story entitled "Lansing health club bars transgender member."

Paid for by Ypsilanti Citizens Wanting YES for Equal Rights, not Special Rights, PO Box 980987, Ypsilanti, MI 48197

Figure 8. Transgender smear tactics used by Ypsilanti Citizens for Equal Rights Not Special Rights in 2002.

Arguments about bathrooms prey "on the false notions that GLBT people are predatory creatures whose elimination and hygiene needs come second to their supposedly voyeuristic desires."[37] Indeed, the women's bathroom is frequently a contested site for gender inclusion, serving as a space in which female masculinity is policed.[38] Scholar Judith Halberstam suggests that women's bathrooms "operate as an arena for the enforcement of gender conformity . . . a sanctuary of enhanced femininity, a 'little girl's room' to which one retreats to powder one's nose or fix one's hair."[39] Gender is more likely to be policed in women's bathrooms than men's bathrooms, and men entering the women's bathrooms are more likely to be perceived as a safety risk or danger. It is also part of what transgender scholar Paisley Currah refers to as the "'transgender sublime' response to unexpected bodies showing up in gender-segregated spaces."[40] For example, when out congressman Barney Frank opposed transgender inclusion in ENDA in 1999, he invoked issues of bathrooms and showers, suggesting that "transgendered people want a law that mandates a person with a penis be allowed to shower with women."[41] Transgender activist Leslie Feinberg describes this as a stereotype that transsexual women are "a Trojan horse trying to infiltrate women's space."[42]

Even before the Religious Right began using transgender smear tactics, LGBT campaigns struggled with transgender visibility in campaigns. According to campaign manager B. J. Metzger, in the 1978 St. Paul referendum, the local campaign "sent out letters advising volunteers to dress straight. They were very caught up in trying to look normal. And that campaign lost."[43] This admonishment to "dress straight" encouraged lesbian volunteers to wear dresses and gay male volunteers to be appropriately masculine. Some scholars have referred to this impulse toward gender normalization as "homonormativity," which Lisa Duggan defines as an impulse within LGBT organizing that "does not challenge heterosexist institutions and values, but rather upholds, sustains and seeks inclusion within them."[44] Susan Stryker, transgender activist, scholar, and public historian, considers homonormativity an apt description of the marginalization of transgender individuals within LGBT politics. For Stryker, this homonormativity "aimed at securing privilege for gender-normative gays and lesbians based on adherence to dominant cultural constructions of gender."[45]

Indeed, reactions to transgender smear tactics may inadvertently reinforce both gender normativity and the representation of the LGBT movement by "gayness" rather than the full LGBT umbrella. Reactions to the use of transgender smear tactics in the 1990s were initially dismissive. When Iowa City activists faced smear tactics about the impending outbreak of cross-dressing in the workplace with the inclusion of transgender protection, local trans-identified activist Brett Beemyn remembered that "the argument took us by surprise at first because it seemed so silly... But when we realized how much of an issue this was for some legislators, we explained... that employers would still be able to have reasonable, equitable dress codes at their places of employment."[46] In cities as diverse as Gainesville, Portland, and Ypsilanti, LGBT activists struggled with how to respond to these tactics, as they become increasingly used by the Religious Right. Many campaigns were blindsided by them. Even if the local ordinance or legislation included transgender protection, LGBT campaigns may have had few discussions and no intergroup education about transgender issues.

Campaign activists have always struggled about how to respond to these smear tactics, because part of disciplined messaging is ignoring the opposition's attempt to derail the campaign's main message. In other words, campaign activists have tried to prevent the Religious Right from convincing them to speak reactively about Boy Scouts, pedophilia, affirmative action, AIDS, or gay sexual practices rather than the substance of their disciplined message. As a consequence, many campaigns ignore transgender smear tactics rather than responding to them.

In addition to avoiding being reactive to the opposition, there was tension about how to represent the LGBT community. Since the early 1990s, most campaign messaging has used *gay* instead of *LGBT* or even *lesbian and gay* to discuss the ballot measure. The reasoning behind this was premised on an understanding of the voters and their ability to comprehend the "alphabet soup" politics that is the contemporary LGBT movement. Many activists referred to voters as "Joe/Joanna on the street" or, more affectionately, "Joe Six Pack." These "Joe Six Pack" voters were often described as uneducated and generally uninformed about the LGBT community. One campaign leader explained to me that campaigns used *gay* because the average voter had a broad understanding of the word *gay* and included many LGBT issues with that word.

During interviews with members of YCFE, which was revived in Ypsilanti to fight the 2002 legal-restrictive initiative, activists suggested that *LGBT* was too confusing and could lead to defeat. One heterosexual ally involved in YCFE explained: "I think there were several people who were sensitive to issues like that about do we use the word *lesbian*? Do we use the word *transgender*? And *it's not that we didn't use those words,* but in general, if you're doing a brochure and you have a headline, you don't include the whole alphabet soup." The LGBT "alphabet soup" was too incomprehensible to voters when messaging needed to be tight and concise. One lesbian activist noted that it would be difficult to include transgender issues in a voter identification effort because "there's too much of a 'what's that?' element to transgender issues." Including transgender messaging would involve educating the voters, a process that was not necessarily a component of either voter identification or narrow messaging.

The use of *gay* rather than *LGBT* created dissension in many campaigns in the 1990s about the politics of comprehensibility versus the politics of representation. One lesbian steering committee member in YCFE framed this gay messaging as implicitly inclusive and stressed the importance of comprehensibility over issues of representation:

> We did talk a lot about just the whole LGBT thing because whenever you're in a situation like this and you have queer people, you have to have the discussion about "well, are we going to say lesbian? Are we going to say lesbian/gay? Are we gonna say LGBT? Are we going to include all the members of the alphabet?" And we had those discussions and what we really ended up with, which may not have been popular with people, I think I was able

to articulate the importance of keeping it simple and that for the vast majority of people the word "gay" encompasses all of those. Now it may. *I understand that a transsexual may not identify as a gay person, but when you look about what we were trying to accomplish, which was win an election, you had to go about that in a way that enables you to win the election.* (Emphasis added)

This activist described voters as comprehending the word *gay* as being inclusive of the entire LGBT community. And indeed, the limited polling and focus-group work done on voters' understanding of transgender issues reflected this activist's understanding. In 1997, when Washington activists were considering their proactive gay rights initiative, the research they conducted on voters suggested that most voters could not differentiate between sexual orientation and gender identity. Many voters in the Washington focus group confused cross-dressing with gay men and lesbians and were uncertain about what *transgender* meant.[47]

In Ypsilanti in 2002, the campaign experienced a lot of pressure from the local transgender community to respond to the transgender smear tactics. Although the campaign did not respond directly, it did issue a flyer that addressed all the attempts of the Religious Right to derail YCFE messaging (Figure 9). This witty flyer framed the bathroom smear tactics as yet another attempt to divert the LGBT movement and avoid questions about real discrimination. Yet it also raised questions within the local LGBT community about who was represented by the campaign and who was included in it.

This lack of inclusion in campaign messaging can raise questions within the local LGBT community about who was represented by the campaign and who was welcome in it. Indeed, when these smear tactics appeared in Religious Right campaigns in Michigan in 2001, editors of the statewide LGBT newspaper, *Between the Lines*, were critical of campaign's responsiveness:

Let's look at the "t." Everyone is great at using the "t," pointing to the "t" and touting "t" inclusiveness. In spite of this, factions of our community remain that are willing to drop the "t" when it's politically expedient. The phenomenon of mainstreaming our issues to fit an antiquated, hetero-dominated ideal of Susie and Mary lesbian and Bobby and Mark gay is increasingly

Figure 9. YCFE response to transgender smear tactics, 2002.

being manipulated by those opposed to rights for all queers. For instance, in this year's campaigns across the state, each city saw literature that directly targeted trans issues in an attempt to scare straight (and lgb) voters into approving anti-gay measures . . . Gay and lesbian leaders of the campaigns scoffed at the trans bathroom idiocy, but, in more than one instance, used the argument, "Look, we gays and lesbians are just like you — we're normal." Sadly, at that moment, the trans-bashing arguments and scare tactics of the religious right and anti-gay campaigns successfully divided the lgb and t communities. The "t" was further marginalized in the campaigns in order to protect the interests of the lgb.[48]

Although this critique occurred before YCFE faced transgender smear tactics it suggests that the lack of response or at times homonormative response to bathroom smear tactics created a legitimacy crisis within the movement. Most campaigns, including YCFE, are open to participation from all members of the LGBT community. However, when transgender community members bring demands for representation or inclusion of their political goals, they are rarely accommodated within LGBT campaigns. In the case of YCFE, LGBT community members were welcome to participate and volunteer, but they did not have ownership over the campaign. The campaign resisted being pulled in multiple directions by community demands that would sidetrack it from its disciplined campaign plan. Some volunteers who worked for the campaign doing phone banking and door-to-door canvassing described feeling alienated by the lack of response of the organization and considered it to be insulting to transgender people. One gay committee member agreed that "we took probably some hits on that from the transgender group. Even though we had trans folks helping us in both campaigns, I think some of them were disappointed that it proceeded to be a gay issue."

Since 2005, these transgender smear tactics have become increasingly common and used more frequently in local referendums than attacks on lesbian or gay life. For example, in referendums in 2008 and 2009, the Religious Right consistently referred to ordinances as the "transgender bathroom ordinance" or the "cross-dressing ordinance." LGBT campaigns have become more proactive about using transgender-inclusive messaging. When the Kalamazoo, Michigan, and Gainesville, Florida, communities faced a referendum on their transgender-inclusive nondiscrimination ordinances, from the beginning campaign messaging referred to the ordinance as providing protections for "gays and transgenders." Kalamazoo campaign manager Jon Hoadley says that the campaign knew what the opposition's playbook was in terms of transgender smear tactics, and they thought it was better to "articulate that it was about gay and transgender people and move forward with it rather than give even the slightest hint that they were hiding something."[49] When faced with the commercial described at the beginning of this chapter, Gainesville's LGBT campaign, Equality Gainesville, responded in a frequently asked questions (FAQ) for voters that "this is a scare tactic with no basis in reality."[50] Local news coverage of transgender smear tactics about bathrooms in both cities also included detailed segments in which campaign leaders differentiated between pedophiles going into women's bathrooms and genuine transgender issues about bathroom use. City council members even reiterated the necessity for transgender protections, providing some education on transgender issues to the voting public.[51]

Transgender smear tactics raise the politics of representation in ballot measure campaigns, a politics that occurs in the broader movement as well. Although many nondiscrimination ordinances include transgender protection, this inclusion is often obscured during referendums and initiatives within implicitly inclusive messaging. This messaging is changing, as LGBT ballot measure campaigns have recently developed language that is more transgender-inclusive. However, when the politics of comprehensibility to moderate voters outweighs the politics of representation, it may create a legitimacy crisis within the LGBT movement.

Fixing the Ship? Making the Hole Larger?

According to the activist quoted near the beginning of this chapter, remedying marginalization within the LGBT movement during ballot measure campaigns is "trying to fix the boat while it's already sailing." Ballot measure campaigns work within a context they did not create — a history of secondary marginalization within the movement. And remedying that marginalization during a fast-paced campaign is indeed like trying to fix a hole in a ship while it is sailing. Ballot measure campaigns implementing model campaign tactics find this hole difficult to repair because of the instrumental focus of most model tactics. When campaigns only include marginalized issues when they are clearly efficacious and contribute to a victory, they may create a legitimacy crisis within the broader LGBT movement. Marginalized movement members may feel shut out and perceive the movement as representing only select community members. For an identity-politics movement, which claims to represent a collective of identities and interests, this can delegitimize the movement.

In ballot measure campaigns there have been clear attempts to remedy marginalization around race and transgender inclusion. Over time, LGBT campaign activists have worked harder to make campaigns more inclusive. However, even the most well-intentioned campaign may inadvertently contribute to secondary marginalization.

THE FUTURE OF GAY RIGHTS AT THE BALLOT BOX

> For months, we have laid out the criteria for moving forward. Like the Obama campaign, we understand that we need a combination of powerful and clear research that informs an expertly run campaign, an unstoppable movement that harnesses the new energy we have seen since the passage of Prop. 8 and the connections through personal stories and outreach in order to win at the ballot box . . . We must build our ultimate victory from the lessons of our recent disappointments. We know that we can change hearts and minds through real conversations with our friends, family, coworkers, and neighbors. This takes time and has to be built to scale—so we can't delay. When we go back to the ballot, we must be strong, clear and embracing.
>
> Rick Jacobs, chair of the Courage Campaign, 2009

BALLOT MEASURE CAMPAIGNS are difficult to fight. They take time, energy, and resources, along with the investment of thousands of volunteers. A victory may propel movement goals forward or stall the opposition. A defeat may demoralize followers, exhaust leaders, and set back movement goals. Although local ballot measures primarily have consequences for the local community, they may be perceived as consequential to the broader movement. National resources and advice pour into local campaigns. A local defeat may allow a strategy to spread across the country, affecting community members elsewhere. A local victory may be hailed as a national victory.

LGBT leaders, organizers, and activists have navigated the tricky terrain of ballot measure campaigns for more than three decades, since the first anti-gay ballot measure in Boulder, Colorado, in 1974. One of the most important reasons for studying anti-gay ballot measures is that they are a significant arena of contention between the Religious Right and the LGBT movement, in which both movements go head to head to get votes.

During this time, the Religious Right has constantly come up with new ways of fighting LGBT rights at the ballot box, switching from referendums on existing LGBT rights laws to legal-restrictive initiatives to same-sex marriage bans. This use of direct democracy by the anti-gay Religious Right has built social movement infrastructure for that movement just as it has for the LGBT movement. By sponsoring ballot measures from Hawaii to Maine, the Religious Right mobilized anti-gay voters, built new organizations, and grew the movement.

This book has analyzed efforts within the LGBT movement to find the best way to fight anti-gay ballot measures. This search for the best way of running ballot measure campaigns has had to constantly balance the goals of the broader LGBT movement with the tactics required to win a political campaign. Ultimately, the relationship between ballot measure campaigns and social movements is both complementary and contradictory.

A Complementary and Contradictory Relationship

In this analysis, the strength and power of ballot measure campaigns and social movements grew together. Initially, ballot measure campaigns were small and underfunded, run on a shoestring budget and able to draw on limited social movement resources. As the LGBT movement grew in size and strength, more resources became available to support campaigns. The study of ballot measures and social movements is inherently a study of the relationship among the national, state, and local levels of a social movement. National (and later statewide) organizations supported local campaigns with money, staff members, training, and advice. Local victories and defeats also buoyed national organizations with new members, leaders, and attention, as was the case, for instance, with the Miami Dade defeat in 1977. In the LGBT movement, campaigns also led to the formation of statewide organizations and, in many cases, launched local and national activists into electoral politics. Ballot measure campaigns often turn into social movement organizations in areas where no SMO existed previously. As activists realized that these ballot issue campaigns were ongoing, the efficiency of developing a statewide organization was evident. Many statewide organizations have moved beyond their focus on campaigns to work on legislative battles and general LGBT issues. Campaigns also built the political savvy of thousands of local campaign activists, which led to significant changes in the LGBT movement. Campaign tactics such as voter identification were increasingly used outside of ballot measure campaigns to further movement goals. Both the movement and ballot measure campaigns became stronger together.

The LGBT movement could also put pressure on ballot measure campaigns to be more than they could be. In many communities, ballot measure campaigns gave rise to the first local or statewide LGBT organization, carrying the weight of LGBT community members' expectations. Many campaign leaders cautioned that campaigns could not both win and incorporate all the demands of the local community. Ballot measure campaigns can also drain resources from the movement and perpetuate secondary marginalization. Within the large and complicated LGBT movement there have been divisions, difficulties, and tensions over the role of mainstream politics, direct-action protest, diversity and marginalization, and whether the movement should engage in single-issue or multiple-issue activism — all of which spill over into ballot measure campaigns. The issues do not start in the campaign, but campaigns may contribute to them, sometimes inadvertently.

Finding Winning Tactics

Whether the relationship is complementary or contradictory, within the LGBT movement there has been a constant search to find the best tactics to win ballot measure campaigns. One of this book's important contributions has been to analyze the development of dominant tactics within a social movement. The LGBT movement has struggled to find the best tactics, trying to establish a set of model campaign tactics that will work in most ballot measure campaigns.

The movement has learned from each victory and defeat, from the first huge defeat in Miami Dade County in 1977 to the victory in Washington State in 2009. Unexpected defeats such as the passage of California Proposition 8 have encouraged everyone from LGBT journalists to leaders to bloggers to pick apart the campaign for evidence of why there was such a big defeat. The interpretation of victories and defeats played a central role in the development of dominant tactics. In early campaigns, LGBT political actors used quasi-social-scientific comparative methods to decide which new tactics should enter the movement's tactical repertoire by examining both victories and defeats. This quasi-scientific reasoning was used in the early 1990s to compare two Oregon campaigns with each other and with the 1992 Colorado Amendment 2 campaign. The victorious Oregon No on 9 campaign in 1992 became the model campaign that solidified both ballot box avoidance tactics and professional campaign tactics as dominant tactics within the LGBT movement. This finding expands on Holly McCammon's research on the role of defeats in tactical changes to suggest that victories and defeats also buoy existing tactical repertoires, providing a supportive role for dominant tactics.[1] Dominant tactics gained ideological power in explaining victories and defeats, a way in which dominant tactics, victories, and defeats had a reiterative relationship. Victories affirmed the power of dominant tactics, and the power of dominant tactics explained victories and defeats.

These dominant tactics were supported by the development of a social movement infrastructure, particularly of strong national and statewide organizations. These organizations also buoyed up local activism between campaigns, building movement power, along with "continuity and historical memory." National organizations, however, did not single-handedly create dominant tactics. Dominant tactics may follow the "bottom-up" approach to institutionalization in which routines are developed by local organizations, disseminated to other organizations, and rapidly become an emergent norm for organizational action.[2] We need to examine more seriously the relationship among different levels within a social movement, particularly the relationships among national, statewide, and local organizations.

With this spread of dominant tactics, there were concerns about the consequence for the LGBT movement as a whole. Activists found themselves debating whether or not campaigns could accommodate direct-action tactics and whether LGBT visibility was an important part of political messaging regardless of the results of professional polling. Activists wondered about the resources being poured into ballot measure campaigns, which often resulted in no gains in LGBT rights.

The Future at the Ballot Box

As I write this in 2011, there is no sign that anti-gay ballot measures are going away anytime soon. Even with promising federal court cases in progress to challenge same-sex marriage bans, the anti-gay Right has an arsenal of potential alternative ballot measures. In addition to Right-sponsored ballot measures, there may be a return to LGBT-sponsored ballot measures in the near future, as constitutional amendment marriage bans are reversed in several states. Whatever the form these ballot measures take, anti-gay ballot box politics is here to stay.

Although the persistence of anti-gay ballot measures continues, the arena of contention has changed in several ways. First, the stakes of these ballot measures have become higher, as evidenced by campaigns in California and Maine, where statewide legal gains have been rolled back at the ballot box. Second, for both the Religious Right and the LGBT movement, these ballot measure campaigns have increased in size, funding, and national focus. Religious Right activists were mobilized on an unprecedented scale for statewide initiatives in California, Maine, and Arizona. What used to be a predominately local, smaller-scale battle has reached epic proportions. Third, there is likely to be a return to LGBT-sponsored ballot measures in the next decade, as there are attempts to rescind and rewrite constitutional amendments in many states. These LGBT-sponsored ballot measures may alter the relationship between ballot measures and the LGBT movement, as ballot measures become less reactive and more intentional.

Regardless of these changes, the questions discussed in this book will continue to be interrogated. How can ballot measure campaigns support the broader social movement? Are the tactics that campaigns use to be victorious harmful to the social movement? And how can the movement run a winning campaign? The answers to these questions are a work in progress for not just the LGBT movement but other movements that are increasingly using the ballot box to meet social movement goals.

NOTES

Introduction

1. A few members of the LGBT movement who read through my manuscript took issue with my use of the word *activist* to describe campaign workers and volunteers because of the way "gay activist" is used pejoratively by the Religious Right. However, other terms such as "organizer" and "political actor" are either inaccurate or too vague. When possible, I try to use more accurate terms such as "organizer" or "leader" when identifying a speaker. In addition, the LGBT movement has gone through several expansive iterations from being the gay movement to now the addition of queer, questioning, ally, and intersex identities to the movement. However, in this text I consistently use LGBT movement for all time periods for simplicity's sake and to acknowledge that even in the early campaigns there were lesbian, bisexual, and transsexual or gender-variant participants.

2. Justin Ewers, "California Same-Sex Marriage Initiative Campaigns Shatter Spending Records," *U.S. News and World Report,* October 28, 2008, http://www.usnews.com.

3. See Ben Ehrenreich, "Anatomy of a Failed Campaign," *Advocate,* December 16, 2008, accessed January 25, 2009, http://www.advocate.com/; Jim Keys, "L.A. Gay Center Responds to Prop 8 Criticism," *Advocate,* November 26, 2008, accessed January 25, 2009, http://www.advocate.com.

4. See Fred Fejes, *Gay Rights and Moral Panic: The Origins of America's Debate on Homosexuality* (New York: Palgrave Macmillan, 2008).

5. Alan S. Yang, "Trends: Attitudes Towards Homosexuality," *Public Opinion Quarterly* 61, no. 3 (1997): 477–502.

6. For a good introduction to the literature on direct democracy, see Shaun Bowler, Todd Donovan, and Caroline Tolbert, eds., *Citizens as Legislators: Direct Democracy in the United States* (Columbus: Ohio State University Press, 1998); David Magleby, *Direct Legislation: Voting on Ballot Propositions in the United States* (Baltimore: Johns Hopkins University Press, 1984).

7. Regina Werum and Bill Winders, "Who's 'in' and Who's 'Out': State Fragmentation and the Struggle over Gay Rights, 1974–1999," *Social Problems* 48, no. 3 (2001): 386–410.

8. There are also legislative referendums, and constitutional amendments that require voter approval, which will be discussed in chapter 1.

9. Mario Diani, "The Concept of Social Movement," *Sociological Review* 40 (1992): 3.

10. Mary Bernstein, "Nothing Ventured, Nothing Gained? Conceptualizing 'Success' in the Lesbian and Gay Movement," *Sociological Perspectives* 46, no. 3 (2003): 353–79.

11. The resource mobilization model stresses the complex, institutional nature of SMOs; however, they can also operate on an informal or ad hoc basis. See John D. McCarthy and Mayer N. Zald, "Resource Mobilization and Social Movements: A Partial Theory," *American Journal of Sociology* 82, no. 6 (1977): 1218; Francesca Polletta, *Freedom Is an Endless Meeting: Democracy in American Social Movements* (Chicago: University of Chicago Press, 2002).

12. Verta Taylor and Nancy Whittier, "Collective Identity and Lesbian Feminist Mobilization," in *Frontiers of Social Movement Theory*, ed. Aldon Morris and Carol Mueller (New Haven: Yale University Press, 1992), 105.

13. Kimberly Clarke Simmons, "Grassroots Goes to the Polls: Citizen Initiatives and Social Movements," Ph.D. dissertation, University of Minnesota, 2002, 194. Research on the relationship between short-lived political events (e.g., campaigns more generally) has also been conducted by other social movement scholars. For example, Suzanne Staggenborg and Josée Lecomte come to similar conclusions as Simmons about the relationship between general campaigns and social movement communities (Suzanne Staggenborg and Josée Lecomte, "Social Movement Campaigns: Mobilization and Outcomes in the Montreal Women's Movement Community," *Mobilization: An International Journal* 14, no. 2 [2009]: 163–80).

14. Simmons, "Grassroots Goes to the Polls," 202–3.

15. Task Force, Memo on Campaigns, November 1993, Box 54, National Gay and Lesbian Task Force records, #7301, Division of Rare and Manuscript Collections, Cornell University Library, 2.

16. Ibid.

17. See Kimberly B. Dugan, *The Struggle over Gay, Lesbian, and Bisexual Rights: Facing Off in Cincinnati* (New York: Routledge, 2005). For other approaches to campaigns, see Staggenborg and Lecomte, "Social Movement Campaigns."

18. For example, see Todd Donovan and Shaun Bowler, "Direct Democracy and Minority Rights: An Extension," *American Journal of Political Science* 42, no. 3 (1998): 1020–24; Daniel A. Smith and Caroline J. Tolbert, *Educated by Initiative:*

The Effects of Direct Democracy on Citizens and Political Organizations in the American States (Ann Arbor: University of Michigan Press, 2004).

19. Ronald T. Libby, *Eco-Wars: Political Campaigns and Social Movements* (New York: Columbia University Press, 1998), 17.

20. Marshall Ganz, "Why David Sometimes Wins: Strategic Capacity in Social Movements," in *Rethinking Social Movements: Structure, Meaning, and Emotion*, ed. Jeff Goodwin and James M. Jasper (New York: Rowman and Littlefield, 2004), 181.

21. Charles Tilly, *From Mobilization to Revolution* (Reading, Mass.: Addison-Wesley, 1978); Charles Tilly, *Regimes and Repertoires* (Chicago: University of Chicago Press, 2006).

22. Ann Swidler, "Culture in Action: Symbols and Strategies," *American Sociological Review* 51 (1986): 273–86.

23. Francesca Polletta, *It Was like a Fever: Storytelling in Protest and Politics* (Chicago: University of Chicago Press, 2006), 55.

24. James M. Jasper, *The Art of Moral Protest: Culture, Biography, and Creativity in Social Movements* (Chicago: University of Chicago Press, 1997).

25. Verta Taylor and Nella Van Dyke, "'Get Up, Stand Up': Tactical Repertoires of Social Movements," in *The Blackwell Companion to Social Movements*, ed. David A. Snow, Sarah A. Soule, and Hanspeter Kriesi (Malden, Mass.: Blackwell Publishing, 2004), 274.

26. Holly J. McCammon, "'Out of the Parlors and into the Streets': The Changing Tactical Repertoire of the U.S. Women's Suffrage Movements," *Social Forces* 81, no. 3 (2003): 787–818.

27. See Bernstein, "Nothing Ventured, Nothing Gained?"

28. David S. Meyer and Suzanne Staggenborg, "Movements, Countermovements, and Political Opportunity," *American Journal of Sociology* 101, no. 6 (1996): 1647.

29. Ibid.

30. Doug McAdam, "Tactical Innovation and the Pace of Insurgency," *American Sociological Review* 48 (1983): 736.

31. Scholars have theorized that social movement organizational readiness, diversity and decentralization, and infrastructure strength impact tactical innovation and flexibility. See Mary Bernstein, "Celebration and Suppression: The Strategic Use of Identity by the Lesbian and Gay Movement," *American Journal of Sociology* 103, no. 3 (1997): 531–65; McAdam, "Tactical Innovation and the Pace of Insurgency"; McCammon, "'Out of the Parlors and into the Streets'"; Aldon Morris, "The Black Southern Sit-in Movement: An Analysis of Internal Organization," *American Sociological Review* 46 (1981): 744–67. Germinal work by Suzanne Staggenborg on social movement organizations suggests that informal, decentralized social movement

organizational structures facilitate innovation, and more formalized, centralized organizational structures lead to narrow strategies and tactics. Debra Minkoff provides evidence to the contrary that older, more formalized social movement organizations may actually be more flexible and adaptive in their strategies. This analysis centers on the changes in the level of professionalization of social movement organizations, at both the national and state level, and its role in the innovation of tactics, building on the multilevel analysis of institutionalization by other scholars, such as Schneiberg and Soule. See Suzanne Staggenborg, "Stability and Innovation in the Women's Movement: A Comparison of Two Movement Organizations," *Social Problems* 36 no. 1 (1989): 75–92; Debra Minkoff, "Bending with the Wind: Strategic Change and Adaptation by Women's and Racial Minority Organizations," *American Journal of Sociology* 104, no. 6 (1999): 1666–1703; Marc Schneiberg and Sarah A. Soule, "Institutionalization as a Contested Multilevel Process: The Case of Rate Regulation in American Fire Insurance," in *Social Movements and Organizational Theory*, ed. Gerald F. Davis, Doug McAdam, W. Richard Scott, and Mayer N. Zald (Cambridge: Cambridge University Press, 2005), 122–60.

32. Tactics cannot become dominant without widespread tactical dissemination or diffusion, and these tactics are spread through channels of diffusion. Tactics can become diffused or spread between organizations through relational ties or direct connections between social movement organizations, including connections between national and local social movement organizations. Other scholars have argued in studies of tactical diffusion that the news media may play a more significant role, particularly in the dissemination of visible tactics such as sit-ins. See Kenneth Andrews and Michael Biggs, "The Dynamics of Protest Diffusion: Movement Organizations, Social Networks, and News Media in the 1960 Sit-Ins," *American Sociological Review* 71, no. 5 (2006): 752–77; Sarah A. Soule, "The Student Divestment Movement in the United States and Tactical Diffusion: The Shantytown Protest," *Social Forces* 75, no. 3 (1997): 855–62; David Strang and John W. Meyer, "Institutional Conditions for Diffusion," *Theory and Society* 22, no. 4 (1993): 487–511.

33. This is less common in the LGBT movement but may be more common in, say, the movements for marijuana legalization and the Equal Rights Amendment.

34. Stephanie L. Witt and Suzanne McCorkle, eds., *Anti-Gay Rights: Assessing Voter Initiatives* (Westport, Conn.: Praeger, 1997), 5.

35. Donald P. Haider-Markel, "Lesbian and Gay Politics in the States," in *The Politics of Gay Rights*, ed. Craig Rimmerman, Kenneth D. Wald, and Clyde Wilcox (Chicago: University of Chicago Press, 2000), 290–346.

36. Glenda M. Russell, Janis S. Bohan, Marya C. McCarroll, and Nathan G. Smith, "Trauma, Recovery, and Community: Perspectives on the Long-Term Impact of Anti-LGBT Politics," *Traumatology* (2010): 1–10, accessed January 2, 2010; doi: 10.1177/1534765610362799.

37. Field Report, "Memo to No on 13," October 15, 1994, Box 224, National Gay and Lesbian Task Force records, #7301, Division of Rare and Manuscript Collections, Cornell University Library.

38. Simmons, "Grassroots Goes to the Polls," 204.

39. Dissent, however, is not always harmful to a social movement. See Amin Ghaziani, *The Dividends of Dissent: How Conflict and Culture Work in Lesbian and Gay Marches on Washington* (Chicago: University of Chicago Press, 2008).

40. Ibid., 130.

41. Jean Hardisty, "What Now? Strategic Thinking about the Progressive Movement and the Right," *Public Eye,* spring 1997, 11.

42. Ibid.

43. Jane Ward, *Respectably Queer: Diversity Culture in LGBT Activist Organizations* (Nashville, Tenn.: Vanderbilt University Press, 2008).

44. Since the late 1980s, *transgender* has come into common use as an umbrella category that includes individuals expressing a wide range of gender variance, including transvestites, transsexuals, and those who identify as no gender, gender queer, or multiple genders. For an excellent account of an ethnography of the category transgender, see David Valentine, *Imagining Transgender: An Ethnography of a Category* (Durham, N.C.: Duke University Press, 2007).

45. Ward, *Respectably Queer,* 2.

1. From Anita Bryant to California Proposition 8

1. See, for example, Jean V. Hardisty, *Mobilizing Resentment: Conservative Resurgence from the John Birch Society to the Promise Keepers* (Boston: Beacon Press, 1999).

2. Smith and Tolbert, *Educated by Initiative.*

3. See the Initiative and Referendum Institute (http://www.iandrinstitute.org) at the University of Southern California for up-to-date information about contemporary initiatives.

4. Magleby, *Direct Legislation.*

5. Ibid.; David McCuan, Shaun Bowler, Todd Donovan, and Ken Fernandez, "California's Political Warriors: Campaigns Professionals and the Initiative Process," in Bowler, Donovan, and Tolbert, *Citizens as Legislators,* 27–54.

6. Susan A. Banducci, "Direct Legislation: When Is It Used and When Does It Pass?" in Bowler, Donovan, and Tolbert, *Citizens as Legislators,* 109–31; Magleby, *Direct Legislation.*

7. Magleby, *Direct Legislation.*

8. Barbara S. Gamble, "Putting Civil Rights to a Popular Vote," *American Journal of Political Science* 41, no. 1 (1997): 248.

9. In 1865, citizens of Washington, D.C., and Georgetown voted on whether blacks should be allowed to vote. In Washington, 6,626 voted against black suffrage and only thirty-five for it; in Georgetown, only one person voted for it. In 1866, Congress overrode these popular votes and by 1874 Congress revoked the forms of voting and home rule for Washingtonians owing to these civil rights issues. Religious Right activists attempted to reinstate the use of referendums and initiatives in Washington, D.C., with the D.C. Referendum, Initiative and Recall Act of 1978 to rescind a recently passed gay rights law (Staff, "Initiative Bill Approved," *The Blade*, April 1978, 6).

10. Alexander Keyssar, *The Right to Vote: The Contested History of Democracy in the United States* (New York: Perseus Books, 2000).

11. Anthony S. Chen, Robert W. Mickey, and Robert P. Van Houweling, "Explaining the Contemporary Alignment between Race and Party: Evidence from California's 1946 Ballot Initiative on Fair Employment," *Studies in American Political Development* 22 (2008): 204–28.

12. Dugan, *The Struggle over Gay, Lesbian, and Bisexual Rights*.

13. John M. Allswang, *The Initiative and Referendum in California, 1898–1998* (Stanford, Calif.: Stanford University Press, 2000).

14. Tina Fetner, *How the Religious Right Shaped Lesbian and Gay Activism* (Minneapolis: University of Minnesota Press, 2008); Glenda M. Russell, *Voted Out: The Psychological Consequences of Anti-Gay Politics* (New York: New York University Press, 2000).

15. These numbers include every time LGBT rights have been voted on, whether the ballot measure was sponsored by the Right or not. These findings echo previous research by political scientists. See Donovan and Bowler, "Direct Democracy and Minority Rights"; Donald P. Haider-Markel, Alana Querze, and Kara Lindaman, "Lose, Win, or Draw? A Reexamination of Direct Democracy and Minority Rights," *Political Research Quarterly* 60, no. 2 (2007): 304–14.

16. Didi Herman, *The Antigay Agenda: Orthodox Vision and the Christian Right* (Chicago: University of Chicago Press, 1997), 9. Unlike other scholars such as Herman, I favor the term "Religious Right" over Christian Right, primarily because of the long and colorful history of Mormon opposition to LGBT rights in the western states.

17. Sara Diamond, *Roads to Dominion: Right-Wing Movements and Political Power in the United States* (New York: Guilford Press, 1995); Hardisty, *Mobilizing Resentment*.

18. Herman, *The Antigay Agenda*.

19. The arena of collective action or conflict is a significant strategic element in movement–countermovement interactions. See David S. Meyer and Suzanne Staggenborg, "Opposing Movement Strategies in U.S. Abortion Politics," in *Research in*

Social Movements, Conflict, and Change, vol. 28, ed. Patrick G. Coy (Bingley, U.K.: Emerald JAI, 2008), 213.

20. Werum and Winders, "Who's 'in' and Who's 'Out.'"

21. Todd Donovan, Jim Wenzel, and Shaun Bowler, "Direct Democracy and Gay Rights Initiatives after *Romer*," in Rimmerman, Wald, and Wilcox, *The Politics of Gay Rights*, 161–62.

22. Harvey Pitman, "In Their Own Words: Conversations with Campaign Leaders," in Witt and McCorkle, *Anti-Gay Rights*, 91.

23. Meyer and Staggenborg, "Movements, Countermovements, and Political Opportunity."

24. John C. Green, "Antigay: Varieties of Opposition to Gay Rights," in Rimmerman, Wald, and Wilcox, *The Politics of Gay Rights*, 121–38.

25. As of 2007, 51.8 percent of the U.S. population was covered by a state, county, and/or city nondiscrimination law and/or broad family recognition law. In 1992, only 33.5 percent of the population was covered (www.thetaskforce.org). Without federal protections against discrimination, these local and statewide nondiscrimination laws are necessary. If the federal Employment Non-Discrimination Act (ENDA) is passed, referendums on nondiscrimination legislation would disappear.

26. Green, "Antigay," 132.

27. Ibid.

28. Donovan, Wenzel, and Bowler, "Gay Rights Initiatives after *Romer*."

29. Donovan and Bowler, "Direct Democracy and Minority Rights"; Gamble, "Putting Civil Rights to a Popular Vote"; Haider-Markel, Querze, and Lindaman, "Lose, Win, or Draw?"

30. Donovan, Wenzel, and Bowler, "Gay Rights Initiatives after *Romer*."

31. I researched these attempts at direct legislation through a variety of methods, including the triangulation of findings from both mainstream and LGBT newspapers and magazines, the newsletters of the Task Force and People for the American Way, and the internal documents of national organizations.

32. These ballot measures do not include campaigns to fight pro-life initiatives or campaigns for the legalization of marijuana that mobilize many LGBT individuals, but not necessarily national movement organizations.

33. "Initiative Use, 1904–2005," Initiative and Referendum Institute, last modified November 2006, http://www.iandrinstitute.org.

34. James W. Button, Barbara A. Rienzo, and Kenneth D. Wald, *Private Lives, Public Conflicts: Battles over Gay Rights in American Communities* (Washington, D.C.: Congressional Quarterly Inc., 1997), 174.

35. This underestimation is unavoidable, particularly for attempted referendums in the 1980s. There is no systematic way of keeping track of attempted ballot measures that got little or no press coverage.

36. These states are followed shortly by Ohio (8), Massachusetts (8), Texas (8), Minnesota (4), and Missouri (4) for attempted direct legislation.

37. Magleby, *Direct Legislation*. Whether or not a state is a swing state may also matter. Florida, Michigan, and Colorado are swing states in presidential elections, although only 20 to 30 percent of all attempted ballot measures in these three states occurred during presidential elections, and many of these attempted measures were local, not state-level, initiatives.

38. "Overview of Initiative Use, 1904–2009," Initiative and Referendum Institute, last updated September 2010, http://www.iandrinstitute.org.

39. Donovan, Wenzel, and Bowler, "Gay Rights Initiatives after *Romer*," 165.

40. Button, Rienzo, and Wald, *Private Lives, Public Conflicts;* Mary Bernstein, "Sexual Orientation Policy, Protest, and the State," Ph.D. dissertation, New York University, 1997, 52.

41. Jerome L. Himmelstein, *To the Right: The Transformation of American Conservatism* (Berkeley: University of California Press, 1990).

42. Diamond, *Roads to Dominion*.

43. Glenda Russell, personal communication with author, May 20, 2010.

44. Judith Cummings, "Homosexual-Rights Laws Show Progress in Some Cities, but Drive Arouses Considerable Opposition," *New York Times*, May 13, 1974, 17. The mayor of Columbus, Ohio, who had been supportive of their newly passed nondiscrimination ordinance, also suffered a recall election, suggesting that this might have been a growing strategy. See Button, Rienzo, and Wald, *Private Lives, Public Conflicts*.

45. Concerned Voters of California Organizing Committee, Press Release on August 3, 1975, Box 5, David Goodstein Papers, #7311, Division of Rare and Manuscript Collections, Cornell University Library.

46. For a full account of Miami–Dade County's campaign, see Fejes, *Gay Rights and Moral Panic*.

47. Hardisty, *Mobilizing Resentment*.

48. And later on, both sexual orientation and gender identity or expression were targeted. Gender identity or expression covers many transgender individuals. For more information, see Paisley Currah and Shannon Minter, "Unprincipled Exclusions: The Struggle to Achieve Judicial and Legislative Equality for Transgender People," in *Regulating Sex: The Politics of Intimacy and Identity*, ed. Elizabeth Bernstein and Laurie Schaffner (New York: Routledge, 2005), 35–48.

49. Hardisty, *Mobilizing Resentment*, 100.

50. John Gallagher and Chris Bull, *Perfect Enemies: The Religious Right, the Gay Movement, and the Politics of the 1990s* (New York: Crown Publishers, 1996), 18.

51. Hardisty, *Mobilizing Resentment*.

52. Diamond, *Roads to Dominion*, 171.

53. Bernstein, "Sexual Orientation Policy, Protest, and the State," 53.

54. Hardisty, *Mobilizing Resentment*, 100.

55. Diamond, *Roads to Dominion*, 205.

56. Gallagher and Bull, *Perfect Enemies*, 20.

57. Ibid.

58. Diamond, *Roads to Dominion*, 231.

59. Leslie Bennetts, "Conservatives Join on Social Concerns," *New York Times*, July 30, 1980, A1; Thomas J. Burrows, "Family Values: From the White House Conference on Families to the Family Protection Act," in *Creating Change: Sexuality, Public Policy, and Civil Rights*, ed. John D'Emilio, William B. Turner, and Urvashi Vaid (New York: St. Martin's Press, 2000), 353.

60. Martin E. Marty, "Morality, Ethics and the New Christian Right," *The Hastings Center Report* 11, no. 4 (August 1981): 16.

61. Diamond, *Roads to Dominion*, 241.

62. Hardisty, *Mobilizing Resentment*, 100.

63. J. Charles Park, "Preachers, Politics, and Public Education: A Review of Right Wing Pressures against Public Schools in America," *Phi Delta Kappan* 61, no. 9 (May 1980): 608–12.

64. Gallagher and Bull, *Perfect Enemies*, 26.

65. Ibid.

66. Joe Baker, "Houston to Vote on Gay Rights Issue," *Advocate*, September 4, 1984, 9.

67. Moral Majority of Santa Clara County, political flyer "Enough Is Enough," 1980, Box 169, National Gay and Lesbian Task Force Records, #7301, Division of Rare and Manuscript Collections, Cornell University Library.

68. Report titled "Austin Housing Ordinance," February 3, 1982, Box 4, Human Rights Campaign Fund records, #7712, Division of Rare and Manuscript Collections, Cornell University Library.

69. Peter Freiberg, "Washington Homophobes Move to Deny Gay Rights," *Advocate*, March 18, 1986, 15. The other two legislative bills that Dobbs tried to sponsor were one quarantining people with AIDS and another reinstating Washington's sodomy law.

70. Bigot Buster/Decline to Sign, Handbook, 2005, Box 224, National Gay and Lesbian Task Force records, #7301, Division of Rare and Manuscript Collections, Cornell University Library.

71. Freiberg, "Washington Homophobes Move to Deny Gay Rights," 11.

72. Mark Vendervelden, "Californians Say 'No on 64,'" *Advocate*, December 9, 1986, 11.

73. Bruce Nichols, "Emotions Tinge Gay Bias Debate in Houston," *Dallas Morning News*, January 6, 1985, 45A.

74. Ironically, Fetner attributes the decline of the Moral Majority to the saturation of direct-mail solicitation. Later groups relied on membership constituencies (Fetner, *How the Religious Right Shaped Lesbian and Gay Activism*, 66).

75. Diamond, *Roads to Dominion*, 244–45.

76. Ibid.; Hardisty, *Mobilizing Resentment*.

77. Diamond, *Roads to Dominion*, 290.

78. Herman, *The Antigay Agenda*.

79. Gallagher and Bull, *Perfect Enemies*, 87–91.

80. The Right won this ballot measure, but the victory was later rescinded by the courts.

81. Staff, "AIDS-Free Zone Proposed," *Eugene Register-Guard*, May 5, 1989, 3C.

82. Dean Congbalay, "The Impact of Concord's AIDS Bias Vote," *San Francisco Chronicle*, November 9, 1989, A5.

83. Susan Kelleher, "Clergymen in Conflict over Gays," *Orange County Register*, October 23, 1989, A1.

84. Hardisty, *Mobilizing Resentment*, 110.

85. Citizens to Retain Fair Employment, "Chronicle of Key Events in the Campaign against Initative 13," 1978, Box 4, Human Rights Campaign Fund records, #7712, Division of Rare and Manuscript Collections, Cornell University Library.

86. Teresa M. Hanafin, "Weld Opposes Push to Repeal Gay Rights Law," *Boston Globe*, August 9, 1991, 18; Staff, "AIDS-Free Zone Proposed." The initiative in Massachusetts was part of a larger attempt to propose four different ballot measures.

87. As legal-restrictive initiatives were being proposed in Colorado and Oregon, one was attempted statewide in Maine as well that would have preempted any future legislation according rights to gay men and lesbians. See Equal Protection Portland, "Background Two," 1992, Box 108, National Gay and Lesbian Task Force records, #7301, Division of Rare and Manuscript Collections, Cornell University Library.

88. Hardisty suggests that OCA was a Christian Coalition affiliate. However, participant observation work done by Vernon Bates suggests instead that there were initial attempts to connect the two organizations and then an "amicable" parting. See Hardisty, *Mobilizing Resentment*, 110; Vernon L. Bates, "Rhetorical Pluralism and Secularization in the New Christian Right: The Oregon Citizens Alliance," *Review of Religious Research* 37, no. 1 (1995): 46–64.

89. See Gallagher and Bull, *Perfect Enemies;* Arlene Stein, *The Stranger Next Door: The Story of a Small Community's Battle over Sex, Faith, and Civil Rights* (Boston: Beacon Press, 2001).

90. Stein, *The Stranger Next Door*, 208. This flyer was likely the work of Scott Lively, an OCA operative who would later write the book *The Pink Swastika*, which suggests that the Nazis were influenced by gay men in implementing the Holocaust.

91. Herman, *The Antigay Agenda,* 138.

92. Hardisty, *Mobilizing Resentment.*

93. Bates, "Rhetorical Pluralism and Secularization in the New Christian Right," 46.

94. For example, part of Anita Bryant's complaints against gay rights in 1977 was the potential for preferential treatment, and in a 1982 campaign in Lincoln, Nebraska, the local Religious Right organization was called the Committee to Oppose Special Rights for Homosexuals (Gallagher and Bull, *Perfect Enemies,* 11).

95. Hardisty, *Mobilizing Resentment,* 106.

96. Tony Marco, "Oppressed Minorities, or Counterfeits?" *Focus on the Family Citizen,* April 20, 1992, 1–4.

97. "Group Planning Counter Attack on Attempt to Repeal Rights Law," clipping from *Pittsburgh Out,* 1991, Box 66, National Gay and Lesbian Task Force Records, #7301, Division of Rare and Manuscript Collections, Cornell University Library; George Foster, "Tacoma's 'Gay' Initiative Wins," *Seattle Post-Intelligencer,* November 14, 1989, B2.

98. Gallagher and Bull, *Perfect Enemies,* 87–94.

99. Diamond, *Roads to Dominion;* Hardisty, *Mobilizing Resentment.*

100. Gallagher and Bull, *Perfect Enemies,* 230.

101. Between 1993 and 1996 there were attempted statewide initiatives in Arizona, Maine, Michigan, and Missouri using the text of Colorado Amendment 2. In addition, groups in Alachua County, Florida, and Cincinnati, Ohio, used initiatives that mimicked Amendment 2 with great success.

102. Comparing the percent of voters supportive of LGBT rights before and after 1992 in referendums, on average 51 percent were supportive after 1992 (and 57 percent after 2000) compared with 39.5 percent on average before 1992.

103. David Douglass, "Taking the Initiative," in Witt and McCorkle, *Anti-Gay Rights,* 17.

104. Stein, *The Stranger Next Door,* 27.

105. Ibid.

106. See Dugan, *The Struggle over Gay, Lesbian, and Bisexual Rights.*

107. When Anita Bryant took the stage in the Miami Dade affair in the late 1970s, the Religious Right was not visibly supportive of the civil rights movement, owing to the sordid links between the contemporary Right and the organized Southern resistance to preserve segregation. Diamond in *Roads to Dominion* describes a shift toward a new racial warfare on the Right. This shift toward secular language about special rights and racial coalition building has not been accompanied by active support of civil rights by the contemporary Right. Indeed, the Religious Right has been supportive of initiatives to rescind affirmative action, starting with the California Proposition 209 in 1996, the California Civil Rights Initiative. Since California

in 1996, the Right has helped sponsor seven additional statewide initiatives to ban affirmative action in states such as Nebraska, Michigan, and Arizona. Apart from visible efforts such as these initiatives, much of the Right's opposition to civil rights progress has been less deliberate and less visible than in the past, replacing a Gramscian "war of position" with the previous "war of maneuver." Rather than a visible fight against civil rights, the Religious Right attack on civil rights has become more insidious, covert, and difficult to identify. See Michael Omi and Howard Winant, *Racial Formation in the United States,* 2d ed. (New York: Routledge, 1994), 81.

108. This data was reported by the *Wall Street Journal* but was collected from surveys of expensive gay men's magazines, thus inflating the median income of gay households. For a full analysis of this data, see M. V. Lee Badgett, "Beyond Biased Samples," in *Homo Economics,* ed. Amy Gluckman and Betsy Reed (New York: Routledge, 1997), 65–72.

109. John D. Skrentny, *The Minority Rights Revolution* (Cambridge: Belknap Press of Harvard University Press, 2002). Many categories included in nondiscrimination ordinances are not immutable, such as religion and political party. Regardless, many LGBT activists have increasingly asserted the immutability of LGBT identities.

110. Didi Herman, "The Gay Agenda Is the Devil's Agenda," in Rimmerman, Wald, and Wilcox, *The Politics of Gay Rights,* 143.

111. Mike Lucas, "A Battle over Gay Rights," *Molalla Pioneer,* September 1, 1993, 2.

112. Jay Croft and Joel Engelhardt, "Hearts, Not Minds, Target of Campaign," *Palm Beach Post,* January 8, 1995, 1A.

113. Dugan, *The Struggle over Gay, Lesbian, and Bisexual Rights.*

114. "Petition Drives: Pros and Cons," undated, Box 225, National Gay and Lesbian Task Force records, #7301, Division of Rare and Manuscript Collections, Cornell University Library, 2.

115. Herman, *The Antigay Agenda,* 110.

116. When voters in Santa Clara County and San Jose, California, considered a referendum in 1980, the local Religious Right warned that passing the ordinance would mean that, among other things, "It would be illegal for you to refuse to hire a babysitter because he or she is a homosexual or transvestite." Early legal-restrictive initiatives in King County, Washington, and Oregon described transvestism as a sexual deviance, and included transvestism in lists of sexual deviance along with homosexuality, pedophilia, and sadomasochism. See Moral Majority of Santa Clara County, "Enough Is Enough."

117. Paisley Currah and Shannon Minter, *Transgender Equality: A Handbook for Activists and Policymakers* (Washington, D.C.: The Policy Institute of the National Gay and Lesbian Task Force and National Center for Lesbian Rights, 2000).

118. Gallagher and Bull, *Perfect Enemies,* 46.

119. Lisa Mottet, personal communication with author, February 18, 2005.

120. Green, "Antigay," 129, 135.

121. Gallagher and Bull, *Perfect Enemies,* 242.

122. Ibid., 260.

123. Stein, *The Stranger Next Door.* This "special rights" messaging was effective in persuading voters to support Colorado Amendment 2 in 1992, where 40 percent of voters surveyed in exit polls asserted that they had voted "yes" because they believed that gay people should not have special rights. However, this statistic may be misleading, as voters may have used "special rights" to avoid being perceived as homophobic. See Lisa Keen and Suzanne B. Goldberg, *Strangers to the Law: Gay People on Trial* (Ann Arbor: University of Michigan Press, 1998).

124. Hardisty, *Mobilizing Resentment,* 114.

125. In 1997, these attempts at stealth initiatives included the Colorado Amendment 17 or the Parental Rights Amendment, which established the right of parents to determine their children's upbringing. This initiative, although it never mentioned sexual orientation, was an unsuccessful test case to determine if such initiatives could be used to control school curriculum and public libraries in the same way as Oregon Ballot Measure 9 had attempted.

126. In the case *In Re Advisory Opinion to the Attorney General,* 632 So.2d 1018 (FL 1994). See Ellen Ann Anderson, *Out of the Closets and into the Courts: Legal Opportunity Structure and Gay Rights Litigation* (Ann Arbor: University of Michigan Press, 2005).

127. Anderson, *Out of the Closets and into the Courts.*

128. See Keen and Goldberg, *Strangers to the Law.*

129. Donovan, Wenzel, and Bowler, "Gay Rights Initiatives after *Romer,*" 169.

130. Fight the Right, "Program Retreat Minutes. February 27 & 28, 1995," Box 226, National Gay and Lesbian Task Force records, #7301, Division of Rare and Manuscript Collections, Cornell University Library, 2.

131. See David L. Chambers, "Couples: Marriage, Civil Unions, and Domestic Partnerships," in D'Emilio, Turner, and Vaid, *Creating Change,* 281–304; Jonathan Goldberg-Hiller, *The Limits to Union: Same-Sex Marriage and the Politics of Civil Rights* (Ann Arbor: University of Michigan Press, 2002).

132. Chambers, "Couples," 294.

133. See Hardisty, *Mobilizing Resentment;* Melanie Heath, "State of Our Unions: Marriage Promotion and the Contested Power of Heterosexuality," *Gender and Society* 23, no. 1 (February 2009): 27–48; Nancy D. Polikoff, *Beyond Straight and Gay Marriage: Valuing All Families under the Law* (Boston: Beacon Press, 2008).

134. Melanie Heath, "Soft-Boiled Masculinity: Renegotiating Gender and Racial Ideologies in the Promise Keepers Movement," *Gender and Society* 17, no. 3 (June 2003): 423–44.

135. Heath, "State of Our Unions."

136. Gallagher and Bull, *Perfect Enemies*, 272; Green, "Antigay," 133. Ex-gay ministries also supported the division of "bad" activist gays from "good" compliant, nonsexual gays.

137. Although Mormon involvement in the California Proposition 8 campaign in 2008 has been well analyzed, Mormon support for same-sex marriage initiatives stretches back to the earliest marriage ban campaigns in Alaska and Hawaii, along with the California Knight Initiative in 2000. See Gallagher and Bull, *Perfect Enemies*, 270.

138. Sean Cahill, *Same-Sex Marriage in the United States: Focus on the Facts*, (Lanham, Md.: Lexington Books, 2004).

139. This is compared to the combined monetary power of the largest thirteen LGBT organizations, which stood at only $54 million at this time (ibid., 20–21).

140. Eventually, San Francisco residents did retain their domestic partnership benefits, but not until after a series of battles.

141. Not all of these initiatives were at the state level. In 2001, voters in Houston, Texas, eliminated domestic partnership benefits for city employees and voters in Miami Beach, Florida, affirmed them.

142. Although Hawaii's Supreme Court case *Baehr v. Lewin* attracted the most media attention, the Alaska Supreme Court also ruled on gay marriage in *Brause and Dugan v. Bureau of Vital Statistics*. See *Baehr v. Lewin*, 852 P.2d 44 (HI 1993); *Brause and Dugan v. Bureau of Vital Statistics*, No. 3AN-95-6562 Civ., 1998 WL 99743 (AK 1998); Goldberg-Hiller, *The Limits to Union*.

143. Alaska Family Coalition, political flyer "The Battle Line Is Drawn," 1998, Box 21, Human Rights Campaign Fund records, #7712, Division of Rare and Manuscript Collections, Cornell University Library.

144. Many of these constitutional amendments were placed on the ballot directly by the legislature, not by Religious Right activists, but they are included in this analysis because of the way they were largely sponsored by the Religious Right and fought by the Religious Right at the ballot box. See Bayliss Camp, "Mobilizing the Base and Embarrassing the Opposition," *Sociological Perspectives* 51, no. 4 (2008): 713–34.

145. Green, "Antigay."

146. The Alliance Defense Fund (ADF) was founded in 1994 by a group of Right leaders that included Dr. James Dobson. But it did not enter anti-gay activism until the 2004 same-sex marriage ballot initiatives. See "About ADF," Alliance Defense Fund, accessed August 2, 2010, http://www.alliancedefensefund.org.

147. NOM was founded in 2007: "in response to the growing need for an organized opposition to same-sex marriage in state legislatures, NOM serves as a national resource for marriage-related initiatives at the state and local level." Most

of NOM"s anti-marriage work has been in California, New Jersey, New York, and Rhode Island ("About NOM," National Organization for Marriage, accessed August 2, 2010, http://www.nationformarriage.org).

148. The Christian Coalition has been slowly declining since 1987, when organizer Ralph E. Reed Jr. resigned as executive director. In 2004, the organization ended its popular Road to Victory conferences, which served to get out the Christian vote. Although it still produces voter guides, other organizations such as Focus on the Family have become more important. See "Profile: Christian Coalition," Political Research Associates, accessed July 1, 2010, http://www.publiceye.org.

149. Camp, "Mobilizing the Base and Embarrassing the Opposition."

150. Surina Khan, "Tying the Not: How the Right Succeeded in Passing Proposition 8," *Public Eye Magazine,* spring 2009, accessed March 19, 2010, http://www.publiceye.org.

151. Ibid., 3.

152. Frank Schubert and Jeff Flint, "Passing Prop 8," *Campaigns and Elections,* February 2009, accessed June 15, 2010, http:// www.Politicsmagazine.com.

153. As of June 23, 2010, People for the American Way reported that this organizing included a series of seven conference calls with anti-gay pastors in an estimated 170–80 locations in Arizona and California and Florida throughout the summer and fall of 2008.

154. Yes on 8, "It's Already Happened," [video] retrieved June 1, 2010 from http:// www.youtube.com.

155. Frequently, however, this messaging was linked. For example, in a 1996 letter to supporters of the Traditional Values Coalition in California, Rev. Sheldon connected the "special rights" argument to same-sex marriage. He suggested that if *Romer v. Evans* rules in favor of the LGBT movement, then "it would directly impact the Hawaiian decision, because, if homosexuality is granted minority status, they must also be granted same-sex marriage rights" (Rev. Louis P. Sheldon, Letter, February 27, 1996, Box 216, National Gay and Lesbian Task Force Records, #7301, Division of Rare and Manuscript Collections, Cornell University Library, 2).

156. Shauna Fisher, "It Takes (at Least) Two to Tango: Fighting with Words in the Conflict over Same-Sex Marriage," in *Queer Mobilizations: LGBT Activists Confront the Law,* ed. Scott Barclay, Mary Bernstein, and Anna-Maria Marshall (New York: New York University Press, 2009), 207–30.

157. Specifically, a gay couple appeared in a television ad on behalf of the Oregon Family Council. See Daniel R. Pinello, *America's Struggle for Same-Sex Marriage* (New York: Cambridge University Press, 2006), 124.

158. Ibid., 161, 175.

159. Yes on 8, "Unnamed Ad," [video] retrieved May 10, 2010 from http:// whatisprop8.com.

160. "Gearing Up for a Fight," People for the American Way article, accessed June 22, 2010, http://www.pfaw.org.

161. Kathleen E. Hull, "The Political Limits of the Rights Frame: The Case of Same-Sex Marriage in Hawaii," *Sociological Perspectives* 44, no. 2 (2001): 216.

162. Schubert and Flint, "Passing Prop 8."

163. Frank Rich, "The Bigots' Last Hurrah," *New York Times*, April 19, 2009, accessed June 23, 2010, http://www.nytimes.com.

164. "Value Voters Summit," Family Research Council Action, accessed June 25, 2010, http://www.valuevotersummit.org.

165. Sean Cahill, "The Anti-Gay Marriage Movement," in *The Politics of Same-Sex Marriage*, ed. Craig Rimmerman and Clyde Wilcox (Chicago: University of Chicago Press, 2007), 156.

166. Meyer and Staggenborg, "Movements, Countermovements, and the Structure of Political Opportunity," 1651; emphasis in the original.

167. McAdam, "Tactical Innovation and the Pace of Insurgency."

2. An Uphill Battle in the 70s and 80s

1. Clyde Wilcox and Robin Wolpert, "Gay Rights in the Public Sphere: Public Opinion on Gay and Lesbian Equality," in Rimmerman, Wald, and Wilcox, *The Politics of Gay Rights*, 409–32.

2. Ghaziani, *The Dividends of Dissent.* Their peers in California a year later, in 1975, did better, as California activists mobilized against the attempted reinstatement of sodomy laws by the Religious Right organization California Coalition of Concerned Citizens. The gay and lesbian activists who mobilized against the ballot initiative before the Right even turned in petitions had already begun hiring a campaign manager, fund-raising, and testing media messages through the campaign management firm Winner, Wagner and Associates. See Concerned Voters of California Organizing Committee, press release, August 3, 1975.

3. For an exception, see Sarah A. Soule, "The Diffusion of an Unsuccessful Innovation," *Annals of the American Academy of Political and Social Science* 566, no. 1 (1999): 120–31.

4. Peter Freiberg, "LaRouche AIDS Initiative," *Advocate*, August 19, 1986, 10–11.

5. NGTF, memo to board of directors, June 1978, Box 153, National Gay and Lesbian Task Force records, #7301, Division of Rare and Manuscript Collections, Cornell University Library.

6. Donovan, Wenzel, and Bowler, "Gay Rights Initiatives after *Romer.*"

7. Report titled "Austin Housing Ordinance," 1; emphasis added.

8. Vendervelden, "Californians Say 'No on 64,'" 11.

9. Fetner, *How the Religious Right Shaped Lesbian and Gay Activism*; Tina Fetner, "Working Anita Bryant: The Impact of Christian Anti-Gay Activism on Lesbian and Gay Movement Claims," *Social Problems* 48, no. 3 (2001): 411–28.

10. Paul Siskind, "C'mon, Folks, This Is Important," *Equal Time*, October 11–25, 1991, 5.

11. Santa Clara campaign leaders, letter to NGTF, January 7, 1980, Box 169, National Gay and Lesbian Task Force records, #7301, Division of Rare and Manuscript Collections, Cornell University Library.

12. For more details on the fair-housing referendum, see Thomas W. Casstevens, *Politics, Housing, and Race Relations: California Rumford Act and Proposition 14* (Berkeley: Institute of Governmental Studies, University of California Berkeley, 1967).

13. NGTF, memo to board of directors, June 1978.

14. Bruce Voeller and Jean O'Leary, Dear Friends letter, April 13, 1978, Box 153, National Gay and Lesbian Task Force records, #7301, Division of Rare and Manuscript Collections, Cornell University Library.

15. Freiberg, "Washington Homophobes Move to Deny Gay Rights," 15.

16. Staff, "Briggs Initiative Qualifies," *The Blade*, July 1978, 6.

17. William E. Adams Jr., "Pre-Election Anti-Gay Ballot Initiative Challenges: Issues of Electoral Fairness, Majoritarian Tyranny, and Direct Democracy," *Ohio State Law Journal* 55, no. 583 (summer 1994).

18. Bigot Buster/Decline to Sign, Handbook, 6.

19. Seattle Committee Against Thirteen, flyer "We CAN Win in Seattle!" (1978), Box 169, National Gay and Lesbian Task Force records, #7301, Division of Rare and Manuscript Collections, Cornell University Library.

20. Their counterleafleting described earlier, which activists declared were "so effective that it resulted in the set-up arrests of three SCAT members by an off-duty police officer hired by SOME [Save Our Moral Ethics]. SCAT has pressed for a jury trial prior to the election, and will utilize this opportunity to expose SOME and its tactics. We are the people on the streets, taking the greatest risks and turning them to our advantage" (ibid).

21. Patricia Jean Young, "Measure 9: Oregon's 1992 Anti-Gay Initiative," master's thesis, Portland State University, 1997.

22. Ibid.

23. Lou Romano, "Move to Block Anita-Type Threat Here," *The Blade*, May 1978, 1.

24. Staff, "Initiative Bill Approved." The later success of this bill in Washington, D.C., may prevent same-sex marriage from getting onto the ballot.

25. Ibid.

26. NGTF, memo to board of directors, June 1978.

27. Thomas J. Collins, "Gay Group Ponders Right Tactics," *St. Paul Pioneer Press*, May 31, 1988, 1A.

28. Ibid.

29. Staff, "From the Ruins of the Charter Amendment," *Star Tribune*, November 15, 1988, 12A.

30. Sarah A. Soule, "Diffusion Processes within and across Movements," in *Blackwell Companion to Social Movements*, ed. David A. Snow, Sarah A. Soule, and Hanspeter Kriesi (Malden, Mass.: Wiley-Blackwell, 2009), 294–310.

31. Staff, "Ypsilanti Voters Defeat Three Ballot Proposals," *Ann Arbor News*, April 8, 1975, 3. The initiative was sponsored by the Human Rights Party, a radical third party that was active in the early 1970s in Ann Arbor, Ypsilanti, and several other Michigan cities with large student populations. For a time the party held several city council seats in Ann Arbor and Ypsilanti. By 1975, the party began to decline, and shortly after this initiative it changed its name to the Socialist Human Rights Party.

32. Fejes, *Gay Rights and Moral Panic*, 203.

33. Ibid.

34. Soule, "The Diffusion of an Unsuccessful Innovation."

35. See Fejes, *Gay Rights and Moral Panic*; Gay Rights Writers Group, *It Could Happen to You: An Account of the Gay Civil Rights Campaign in Eugene, Oregon* (Boston: Alyson Publications, 1983).

36. Whether or not they used petitions in this way depended on the level of organization of the Religious Right campaign.

37. Citizens to Retain Fair Employment, memo "Synopsis of Preliminary Campaign Strategies," July 8, 1978, Box 153, National Gay and Lesbian Task Force records, #7301, Division of Rare and Manuscript Collections, Cornell University Library, 2.

38. Lisa M. Keen, "Denver Defeats Move to Remove Protections for Gays," *Washington Blade*, May 24, 1991, Box 223, National Gay and Lesbian Task Force records, #7301, Division of Rare and Manuscript Collections, Cornell University Library.

39. Eugene Citizens for Human Rights, canvassing packet, 1978, Box 153, National Gay and Lesbian Task Force records, #7301, Division of Rare and Manuscript Collections, Cornell University Library.

40. Mark Kasel, "Victory! Human Rights to Stand in St. Paul," *Equal Time*, November 22–December 6, 1991, 1.

41. Siskind, "C'mon, Folks, This Is Important," 5.

42. Mark Kasel, "St. Paul Election to Test Gay Political Clout," *Equal Time*, October 25–November 8, 1991, 8.

43. Scot Nakagawa, "Email Re: PFAW Meeting, etc.," 1994, Box 222, National Gay and Lesbian Task Force Records, #7301, Division of Rare and Manuscript Collections, Cornell University Library.

44. "Austin Housing Ordinance," 2.

45. Ibid.

46. It was still uncommon at this time to use the phrase "gay or lesbian."

47. Citizens to Retain Fair Employment, flyer "In America," 1978, Box 153, National Gay and Lesbian Task Force Records, #7301, Division of Rare and Manuscript Collections, Cornell University Library.

48. Some of the political flyers and ads used in St. Paul in 1978 never used the word *gay* or *homosexual* and instead asserted that "each of us knows that discrimination is wrong. Each of us knows that every human being is entitled to basic human rights and basic human respect."

49. Seattle Committee Against Thirteen, "We CAN Win in Seattle!"

50. Eugene Citizens for Human Rights, canvassing packet.

51. Live and Let Live Committee, press release, May 30, 1980, Box 169, National Gay and Lesbian Task Force Records, #7301, Division of Rare and Manuscript Collections, Cornell University Library.

52. St. Paul Campaign, flyer "Sure, Parents Have Rights," 1978, Box 4, Human Rights Campaign Fund records, #7712, Division of Rare and Manuscript Collections, Cornell University Library.

53. Staff, "NGTF Sponsors Conference of Referenda Campaign Leaders," *It's Time,* October 1978, 2.

54. Keen, "Denver Defeats Move to Remove Protections for Gays."

55. Live and Let Live Committee, press release, May 30, 1980.

56. Scott Maier, "Initiative 35's Backers Critical of Foe's Slogan," *Seattle Post-Intelligencer,* October 29, 1990.

57. McCammon, "'Out of the Parlors and into the Streets,'" 799.

58. Soule, "The Diffusion of an Unsuccessful Innovation."

59. Staff, "NGTF Sponsors Conference of Referenda Campaign Leaders."

60. John Loughery, *The Other Side of Silence: Men's Lives and Gay Identities, a Twentieth-Century History* (New York: Henry Holt and Company, 1998).

61. "Austin Housing Ordinance," 2.

62. Kenneth T. Andrews, *Freedom Is a Constant Struggle: The Mississippi Civil Rights Movement and Its Legacy* (Chicago: University of Chicago Press, 2004), 22.

63. Donald P. Haider-Markel, "From Bullhorns to PACs: Lesbian and Gay Politics, Interest Groups, and Policy," Ph.D. dissertation, University of Wisconsin Milwaukee, 1997.

64. Anderson, *Out of the Closets and into the Courts,* 2.

65. John D'Emilio, "Organizational Tales: Interpreting the NGLTF Story," in D'Emilio, Turner, and Vaid, *Creating Change*, 482.

66. This account of national organizations ignores important national groups such as the National Black Lesbian and Gay Leadership Forum, the Gay, Lesbian, and Straight Teachers Network (GLSTN), the National Center for Lesbian Rights, and Parents and Friends of Lesbians and Gays (PFLAG). These organizations are important in the development of the LGBT movement but were only minimally involved in the spread of campaign tactics.

67. Fetner, *How the Religious Right Shaped Lesbian and Gay Activism*.

68. D'Emilio, "Organizational Tales: Interpreting the NGLTF Story," 475.

69. Staff, "NGTF Assists Dade County," *It's Time*, April–May 1977, 3.

70. Staff, "Voeller Speaks at Harvard; Assists Wichita Gays," *It's Time*, February 1978, 3.

71. Keen, "Denver Defeats Move to Remove Protections for Gays."

72. Staff, "NGLTF Assists Dade County," 3.

3. Fighting the Right in the 90s

1. Fetner, *How the Religious Right Shaped Lesbian and Gay Activism*, 85.

2. Ibid.

3. John Gallagher, "The Right's New Strategy" (*Advocate*, 1992), Box 221, National Gay and Lesbian Task Force records, #7301, Division of Rare and Manuscript Collections, Cornell University Library, 46.

4. The Religious Right won at the ballot box. However, this initiative was overturned in *Merrick v. Board of Higher Education* with the assistance of national organizations such as Lambda Legal. See Anderson, *Out of the Closets and into the Courts; Merrick v. Board of Higher Education*, 841 P2d 646 (OR 1992).

5. Gallagher and Bull, *Perfect Enemies*, 43; Young, "Measure 9."

6. Thalia Zepatos, "No on 9 Campaign Field Strategy," in Task Force Fight the Right Action Kit, 1993, Box 154, National Gay and Lesbian Task Force records, #7301, Division of Rare and Manuscript Collections, Cornell University Library.

7. Gallagher and Bull, *Perfect Enemies*.

8. Sue Anderson, interview with author, June 3, 2010.

9. Ibid.

10. Creating Change, audiotapes from the 1992 Task Force meeting, Box 178, National Gay and Lesbian Task Force records, #7301, Division of Rare and Manuscript Collections, Cornell University Library.

11. Ibid.

12. Scot Nakagawa, interview with author, June 26, 2009.

13. Idaho activists attributed their unlikely victory to campaign techniques. See Pitman, "In Their Own Words," 89.

14. Lesbian Avengers, "Out against the Right: An Organizing Handbook," accessed May 10, 2010, http://www.octobertech.com.

15. Show Me Equality, Missouri Activists' Handbook, April 1994, Box 224, National Gay and Lesbian Task Force records, #7301, Division of Rare and Manuscript Collections, Cornell University Library, 5.

16. Ibid.

17. Nicole LeFavour, interview with author, May 12, 2010.

18. Pacy Markman worked on Ballot Measure 9 (1992), Proposition 6 (1978), and Proposition 102 (1988). See Pacy Markman, "The Message and the Media," 1993, Box 224, National Gay and Lesbian Task Force records, #7301, Division of Rare and Manuscript Collections, Cornell University Library.

19. Lake Research, "Executive Summary," 1995, Box 224, National Gay and Lesbian Task Force records, #7301, Division of Rare and Manuscript Collections, Cornell University Library, 6.

20. Markman, "The Message and the Media," 5.

21. Bob Dunn, "Winning at the Polls Is Not Necessarily a Victory," December 1994/January 1995, Box 225, National Gay and Lesbian Task Force records, #7301, Division of Rare and Manuscript Collections, Cornell University Library, 4.

22. Task Force, e-mail from a consultant Re: Idaho "No on One," November 3, 1994, Box 225, National Gay and Lesbian Task Force records, #7301, Division of Rare and Manuscript Collections, Cornell University Library, 3.

23. Save Our Communities, "The Campaigns against Anti-Gay Initiatives in Keizer, Oregon, and Marion County, Oregon," April 1994, Box 224, National Gay and Lesbian Task Force records, #7301, Division of Rare and Manuscript Collections, Cornell University Library, 3.

24. Sara Pursley, "Lesbian Avengers Battle the ICA [Idaho Citizens Alliance] in Northern Idaho," *Diversity,* December 1994/January 1995, Box 225, National Gay and Lesbian Task Force records, #7301, Division of Rare and Manuscript Collections, Cornell University Library.

25. Evan Gerstmann, *The Constitutional Underclass: Gays, Lesbians, and the Failure of Class-Based Equal Protection* (Chicago: University of Chicago Press, 1999), 105.

26. See Anderson, *Out of the Closets and into the Courts,* 144–45.

27. Ibid.

28. Keen and Goldberg, *Strangers to the Law,* 237–38.

29. Sue Anderson, interview with author, June 3, 2010.

30. See, for example, No on 9, "Measure 9 Impact Statement #2," 1992, Box 34, Federation of Parents, Families, and Friends of Lesbians and Gays (PFLAG)

Records, #7616, Division of Rare and Manuscript Collections, Cornell University Library.

31. Donna Minkowitz, "Scenes from the Mall," *Village Voice,* May 11, 1993, Box 222, National Gay and Lesbian Task Force records, #7301, Division of Rare and Manuscript Collections, Cornell University Library.

32. Dugan, *The Struggle over Gay, Lesbian, and Bisexual Rights,* 64.

33. Dave Fleischer, interview with author, July 3, 2009.

34. Ibid.

35. See Fetner, *How the Religious Right Shaped Lesbian and Gay Activism.*

36. NGLTF Policy Institute, Fight the Right 1993 action kit, Box 154, National Gay and Lesbian Task Force records, #7301, Division of Rare and Manuscript Collections, Cornell University Library.

37. Scot Nakagawa, interview with author, June 26, 2009.

38. Dave Fleischer, interview with author, July 3, 2009.

39. HRC, "HRC's Involvement in Statewide Ballot Initiatives Campaigns," 1995, Box 23, Human Rights Campaign Fund records, #7712, Division of Rare and Manuscript Collections, Cornell University Library.

40. HRCF, Americans Against Discrimination draft, 1994, Box 21, Human Rights Campaign Fund records, #7712, Division of Rare and Manuscript Collections, Cornell University Library.

41. Ibid.

42. HRCF, memo Re: Ballot Initiative Component of Field, July 3, 1995, Box 27, Human Rights Campaign Fund records, #7712, Division of Rare and Manuscript Collections, Cornell University Library.

43. Anderson, *Out of the Closets and into the Courts.*

44. NGLTF Policy Institute, Fight the Right 1992 action kit, Box 154, National Gay and Lesbian Task Force records, #7301, Division of Rare and Manuscript Collections, Cornell University Library.

45. NGLTF Policy Institute, Fight the Right 1993 action kit.

46. D'Emilio, "Organizational Tales," 485.

47. Minkowitz, "Scenes from the Mall."

48. Campaign leaders, letter to Radecic and McFeeley re: state initiatives, February 6, 1994, Box 222, National Gay and Lesbian Task Force records, #7301, Division of Rare and Manuscript Collections, Cornell University Library.

49. Gallagher and Bull, *Perfect Enemies;* Urvashi Vaid, *Virtual Equality: The Mainstreaming of Gay and Lesbian Liberation* (New York: Anchor Books, 1995); Haider-Markel, "From Bullhorns to PACS."

50. Thalia Zepatos, interview with author, July 8, 2009.

51. Simmons, "Grassroots Goes to the Polls"; Witt and McCorkle, *Anti-Gay Rights.*

52. Dave Fleischer, interview with author, July 3, 2009.

53. Jeff Wunrow, interview with author, June 2, 2010.

54. Andrew Sullivan, *Virtually Normal: An Argument about Homosexuality* (New York: Vintage Books, 1996); Vaid, *Virtual Equality.*

55. Vaid, *Virtual Equality,* 147.

56. Ibid., 106.

57. Ward, *Respectably Queer.*

58. Vaid, *Virtual Equality,* 104.

59. Deborah B. Gould, *Moving Politics: Emotion and ACT UP's Fight against AIDS* (Chicago: University of Chicago Press, 2009), 276.

60. Gallagher, "The Right's New Strategy," 47.

61. Bigot Buster/Decline to Sign, Handbook.

62. One example of a satirical flyer was a mock press release sent out by the Bend Alliance of Religious Fundamentalists (BARF) and Oregonians Against Cunnilingus (OAC) after 1992. In this press release, BARF and OAC propose "an intensive petition drive to place Measure 69 on Oregon's June ballot. In addition to squandering monetary resources, and making the state a bigger laughing stock than it already is, Measure 69 will accomplish the following . . . declare a felony, and label as 'abominations,' all sexual activity except for bi-weekly heterosexual coitus in the missionary position . . . Should you want more information about OAC, simply contact any Oregonian who is still displaying a 'Yes on 9' campaign sign or bumper sticker from the November election. Measure 9 backers were the true inspiration for proposed Measure 69, and for OAC's efforts to bring harmony, understanding, and tolerance to the Oregon community" (Oregonians Against Cunnilingus, mock press release, 1992/1993, Box 106, National Gay and Lesbian Task Force records, #7301, Division of Rare and Manuscript Collections, Cornell University Library).

63. Task Force, e-mail from a consultant re: Idaho "No on One."

64. Lesbian Avengers, "Out against the Right."

65. Ibid.

66. Task Force, Lewiston Fieldnotes, 3.

67. A Task Force consultant was critical of this "happy homosexual protest" because "Clearly having a 'happy homosexual' action at a vehemently anti-gay church is not intended to change any hearts and minds of church members (although it might be personally entertaining). Instead, it was meant to be a media event, since the Avengers planned to invite the media. If media is the major goal, then media impact should be critically assessed. What sort of media will such an event generate, one week before the election? . . . it made me question [the Avengers'] motives and their media judgment. I also, however, believe there should be a limit on how far we should go to stop actions with which we disagree. Win or lose on

November 8, the gay/lesbian community in Idaho needs to live with and work with one another after it's all over" (Task Force, e-mail from a consultant re: Idaho "No on One,"3).

68. Fetner, *How the Religious Right Shaped Lesbian and Gay Activism*, 91.

69. Equal Rights PAC [Political Action Committee], letter to Task Force, undated, Box 224, National Gay and Lesbian Task Force records, #7301, Division of Rare and Manuscript Collections, Cornell University Library.

70. Ibid.

71. Save Our Communities, "The Campaigns against Anti-Gay Initiatives."

72. Ibid., 6.

73. Ibid., 7.

74. Save Our Communities, fund-raising letter, "Communicate. Organize. Act" (1993), Box 224, National Gay and Lesbian Task Force records, #7301, Division of Rare and Manuscript Collections, Cornell University Library.

75. Inga Sorensen, "From Klamath Falls to Astoria, Rural Activists Are on the Cutting Edge," *Lavender Network Newsletter*, September 1994, 1, 4.

76. Ibid.

77. See Stein, *The Stranger Next Door*, for more details and a critique of the exhibit.

78. Meyer and Staggenborg, "Movements, Countermovements, and Political Opportunity," 1649.

4. A Winning Streak

1. Ghaziani, *The Dividends of Dissent*.

2. William A. Gamson, *The Strategy of Social Protest* (Homewood, Ill.: Dorsey Press, 1975); Jack Goldstone, "The Weakness of Organization: A New Look at Gamson's *The Strategy of Social Protest*," *American Journal of Sociology* 85, no. 5 (1980): 1017–42.

3. Camp, "Mobilizing the Base and Embarrassing the Opposition"; Rory McVeigh and Maria-Elena D. Diaz, "Voting to Ban Same-Sex Marriage," *American Sociological Review* 74, no. 6 (2010): 891–915.

4. Camille Colatosi, newspaper clipping titled "The Bad Habits of Homos" from unknown newspaper, 1993, James W. Toy Papers, Bentley Historical Library, University of Michigan.

5. Michigan Campaign for Human Dignity, newsletter, July 25, 1993, James W. Toy Papers, Bentley Historical Library, University of Michigan.

6. Although *Romer v. Evans* invalidated state-level legal-restrictive initiatives on multiple grounds, a similar suit for Cincinnati Issue 3 was upheld by a district

court that served the state of Michigan as well, calling into question the ability of Michigan activists to pass legal-restrictive initiatives. See *Equality Foundation of Greater Cincinnati v. City of Cincinnati,* 128 F. 3d 289 (6th Circ. 1997).

7. For a full account of how transgender protections became included in the Ypsilanti nondiscrimination ordinance, see Amy L. Stone, "Like Sexual Orientation? Like Gender? Transgender Inclusion in Non-Discrimination Ordinances," in Barclay, Bernstein, and Marshall, *Queer Mobilizations,* 142–57.

8. Before calling itself YCFE this group went by the name Citizens for Community and was not a registered campaign organization. It was much more loosely structured, had no leadership, and was not hierarchical.

9. Beth Bashert, interview with author, January 25, 2005. Only a few interviews in this chapter have a clear, named source. Most interviews were either conducted under IRB requirements of confidentiality or the activist in question asked for confidentiality.

10. Paul Heaton, interview with author, January 20, 2005.

11. See Paul Heaton, "Lessons from Ypsilanti," *Advocate,* July 7, 1998, 11.

12. See, for example, Andrews and Biggs, "The Dynamics of Protest Diffusion"; Soule, "The Student Divestment Movement in the United States and Tactical Diffusion"; Soule, "Diffusion Processes within and across Movements."

13. E-mail to staff members. Subject: Victory 101 for Hawaii, May 7, 1997, Box 25, Human Rights Campaign Fund records, #7712, Division of Rare and Manuscript Collections, Cornell University Library.

14. Ibid.

15. Thalia Zepatos, interview with author, July 8, 2009.

16. "Task Force Organizing and Training Staff Complete Record-Breaking Training in New Mexico," National Gay and Lesbian Task Force press release, August 1, 2003, http://www.thetaskforce.org.

17. Simmons, "Grassroots Goes to the Polls," 212.

18. Georg Ketelhohn, Liebe Gadinsky, and Dave Fleischer, "How to Win an Election — Even in Florida: Lessons from the 2002 Victory in Miami," handout obtained by author at the 2002 Creating Change conference in Portland, Oregon.

19. "Task Force History," National Gay and Lesbian Task Force, accessed December 20, 2010; http://www.taskforce.org.

20. Polletta, *It Was like a Fever,* 54.

21. Jasper, *The Art of Moral Protest,* 237.

22. Elisabeth Clemens, "Organizational Repertoires and Institutional Changes: Women's Groups and the Transformation of U.S. Politics, 1890–1920," *American Journal of Sociology* 98, no. 4 (1993): 758; Bernstein, "Celebration and Suppression."

23. See Jasper, *The Art of Moral Protest.*

24. Ann-Marie E. Szymanski, *Pathways to Prohibition: Radicals, Moderates, and Social Movement Outcomes* (Durham, N.C.: Duke University Press, 2003).

25. These ordinances were also transgender inclusive. See Stone, "Transgender Inclusion in Non-Discrimination Ordinances."

26. Ferndale City Council, videotape of city council public hearing, July 8, 1991, copy in author's possession courtesy of Rudy Sera.

27. Royal Oak activists had been working for a local LGBT rights ordinance at the same time as their Ferndale neighbors. Royal Oak City Commission members initially passed the ordinance and then, after being pressured by the local Religious Right, rescinded their decision by sending the ordinance to the public in a binding advisory vote. The Royal Oak opposition pushed for an additional charter amendment, but failed to turn in the required signatures on time (Staff, "Antigay Proposal Won't Make Ballot," *Detroit Free Press*, August 10, 2000, 6B).

28. Sarah Mieras, "Royal Oak: Lessons to Learn," *Between the Lines*, January 3–9, 2002, 7.

29. Dave Fleischer, "Strangers in Paradise: Royal Oak Offers a Lesson," *Between the Lines*, September 6–12, 2001, 9.

30. Carol Anderson, interview with author, June 25, 2009.

31. Sam Smith, "Why Question 6 Failed," *Portland Phoenix*, December 14–21, 2000, accessed May 4, 2010, http://portlandphoenix.com.

32. HRC, memo to: Public Policy Committee, July 30, 2002, Box 29, Human Rights Campaign Fund records, #7712, Division of Rare and Manuscript Collections, Cornell University Library.

33. Carol Anderson, interview with author, June 25, 2009.

34. Dave Fleischer, interview with author, July 3, 2009.

35. Beth Bashert, interview with author, January 25, 2005.

36. Bashert started working for Michigan pro-choice group NARAL (formerly known as the National Abortion Rights Action League) shortly after the Ypsilanti campaign and learned of the extensive statewide voter identification efforts of both the pro-choice movement and pro-conservation hunters. She also attended a Task Force workshop with Dave Fleischer on campaign techniques. For Bashert, "those voters meant power" and led her to wonder "what if the gay community had that voter strength?" (ibid.).

37. Michigan Equality, Strategic Plan, April 7, 2001, Beth Bashert Papers, Bentley Historical Library, University of Michigan, 3.

38. Using funding from local right-wing benefactors such as Tom Monaghan, the former Domino's Pizza owner, professional petitioners gathered signatures in cities such as Grand Rapids, Flint, Grand Ledge, Kalamazoo, Ypsilanti, and Traverse City throughout 2000 and 2001 (ibid.; Mike Martindale, "Family Group to Challenge Gay Law," *Detroit News*, March 8, 2001, 1, 3).

39. Petitions were gathered for an anti-gay charter amendment in Ypsilanti for the same election but it was pushed back to the November 2002 election because of a missed deadline.

40. In cities where there were signs of circulating petitions, activists formed such preemptive organizations as Flint United Against Discrimination and Grand Rapids Against Discrimination.

41. Sharon Gittleman, "Woods Residents Organize for Rights Battle," *Between the Lines*, August 2–8, 2001, 31, 7.

42. Sarah Mieras, "Counting Continues in Kalamazoo Petition Drive," *Between the Lines*, February 15–21, 2001, 7, 9–10.

43. Sarah Mieras, "From Benefits to Votes: Kalamazoo under Siege," *Between the Lines*, January 3–9, 2002, 3.

44. Ghaziani, *The Dividends of Dissent.*

45. Ibid., 226–27.

46. Alexandra Chasin, *Selling Out: The Gay and Lesbian Movement Goes to Market* (New York: St. Martin's Press, 2000).

47. Ghaziani, *The Dividends of Dissent.*

48. Ibid., 230.

49. HRC, Notes from Field Department Mini-Retreat, November 8, 1999, Box 55, Human Rights Campaign Fund records, #7712, Division of Rare and Manuscript Collections, Cornell University Library.

50. HRCF, memo from Tony Re: Ballot Initiative Component of Field, July 3, 1995, Box 27, Human Rights Campaign Fund records, #7712, Division of Rare and Manuscript Collections, Cornell University Library.

51. SAVE DADE, "Special Election Issue," 1996, Box 25, Human Rights Campaign Fund records, #7712, Division of Rare and Manuscript Collections, Cornell University Library.

52. D'Emilio, "Organizational Tales."

53. This federation grew out of a meeting of statewide organizations at the November 1996 Task Force Creating Change Conference. Originally named the Federation of Statewide Lesbian, Gay, Bisexual and Transgender Political Organizations, the federation is now called the Equality Federation and operates independently of the Task Force.

54. Craig A. Rimmerman, *From Identity to Politics: The Lesbian and Gay Movements in the United States* (Philadelphia: Temple University Press, 2002), 34.

55. Ghaziani, *The Dividends of Dissent*, 228.

56. Memo to Elizabeth Birch Re: Oregon Background Information, May 11, 1997, Box 27, Human Rights Campaign Fund records, #7712, Division of Rare and Manuscript Collections, Cornell University Library.

57. Statewide Federation, Minutes from Highlander Meeting, July 13, 1997,

Box 221, National Gay and Lesbian Task Force records, #7301, Division of Rare and Manuscript Collections, Cornell University Library.

58. Memo to Elizabeth Birch Re: Washington State Background Info, May 10, 1997, Box 23, Human Rights Campaign Fund records, #7712, Division of Rare and Manuscript Collections, Cornell University Library, 6.

59. Human Rights Task Force, "Winning on Our Terms," 1994, Box 223, National Gay and Lesbian Task Force records, #7301, Division of Rare and Manuscript Collections, Cornell University Library, 3.

60. Inga Sorensen, "Just Do It?" *Just Out,* September 5, 1997, 1997, 11.

61. HRC, memo "Why the Oregon Project and Not an Initiative Campaign?" (undated), Box 27, Human Rights Campaign Fund records, #7712, Division of Rare and Manuscript Collections, Cornell University Library.

62. Robert Salladay, "Pro-Gay Marriage Ballot Initiative Launched," *Press-Telegram,* December 3, 1999, A21.

63. Dave Fleischer, "Building Our List of Supporters (Voter I.D.) Gives Us the Power," 1999, handout obtained at the 2002 Creating Change conference in Portland, Oregon.

64. E-mail to staff members. Subject: Victory 101 for Hawaii.

65. Idea Idaho, Proposal "Voter ID Project," 1996, Box 25, Human Rights Campaign Fund records, #7712, Division of Rare and Manuscript Collections, Cornell University Library.

66. Memo Re: HRC Participation in Ron Wyden for U.S. Senate, December 17, 1996, Box 27, Human Rights Campaign Fund records, #7712, Division of Rare and Manuscript Collections, Cornell University Library.

67. Letter to Senatorial Campaign Committee, February 3, 1996, Box 27, Human Rights Campaign Fund records, #7712, Division of Rare and Manuscript Collections, Cornell University Library.

68. "$500,000 Awarded by Task Force to Gay Advocacy Groups across the Country to Build Public Support for Equal Rights," National Gay and Lesbian Task Force, press release, October 27, 2003, http://www.thetaskforce.org.

69. Protect Our Children, campaign briefing, November 22, 1996, Box 24, Human Rights Campaign Fund records, #7712, Division of Rare and Manuscript Collections, Cornell University Library.

70. "Activist Story—Stephanie Anderson," National Gay and Lesbian Task Force, accessed March 25, 2010, http://www.taskforce.org.

71. Before 1997, the LGBT movement had won eight statewide ballot measures and lost only three, two of which were overturned in the courts.

72. PFLAG, "No on Prop. 22/No on Knight Action Pack," 2000, Box 54, Federation of Parents and Friends of Lesbians and Gays records, #7616, Division of Rare and Manuscript Collections, Cornell University Library.

73. Simmons, "Grassroots Goes to the Polls," 120.

74. Smith, "Why Question 6 Failed."

75. Ibid.

76. See Ward, *Respectably Queer.*

77. Simmons, "Grassroots Goes to the Polls," 210.

78. Ibid., 209.

79. Smith, "Why Question 6 Failed."

80. Two of these ballot measures were in Nevada in 2000 and 2002. Nevada requires constitutional amendments to be passed in two consecutive general elections.

81. Defend Alaska's Privacy, letter, July 16, 1998, Box 25, Human Rights Campaign Fund records, #7712, Division of Rare and Manuscript Collections, Cornell University Library, 10.

82. Donna Red Wing and Nancy Buermeyer, article from *HRC Quarterly,* spring 1997, Box 25, Human Rights Campaign Fund records, #7712, Division of Rare and Manuscript Collections, Cornell University Library, 10–11.

83. Protect Our Constitution, memo, June 4, 1997, Box 55, Human Rights Campaign Fund records, #7712, Division of Rare and Manuscript Collections, Cornell University Library.

84. HRC, "Campaign Hawaii: The Blue Print," undated, Box 55, Human Rights Campaign Fund records, #7712, Division of Rare and Manuscript Collections, Cornell University Library.

85. HRC, memo to: Faith and Fairness Coalition, May 6, 1998, Box 24, Human Rights Campaign Fund records, #7712, Division of Rare and Manuscript Collections, Cornell University Library.

86. Michael Gordon, interview with author, May 7, 2010.

87. Ibid.

88. The emphasis on marriage and other mainstream goals during the 2000 Millennium March on Washington was controversial. The 2000 March platform included "equal marriage rights" as a demand (Ghaziani, *The Dividends of Dissent,* 270–74).

89. PFLAG, "No on Prop. 22/No on Knight Action Pack."

90. Andrews and Biggs, "The Dynamics of Protest Diffusion."

5. Losing at Same-Sex Marriage

1. John D'Emilio, "The Marriage Fight Is Setting Us Back," *Gay and Lesbian Review* 12, no. 6 (November 10, 2006): 10.

2. "Beyond Same-Sex Marriage: A New Strategic Vision for All Our Families and Relationships," accessed August 29, 2010, http://www.beyondmarriage.org.

3. McCammon, "'Out of the Parlors and into the Streets.'"

4. "Relationship Recognition Map for Same-Sex Couples in the United States," National Gay and Lesbian Task Force, last modified September 13, 2010, http://www.thetaskforce.org.

5. Evan Wolfson, "Moving Marriage Forward: The Tools to Keep Winning," speech at Creating Change conference in Dallas, February 4, 2010.

6. Jon Hoadley, interview with author, May 18, 2010. In this chapter, many interviews do not have a clear, named source. This is often because of a request for confidentiality. Also, I do not disclose the identity of any interviewees who currently work for the Task Force or HRC.

7. Sandeep Kaushik, "Gay Marriage Backers Focus on Oregon Battle," *Boston Globe*, September 27, 2004, A3.

8. Jeff Wunrow, interview with author, June 2, 2010.

9. Doug Gray, interview with author, June 3, 2010.

10. Jen Christensen, "Straight Talk Wins in Arizona," *Advocate*, December 19, 2006, 2.

11. Ibid.

12. Cynthia Leigh Lewis, interview with author, June 25, 2010.

13. Jon Hoadley, interview with author, May 18, 2010.

14. Joshua Friedes, "A Debrief of LGBT Initiative Campaigns from 2009," workshop February 5, 2010, at Creating Change conference in Dallas. Referendum 71 passed 53 percent to 47 percent, or a margin of 113,000 votes, some 104,000 of which came from the Seattle area. See Dick Morrill, "We Are Two States: Seattle and Washington," *Seattle News Online*, December 11, 2009, accessed June 23, 2010, http://crosscut.com.

15. Joshua Friedes, "A Debrief of LGBT Initiative Campaigns from 2009."

16. Cynthia Leigh Lewis, interview with author, June 25, 2010.

17. Jon Hoadley, interview with author, May 18, 2010.

18. "As Goes California, So Goes the Nation," last modified October 30, 2008, http://gayblogger.com.

19. John Gallagher and William Henderson, "For Arizona, Three's a Crowd," *Advocate*, September 23, 2008, 26.

20. Ehrenreich, "Anatomy of a Failed Campaign," 2.

21. Ibid.

22. Dan Aiello, "No on Prop 8 Official Grilled over Campaign," *Bay Area Reporter*, November 13, 2008, 40.

23. Ehrenreich, "Anatomy of a Failed Campaign," 2.

24. James Kirchick, "The New Religious Right," *Advocate*, September 18, 2009, accessed August 1, 2010, http://www.advocate.com.

25. Aiello, "No on Prop 8 Official Grilled over Campaign."

26. Betsy Smith, "A Debrief of LGBT Initiative Campaigns from 2009," workshop, February 5, 2010, at Creating Change conference in Dallas.

27. Ibid.

28. Ibid.

29. Cynthia Leigh Lewis, interview with author, June 25, 2010.

30. Dave Fleischer, interview with author, July 3, 2009.

31. This messaging was used in Houston in 2005.

32. Task Force, handbook obtained by author at the 2006 Midwest LGBT Power Summit, April 7–9, 2006, Milwaukee, 112.

33. Dave Fleischer, interview with author, July 3, 2009.

34. Ibid.

35. "Proposition 8: Post-Election California Voter Survey," David Binder Research, accessed July 1, 2010, http://www.eqca.org.

36. Patrick McCreery, "Save Our Children/Let Us Marry: Gay Activists Appropriate the Rhetoric of Child Protectionism," *Radical History Review* no. 100 (2008): 196.

37. Equality California, "Winning Back Marriage Equality in California: Analysis and Plan," Equality California, accessed July 1, 2010, http://www.eqca.org, 14.

38. Seth Kilbourne, interview with author, July 14, 2010.

39. "About Vote for Equality," Gay and Lesbian Center, accessed August 1, 2010, http://www.vote4equality.org.

40. Equality California, "Winning Back Marriage Equality in California," 17.

41. Basic Rights Oregon, "Summary of Findings of the Oregon Marriage Persuasion Experiment 2009," handout received at 2010 Creating Change in Dallas.

42. Ibid.

43. Wolfson, "Moving Marriage Forward."

44. "Restore Equality 2010," accessed August 1, 2010, http://www.restoreequality2010.com.

45. Memo from Dave Fleischer to Marc Solomon Re: When to Return to the Ballot, Equality California, last modified July 17, 2009, http://www.eqca.org, 9.

46. Memo from Gale Kaufman to Marc Solomon Re: Overturning Prop 8 Ballot Measure, Equality California, last modified July 17, 2009, http://www.eqca.org, 6.

47. "LGBT Equality," Ballot Initiative Strategy Center, accessed August 1, 2010, http://www.ballot.org.

6. Smears, Tears, and Queers

1. Citizens for Good Public Policy, *Bathrooms Video,* retrieved September 3, 2009, from http://citizensforgoodpublicpolicy.org.

2. Ward, *Respectably Queer,* 132.

3. Armstrong, *Forging Gay Identities*, 18.

4. Randi Romo, interview with author, May 17, 2010.

5. Ibid.

6. See Ghaziani, *The Dividends of Dissent*, for a discussion of single and multi-issue politics in the LGBT movement.

7. Sue Anderson, interview with author, June 3, 2010.

8. Cathy Cohen, *The Boundaries of Blackness: AIDS and the Breakdown of Black Politics* (Chicago: University of Chicago Press, 1999).

9. Armstrong, *Forging Gay Identities*, 102.

10. Ibid., 135; emphasis in the original.

11. Vaid, *Virtual Equality*; Keith O. Boykin, "Where Rhetoric Meets Reality: The Role of Black Lesbians and Gays in 'Queer' Politics," in Rimmerman, Wald, and Wilcox, *The Politics of Gay Rights*, 79–96.

12. Armstrong, *Forging Gay Identities*; Ghaziani, *The Dividends of Dissent*.

13. Boykin, "Where Rhetoric Meets Reality"; Vaid, *Virtual Equality*.

14. Allan Bérubé, "How Gay Stays White and What Kind of White It Stays," in *The Making and Unmaking of Whiteness*, ed. Brigit Brander Rasmussen, Eric Klinenberg, Irene J. Nexica, and Matt Wray (Durham, N.C.: Duke University Press, 2001), 246.

15. Ward, *Respectably Queer*.

16. Similar to other politicized identities, there is individual variation within these groups as to whether or not they self-identify as transgender, particularly among heterosexual-identified cross-dressers and other gender-variant identities such as butches and drag queens. See Gayle Rubin, "Of Catamites and Kings: Reflections on Butch, Gender, and Boundaries," in *The Persistent Desire: A Butch Femme Reader*, ed. Joan Nestle (Boston: Alyson Publications, 1992); Leila J. Rupp and Verta Taylor, *Drag Queens at the 801 Cabaret* (Chicago: University of Chicago Press, 2003); Valentine, *Imagining Transgender*.

17. Joanne Meyerowitz, *How Sex Changed: A History of Transsexuality in the United States* (Cambridge: Harvard University Press, 2002).

18. See Susan Stryker, "Transgender History, Homonormativity, and Disciplinarity," *Radical History Review* 100 (winter 2008): 145–57.

19. Valentine, *Imagining Transgender*.

20. The dissent over the inclusion of gender identity in proposed versions of the Employment Non-Discrimination Act (ENDA) illustrates the tensions about transgender issues. ENDA, which has a history dating back to the early 1970s, would prohibit discrimination in the workplace based on sexual orientation. In 2003, transgender rights advocates persuaded national organizations in Washington to support a "transgender-inclusive" ENDA. However, in 2007, Repre-

sentative Barney Frank and House Speaker Nancy Pelosi, supported by HRC, excluded transgender protections from a version of ENDA that was considered highly likely to pass through a Democratic-majority House. National activists and transgender advocates objected strongly to this exclusion, causing rifts within the LGBT movement. Whether to settle for nothing but full inclusion or what was easily attainable was part of this rift. See Paisley Currah, "Expecting Bodies: The Pregnant Man and Transgender Exclusion from the Employment Non-Discrimination Act," *Women's Studies Quarterly* 36, nos. 3–4 (fall/winter 2008): 330–36.

21. Shane Phelan, *Sexual Strangers: Gays, Lesbians, and Dilemmas of Citizenship* (Philadelphia: Temple University Press, 2001), 125.

22. Shannon Price Minter, "Do Transsexuals Dream of Gay Rights? Getting Real about Transgender Inclusion," in *Transgender Rights*, ed. Paisley Currah, Richard M. Juang, and Shannon Price Minter (Minneapolis: University of Minnesota Press, 2006), 153.

23. Cohen, *The Boundaries of Blackness*; Keith Boykin, *One More River to Cross: Black and Gay in America* (New York: Anchor Books, 1996).

24. Barbara Smith, "Where Has Gay Liberation Gone?" in Gluckman and Reed, *Homo Economics*, 200.

25. Scot Nakagawa, "Email Re: PFAW Meeting," 1994, Box 222, National Gay and Lesbian Task Force Records, #7301, Division of Rare and Manuscript Collections, Cornell University Library.

26. Darren Lenard Hutchinson, "'Gay Rights' for 'Gay Whites'?: Race, Sexual Identity, and Equal Protection Discourse," *Cornell Law Review* 85 (July 2000): 1358; Bérubé, "How Gay Stays White and What Kind of White It Stays"; Paisley Currah, "Searching for Immutability: Homosexuality, Race, and Rights Discourse," in *A Simple Matter of Justice?: Theorizing Lesbian and Gay Politics*, ed. Angelia R. Wilson (London: Cassells, 1995), 51–90.

27. Reverend Eric Lee, "Travesty of Justice," *Huffington Post*, August 26, 2010, accessed September 1, 2010, http://www.huffingtonpost.com.

28. Bernstein, "Sexual Orientation Policy, Protest, and the State."

29. Scot Nakagawa, memo Re: FTR Presentation, May 17, 1994, Box 222, National Gay and Lesbian Task Force Records, #7301, Division of Rare and Manuscript Collections, Cornell University Library, 3.

30. Debbie and Angie Winans were promoting their anti-gay song "Not Natural," which had been released in summer 1997. This rally was technically sponsored by the Ministers Alliance and the conservative organization Citizens for Traditional Values; however, COST promoted the rally and it was clearly centered on the ordinance.

31. Khan, "How the Ex-Gay Movement Serves the Right's Attack on Democracy"; Joan Nestle, Clare Howell, and Riki Wilchins, *Gender Queer: Voices from beyond the Sexual Binary* (Los Angeles: Alyson Books, 2002); Jan Stevenson, "Reggie White to Appear at Ypsilanti Anti-Gay Rally," *Between the Lines,* April 30–May 13, 1998, 1, 7.

32. Joshua Gamson, "Messages of Exclusion: Gender, Movements, and Symbolic Boundaries," *Gender and Society* 11, no. 2 (1997): 178–99; Phelan, *Sexual Strangers;* Jillian Todd Weiss, "GL vs. BT: The Archaeology of Biphobia and Transphobia within the U.S. Gay and Lesbian Community," in *Bisexuality and Transgenderism: Intersexions of the Others,* ed. Jonathan Alexander and Karen Yescavage (New York: Harrington Park Press, 2003), 25–56.

33. Jen Christensen, "Fear and Loathing in Gainesville," *Advocate,* April 2009, 16.

34. The Gainesville referendum included an elimination of both gender identity and the long-existing protection for sexual orientation.

35. Ypsilanti Citizens Voting Yes for Equal Rights Not Special Rights, flyer, in author's possession courtesy of the YCFE private files.

36. Linda Caillouet, letter to voters on behalf of Ypsilanti Citizens Voting Yes for Equal Rights Not Special Rights, 2002, in author's possession courtesy of the YCFE private files.

37. Currah and Minter, *Transgender Equality,* 59.

38. Judith Halberstam, *Female Masculinity* (Durham, N.C.: Duke University Press, 1998).

39. Ibid., 24.

40. Currah, "Expecting Bodies," 333.

41. Mubarak Dahir, "Whose Movement Is It?" *Advocate,* May 26, 1999, 50.

42. Leslie Feinberg, *Transgender Warriors: Making History from Joan of Arc to RuPaul* (Boston: Beacon Press, 1996), 117.

43. Currah and Minter, *Transgender Equality,* 21.

44. Lisa Duggan, *The Twilight of Equality?* (Boston: Beacon Press, 2003), 50.

45. Stryker, "Transgender History, Homonormativity, and Disciplinarity," 147–48.

46. Currah and Minter, *Transgender Equality,* 54.

47. Hands Off Washington, memo to HRC Re: Funding Needs for I-677, August 19, 1997, Box 23, Human Rights Campaign Fund records, #7712, Division of Rare and Manuscript Collections, Cornell University Library.

48. Staff, "In Support of Queer Alphabet Soup," *Between the Lines,* December 20–26, 2001, 6.

49. Jon Hoadley, interview with author, May 18, 2010.

50. "FAQ," Equality Gainesville, accessed September 3, 2009, http://equalitygainesville.com.

51. Local news coverage, [video] retrieved September 3, 2009, http://www
.bilerico.com/2009; local news coverage, [video] retrieved September 3, 2009,
http://www.livevideo.com.

Conclusion

1. McCammon, "'Out of the Parlors and into the Streets.'"
2. Schneiberg and Soule, "Institutionalization as a Contested Multilevel
Process."

INDEX

Amy L. Stone is assistant professor of sociology at Trinity University in San Antonio, Texas.